PLANE SPEAKING

Patrick Stephens Limited, a member of the Haynes Publishing Group, has published authoritative, quality books for enthusiasts for more than twenty years. During that time the company has established a reputation as one of the world's leading publishers of books on aviation, maritime, military, model-making, motor cycling, motoring, motor racing, railway and railway modelling subjects. Readers or authors with suggestions for books they would like to see published are invited to write to: The Editorial Director, Patrick Stephens Limited, Sparkford, Nr Yeovil, Somerset, BA22 7JJ.

Bill Gunston
PLANE
SPEAKING

A personal view of aviation history

Patrick Stephens Limited

© Bill Gunston 1991

First published 1991

British Library Cataloguing in Publication Data

Gunston, Bill, *1927-*
Plane speaking
1. Aviation, history
I. Title
619.1309

ISBN 1-85260-166-3

Patrick Stephens Limited is a member of the Haynes Publishing Group, Sparkford, Nr Yeovil, Somerset BA22 7JJ.

Typeset by Harper Phototypesetters Limited, Northampton
Printed in Great Britain by . . .

1 3 5 7 9 10 8 6 4 2

Contents

Acknowledgements

A lot of people have helped me to collect illustrations, including Phil Jarrett, Mike Hooks, Ann Tilbury, John Stroud, Jack Bruce, Nigel Eastaway, Richard Almond, Geoff Norris, Harry Holmes, Fred Adkin, Ken Munson, Hugo Hooftman, Derek Brown, Robert B. Stratton, Don Forsyth, and a man in New Zealand who does not wish to be identified. I am deeply grateful to all of them.

Introduction

This book is a collection of 45 stories about aircraft that I find interesting. They are picked at random. I apologize if some are judged to be pot-boilers, already done to death and unlikely to throw up any new information. Most, I think, have received little publicity, or I have approached well-known stories from a new angle. Almost all are in some way controversial. Some are simply tales of remarkable happenings, often to be explained only on the basis of extraordinary luck (good or bad). Others argue around a particular subject. Quite a few point an accusing finger and draw attention to what in World War Two was called 'finger trouble', meaning stupidity or incompetence. It is easy to criticize with the benefit of hindsight, but when you read some of these stories you wonder whose side some people were on.

When relating something that you were not personally involved in you have to do your best to get it right. Often the readily available account turns out to be dangerously biased, and perhaps even wrong in some of its facts. The way of the commentator with hindsight is perilous, and this is especially the case when he feels justified in being critical. In some of the stories in this book I have adopted the attitude 'How could we have got it so wrong?' For example, we (that is, Britain and her Allies) could hardly have been more inept before 1939 in assessing the equipment of Hitler's Luftwaffe, or before 1941 in our knowledge of Stalin's 'Red air fleet' or Hirohito's imperial army and navy air forces. Could it all have been cunning double-bluff? Hardly.

I have arranged these stories in chronological order, but often each is a potpourri of several related tales, of things that happened at different times. Obviously, they can be read in any order, and the chronological sequence merely gives the book an element of structure.

A few of the tales are, in my opinion, of considerable historical importance. They deserve to have at least a small spotlight trained on them, in the hope that new light may thereby emerge. There are hundreds more, waiting to be discussed.

A book of this nature inevitably tends to generate differing emotions, including amusement, disbelief (or at least incredulity, which is not quite so strong), and anger—anger at what happened or anger at the author for in some way getting it wrong. It is incredibly difficult to be truly impartial and objective, especially when you feel strongly about something. I assure you that I have tried to be, and that my expressed opinions are held sincerely.

BILL GUNSTON
Haslemere, Surrey

1

Nineteenth Century

The Flying Machine

Nothing is more pointless than trying to be clever with the benefit of hindsight, but the failure of would-be aviators to build a practical flying machine until the twentieth century seems to me astonishing. Virtually all the basic principles were laid down at the very start of the nineteenth century by Sir George Cayley. In particular, he addressed the crucial problem of control; yet this was to varying degrees ignored by all subsequent workers until Lilienthal and the Wright Brothers.

This lack of control would almost certainly have killed any of the nineteenth-century pioneers had they really been able to fly—in other words, had they been able to obtain enough sustained thrust and lift. One who just about managed it was Félix Du Temple in 1874. Others were Aleksandr Mozhaiski in 1884, Clément Ader in 1890, and Sir Hiram Maxim in 1894—the last named with a giant twin-engined machine with the same wing area as a B-52. The point is, had any of these really flown, they would have pitched nose-up or nose-down, or (even more likely) rolled over sideways, without the pilot being able to do anything about it.

The problem of lateral control is discussed in a separate story (No 12). But this is just one aspect of the overall control problem. Today we are so used to the fact that you need control about all three axes that it is difficult for us to put ourselves in the position of the nineteenth-century workers. They had little to go on except the visible proof that birds can fly. They could see that birds had tails, so virtually all the nineteenth-century flying machines were designed with some kind of tail (though often the inventor was uncertain of its function). The fact that bird wings are flexible, and together with flight feathers provide perfect lateral control, was less obvious.

Another factor that for a long time lay hidden was the importance of aspect ratio. This, the 'slenderness' of a wing, is for a rectangular wing merely the numerical value of the span divided by the chord (distance from leading edge to trailing edge). For a tapered wing it is span^2 divided by area. Many early designers thought that area was all that mattered; but, for the modest speeds that they might have hoped to attain, the ideal aspect ratio would be in the range of 15 to 30, like a modern sailplane. Doubtless such a wing could not then have been built, but to select an aspect ratio of less than 2 would have put paid to the idea of ever getting off the ground. One who did this was Mozhaiski, whose wing looked square. Cayley's triplane of 1849 appeared to have an aspect ratio of less than unity, but this was no doubt due to foreshortening in the only known illustration. Cayley's famous 1852 glider, a replica of which was flown many times under tow in the 1980s, with brilliant success, had an aspect ratio of about 1.7, span and root chord being about equal. This wing worked so well because, like the Rogallo and subsequent 'parawings', the fabric billowed out under aerodynamic load to form a curved lifting surface. I do not know if Cayley appreciated that this would happen. Certainly many subsequent designers regarded their wings as mere two-dimensional inclined planes.

The 1852 glider was one of the very few nineteenth-century designs for a flying machine to have a clear-cut vertical tail as well as a horizontal one. As ships have rudders, this is surprising, but the fact remains that hardly any of the known designs have a fin or rudder, and many have no tail controls at all. Mozhaiski appears to have benefited from the additions of subsequent artists and model-makers, who give his crude machine a proper tail, 1910-style. As actually built, it had just a tiny pair of elevators. Not one designer thought of providing lateral control, and this probably stemmed from an inability to sit in an armchair and simply imagine what might happen, should their creation ever get off the ground. Had they done so, and in their mind's eye watched their uncontrollable brainchild pitch or roll into the ground (they could hardly have been expected to imagine a stall), they would surely have leaped up shouting 'Eureka!'

This lack of imagination, which I find astonishing, went so far as to divide aviators into two streams, which Charles Gibbs-Smith called the 'airmen' and the 'chauffeurs'. You have only to look at the heavier-than-air machines designed or built after 1880 to see into which category the inventor belonged. The airmen recognized that, before you can fly an aeroplane, you have to learn to fly. To them it seemed sensible to start flying simple gliders. In doing so they expected to learn how to fly, and also how to make a machine controllable. The simplest method of control is what I have been told is known as body-English, though I cannot find this term in various Oxford, Webster's, and other dictionaries. It means controlling the aircraft by moving one's own body to alter the position of the CG (centre of gravity). Lilienthal's many hundreds of glides using this method had brought him to the point where he had designed control surfaces for a definitive aircraft when, tragically, he was killed. He was the chief pioneer of the airmen, and the world's first pilot. The Wrights had to go through the same process before they could design their powered Flyer.

The chauffeurs must simply have lacked imagination. They thought of an aeroplane as merely another kind of horseless carriage. Like a car, they expected it just to be driven around the sky. Their brains never for a moment envisaged a stall, a roll, a dive, a loop, or anything else except a serene onward progress supported by wings. So they ignored control and devoted all their attention to lift and thrust. In the matter of lift nobody knew whether it was better to use one big wing, or two, or (as Horatio Phillips used) up to 200, looking like a Venetian blind. Phillips was one of the very few to undertake effective research into wing sections (aerofoils). Some designers merely put a bit of curvature on their wings, while a few made them flat.

So what about propulsion? Leonardo da Vinci sketched a helical screw helicopter, but for some reason all the designers of propelled balloons could think of, in the period from 1785 onwards, were oars! You have only to think about it to appreciate that, even with larger than normal paddle ends, oars are not very effective in the atmosphere. Many workers clung to the belief that, to fly, man had to emulate the birds and build a flapping-wing machine. Such contraptions, called ornithopters, have done little except leave us with some hilarious ciné films. Not one has ever flown.

I am uncertain when the screw propeller was first applied, in sketch or in practice, to aircraft. Certainly de Launoy and Bienvenue used the invention in their helicopter design of 1796, and of course the screw propeller goes back into antiquity, the Chinese using hot-air-driven propeller lamp covers in 150 BC. Henson's 'Aerial Steam Carriage' of 1843—a most remarkable design for its day— had two pusher propellers. From then onwards most designers used one or more screw propellers, and seemed unconcerned at the weight and bulk of the machinery needed to drive it. Sir Hiram Maxim, the inventor of many things, including a famed machine gun, had the wealth needed to indulge his aeronautical interests to the full, and his monster machine of 1894 lacked any form of lateral control but had two stokers pumping fuel into a boiler! So despite the outstanding power/weight ratio of his twin engines his overall propulsion system was ponderous. Amazingly, it even had a large condenser above the upper wing, just as if he wanted to go non-stop to Australia. Several other early designers used condensers, among them Mozhaiski and Ader. Obviously, they reckoned the weight of the condenser would be more than outweighed by the saving in weight of water needed, but this is utter nonsense unless they thought they were going to fly for an hour or two at a time. To me the nineteenth-century idea of trying to defeat gravity with water-filled boilers and condensers is ludicrous.

When you sit back and think for a minute you surely see that 100 years ago you didn't need propulsion for very long. Once aviators actually started to fly, in this century, they were delighted to get a brief bit of 'daylight under the wheels'. The 24 flights that were made by various experimenters between 1906 and April 1908 were all of less than two minutes' duration. So there was certainly a case for some kind of stored energy. Many of the pioneers were French, and two who thought of stored energy were Alphonse Pénaud (twisted-elastic model, 1871) and Victor Tatin (twin compressed-air-driven propeller model, 1879). But we could do better even than this. All that was needed was a bit of thrust. This could be provided, cheaply and reliably, by a rocket. Congreve's army rockets had been made by the thousand at the very start of the nineteenth century, and were completely known quantities. It should not have been difficult to arrange for each rocket in a group to fire the next. Four of the 32-lb size would have given reliable thrust without overstressing the structure. The low propulsive efficiency would have been of no consequence.

Of course, most writings about 'who was first' are riddled with nationalism. To the Russians, Mozhaiski was first, not the Wrights. To the French, Ader stands supreme—a ridiculous claim which was to some degree upheld by that great aviator and editor, Major Oliver Stewart MC. He and I had many heated arguments about the undoubted fact (he would say, 'my contention') that, had Ader ever really flown, his totally uncontrollable *Eole* would have crashed. The reader is referred to contemporary writings, or the scholarly books of Gibbs-Smith.

2

1849

Taildraggers

1849 is merely the year of Sir George Cayley's sketch of a man-carrying triplane. This is the earliest picture I know of a taildragger, the colloquial term (of post-1955 US origin?) for an aeroplane with a tailwheel-type landing gear. (Henson's wonderful drawing of an 'aerial steam carriage' of 1843 had tricycle, nosewheel, landing gear.) When the pioneer aviators got going in the first decade of this century some used tailwheels, some nosewheels, a lot used floats, the Romanian Vuia fitted 'a wheel at each corner', and Robert Esnault-Pelterie anticipated the Harrier by using tandem wheels plus other wheels at the wingtips. Early Antoinettes rode on four wheels like a pram, Curtiss consistently favoured the nosewheel arrangement, and Cody used belt and braces in having wheels everywhere his clumsy machines might contact the ground.

By 1912 the aeroplane had pretty well settled down to having the main wheels well in front of the centre of gravity and a tailskid (sometimes a wheel) at the back. In World War One tens of thousands of aircraft were built to this formula. Some French and big German bombers had nosewheels, but these were only to protect the nose and normally never touched the ground. Apart from the RE.5 and RE.7, most of the rare nosewheel aircraft were pushers, such as Voisin and early Breguet bombers. Few pilots thought much about it.

For an activity supposedly founded on numerical answers to technical problems, and where all the answers must obey the laws of physics, aviation is surprisingly prone to the dictates of fashion. After 1918 the nosewheel virtually disappeared. Apart from one or two experimental aircraft I cannot think of anything that used such landing gear again until 1935. Then, quickly, it caught on in the United States. By 1938 nearly half the new designs on American drawing boards had what became known as 'tricycle' landing gears (though there is no reason why a tricycle should have the single wheel at the front). From this point on, there was no looking back; the nosewheel was on balance preferable to the tailwheel, except for certain specific applications. Most other countries did little or nothing before World War Two. Exceptions included General Aircraft's Monospar ST.25U built for the Air Ministry in 1936 with a clumsy 'tricycle', which proved so good that almost every subsequent GAL design used a nosewheel; the Dutch Fokker D.23 fighter; Tolstikh's rebuilt SB-2 bomber at TsAGI (Soviet Union) in 1940; and the Soviet

Moskalyev SAM-13 fighter designed in 1937 but not flown until 1940. Several reports describe the tailless KhAI-4 of 1934 as the first Soviet aircraft with a nosewheel, but the only drawings I have seen show the main wheels in front.

Thus by the middle of World War Two the United States had production lines pouring out aircraft with nosewheels, while the rest of the world still had only a few prototypes. There were just a few exceptions. At Easter 1944, as a 17-year-old ATC cadet, I spent one of my happiest weeks at RAF Brize Norton. A Heavy Glider Conversion Unit was teaching army pilots to fly giant Horsa gliders, the tugs being Albemarles. Both had nosewheel type landing gear, and nobody even thought about it.

Digressing from the main point, I was lucky enough to have 16 trips in the tugs and a few more nervous ones in the creaking wood-smelling gliders, which gave a very rough ride in turbulent air. At dawn there might be 60 huge tow-ropes laid out beside the downwind end of the runway. Albemarles would queue to be coupled to a Horsa and would then taxi gently forward until a batsman signalled 'All out', in other words that the slack had been taken up; then the throttles were firewalled. It was a tough life for the Hercules sleeve-valve engines, which had not been designed for sustained high powers at about 100 knots, and on return they poured smoke from overheated oil. In those days the sky was literally full, and you had to keep a sharp look-out in all directions. After the glider had cast off, the tug would dive on a particular field and I would be detailed to 'pull the tit' and release the rope. 'Erks' in the field, whose faces all looked white, would contrive to dodge the massive forged aluminium fitting on the end of the rope, which sometimes (I did this too) had to be dug out with a spade. At lunchtime the field party would drive back to Brize with a truck full of ropes. They really were hefty. They were 'nine-inch Manila', this being the circumference. One day a Yank appeared with the newly invented nylon rope. It looked about an inch across. We connected his C-47 to a CG-4 and watched him thunder off into the distance. The glider never moved, but the rope grew visibly thinner. Suddenly, whoosh! The CG-4 rushed after the tug like greased lightning.

So why am I eager to pontificate on nosewheels? For several reasons. One is that, as well as fashion, aviation is susceptible to strong nationalist feelings which occasionally cause seriously warped judgement. Another is that the kind of landing gear you have dictates how you land the aircraft, or perhaps how you ought to. Strangest of all, the nosewheel has been around since the dawn of aeroplane flight, and is demonstrably superior in almost all applications, so why did it virtually disappear between the wars?

To consider how you fly, to some degree the nosewheel aircraft can just be flown off and flown back on. The aircraft designer has to make judgements regarding the incidence of the wing and the length of the nose leg, which determines the ground attitude. It is usual to design the aircraft so that in the normal ground attitude lift is zero, or even slightly negative. This has to be so in order for the aircraft not to 'balloon' back into the sky on a bumpy landing. Therefore on takeoff you have to lift the nosewheel well off the ground. When modern jetliners rotate, their attitude can change by 15° or more. This gives a measure of how far away from lifting the aircraft the wing is on landing with the nose lowered, even without using lift dumpers. On the other hand, some aircraft, such as the F-15, are held fully nose-high after landing to increase drag and save wear on the highly stressed wheel brakes.

A few of today's enthusiasts may have the chance to sit in some World War Two fighter cockpits. If they sit in a Spitfire cockpit (especially a Griffon-Spitfire) and then sit in a P-38 Lightning they will see that the tailwheel aircraft offered no forward view at all, except out to one side, while the P-38 view was almost perfect. Taxiing the nosewheel aircraft was thus simple, whereas the tailwheel fighter had to proceed in a series of doglegs, or else someone had to sit on the lurching wing and direct the pilot, as was often done at forward airstrips. At least with a Spit or Typhoon this chap had cannon he could hang on to!

Arrived at the start of the takeoff run, the tailwheel pilot then had to pick a distant point on the horizon, unless there was a clearly marked runway, and uncage his directional gyro. He had to check in advance that the takeoff path was clear, because during the early part of the run he could see nothing. Worse, many aircraft and especially the powerful fighters, had a strong tendency to swing when the throttle was opened. In other words, they tried to make an uncommanded turn to left or right. Unless extremely promptly and firmly corrected, this turn got swiftly more violent until it resulted in a ground loop and, unless speed was low, an aircraft sitting on its belly and probably not worth repairing.

Swing is a characteristic of most taildraggers, and especially the high-power ones, even those with two or more engines. I do not have the slightest doubt that the number of Spitfires, Bf 109s, Typhoons, Beaufighters, Mosquitoes, and many other types that were written off because of swinging and ground-looping was greater than the number written off as the result of air combat. Swing results from the relative positions of the three wheels and the centre of gravity, which can make the aircraft highly unstable directionally. It can also be strongly affected by tailwheel geometry and leg angle, the effect of powerful spiralling slipstream, propeller torque forcing one mainwheel into the ground far more heavily than the other, and several other factors. Both on takeoff and landing the effect can be sudden, violent, and, unless response is instant, swiftly embarrassing. In World War Two many thousands of pilots said things like, 'I had full brake and full rudder and still I couldn't hold her.' Even today's cosseted warbirds are occasionally seriously damaged by uncontrolled swinging.

Today's pilots are used to nosewheels, or (if they fly a taildragger) to something with modest engine power. They will probably never have experienced a swing, and not be quite clear what it's all about. Believe me, it was an ever-present and very real hazard. High-power tailwheel aircraft often were so unstable directionally, on takeoff or landing, that they could get into a swing before the pilot could catch it. Then all that happened was that the turn got ever-tighter; the landing gear might collapse within two seconds of the start of the turn, and you ended up facing the way you came, on your belly, or possibly even inverted. It was not a thing to make light of.

All this sounds like more powerful reasons for fitting nosewheels, but in World War Two nationalism reared its head. In 1943 Sir Roy Fedden led an important technical mission to the United States. He left behind a country absolutely convinced of its aircraft superiority over the United States—except perhaps in terms of sheer numbers—and exceedingly reluctant to believe that anything could be learned by going there. Fedden, who actually knew a little about the USA, did not subscribe to this view. He wrote up his visit in a report of over 600 pages, with numerous diagrams and photographs, most showing things that we in Britain had never done and had often never heard of. Instead of the British industry being grateful for having some of their ignorance removed, Fedden's report caused incredulity, mirth, and quite a lot of resentment. For example, a few weeks after Fedden returned, Mr Wellwood Beall of Boeing came to Britain. One of the top British planemakers—Sir Fred—buttonholed him and asked: 'Have you seen this ridiculous report of Fedden's? We've called it Fedden's Folly. He says you have 3,200 qualified technical staff! We've made it a laughing stock.' Beall replied, 'You are quite right, the figure is not accurate. It was correct in January 1943, but today the figure is 3,880.' The laughter suddenly stopped, because that was more than could be mustered by the entire British industry.

To return to landing gears, Fedden naturally reported that 'Nosewheel undercarriages have come to stay, and perhaps to spread.' He devoted a major section of his massive report to an analysis of US landing gears, which contained an enormous amount of educational material for the backward British. Far from for a single instant considering there might be anything to learn, the British landing-gear managements were incensed. Dowty even published a major rebuttal, issued in the form of a 12-page brochure called 'Comments on the Fedden Mission Report'. It sought by every means possible to prove that nosewheel-type landing gears were nonsense, that almost all Fedden's findings were flawed or in some way inappropriate to Britain, and that in fact the Americans ought to copy Britain. So for nearly ten years after the war US airliners had 'tricycle' gear, with single legs resting on twin wheels and level cabins, while British aircraft had tailwheels, with twin legs resting on huge single wheels and sharply sloping cabins.

In 1979 I had a letter from a man of vast experience who wrote, 'There seems no doubt that the tailwheel always comes into the ground-looping act . . . My own flying stopped in 1929 at the time of the NY stock market crash, and started again in September 1939. What strange things had happened in the meanwhile! I found DC-3s being wheeled in for tail-up touchdowns, while Harvards were being dragged in under power with full flap. I was told "The airspeed is controlled by the elevators, and the rate of climb or descent by the throttle". In 1929 it was considered bad form to "rumble" the engine on the approach, this being considered misjudgement; now I was told to come in under power and land by closing the throttle.'

When I was a pupil and then an instructor on Harvards we adhered to the old method; we made steep gliding approaches with full flap, aimed to hold off just above the ground near stalling speed, and finally haul back hard enough to do a three-pointer. Then, of course, you had to be alert for the slightest incipient swing. Doing a 'wheeler' is often much easier, and this closely parallels the technique with a nosewheel. You fly the aircraft on to the ground whilst still having a good forward view, and rely on brakes, lift dumpers, full flap, reverse-pitch or jet reverse, and whatever else you may have to pull up. One could go on indefinitely discussing the pros and cons, but the remarkable facts are the long time it took for nosewheel gears to be accepted, and the bitter rearguard action fought against them in Britain.

3

7 October 1903

The First Aerodromes

In the late nineteenth century the Secretary of the Smithsonian Institution in Washington, the premier scientific body in the United States, was Dr Samuel Pierpont (not Pierpoint) Langley. A famed astronomer, he seemed to go slightly mad in 1886 by becoming captivated by the idea that man could build a workable man-carrying flying machine. For a reputable scientist to cherish such a belief was almost tantamount to professional suicide, but Langley's established stature gave the derided notion at least a modicum of respectability. What nobody would ever have expected is that the resulting full-scale machine would be the subject of endless heated argument, plus a much later attempt to prove it could fly, a surprisingly unscientific project carried through with the full knowledge of the Smithsonian.

At first Langley did very well. He wisely studied what previous workers had done, and settled on the configuration of a tandem monoplane, as advocated in the 1870s by D.S. Brown in England. He made a succession of models, with widely separated front and rear wings of equal size, using considerable dihedral in order to obtain natural lateral stability. The fifth and sixth models had small steam engines driving twin propellers carried outboard on each side just behind the front wing. They flew well, reaching distances up to 4,200 ft. They were probably the best model flying machines constructed up to that time, though Langley never did anything about the problem of flight control. He fell firmly into what was later called the 'chauffeur' class, who somehow believed all you had to do was make the flying machine. Then you just got in and rode in it.

Langley called his models Aerodromes, from the Greek *dromos*, meaning running or a racecourse. By 1897 he considered he had at least proved how an 'Aerodrome' should be designed, and—perhaps spurred by the thought that such activities were in the public mind associated with lunatics—he stopped further experiments. But in 1898 the Spanish-American war broke out. Such was Langley's stature that the US War Department requested that he should build them a full-scale Aerodrome. Bearing in mind both the experience of the Wrights in 1905–8 and the uncompromising view of military and naval staffs almost everywhere that the flying machine could not be of the slightest practical use, it is amazing that the hidebound people in Washington not only thought a Langley Aerodrome might be useful to help fight the Spanish but were prepared to back this belief with substantial official funding. Not surprisingly, because he had no doubt of eventual success, Langley accepted.

Of course, he merely scaled up his No 5 and No 6 model Aerodromes, at first to quarter-scale. This was completed in 1901, and was the first petrol-engined aeroplane ever to fly. Meanwhile, his gifted mechanic and pilot, Charles M. Manly, designed and built an outstanding engine for the full-size machine. Based on the car engine of Stephen M. Balzer, it was a five-cylinder water-cooled radial (not rotary), rated at just over 52 horsepower. It weighed 3.96 lb per hp, a ratio that was never again equalled until after 1914. As before it drove twin propellers behind the front wing. An addition in the full-size, piloted, Aerodrome was a cruciform tail which in theory was to give control in pitch and yaw.

What Langley did not do was build simple gliders in order to find out how such a machine should actually be controlled in practice. Lilienthal and Pilcher had by this time made hundreds of glides, so that—having become pilots—all they needed to do was add an engine. Tragically, Pilcher, a Scot, was killed in 1899 just as he was in the process of doing this. But for this quirk of fate the most famous name in aviation would be Percy Pilcher, and not Wright. But Langley never thought about control. Today we would be horrified at the thought of a man who was not a pilot being asked to fly an aeroplane with no proper control system, but that is just one of the causes for argument over Langley's Aerodromes.

What is more strange is why, having the obvious possibility before him of fitting his machine with wheels for taking off and landing on any fairly smooth stretch of ground, Langley should have hit on (what seems to us as) the ridiculous idea of launch by catapult from a ponderous structure built on top of a houseboat moored in the River Potomac. Why go to all the expense? What was the advantage of such an arrangement? Suppose the Aerodrome worked as predicted, and climbed away, how was Manly ever to land again, since there was no provision for a successful landing on land or in the river? Why adopt a scheme virtually guaranteed to require rebuilding of the machine after each flight (not a very good idea for a military aeroplane in wartime)?

The date above is that of the first launch. (Incidentally, by this time the Wrights were busy completing their first powered Flyer at Kitty Hawk.) After seemingly endless preparations the Aerodrome was launched. It nosed sharply down the moment it left the catapult, and plunged straight into the water not much more than its own length away from the houseboat. Fortunately Manly was unhurt, and both he and the Aerodrome were fished out and rehabilitated. It was generally agreed that the machine had fouled the launch mechanism, though there does not seem to have been any detailed investigation and it is hard to see on what evidence this belief was based.

The second launch took place, without significant modification to either the machine or catapult, on 8 December 1903. It resulted in instant disaster. Photographs of the launch show the frail machine twisting catastrophically and breaking up in the air before even fully clearing the end of the catapult. The wreckage naturally fell into the Potomac, and on this occasion Manly was trapped and almost drowned.

This served merely to confirm what almost everyone had known all along. The US Government withdrew its support, and henceforth totally disbelieved in flying machines. After all, if the great Langley, with almost limitless backing, couldn't make one work, who could? The *New York Times* summed it up with 'The flying machine which will really fly might be evolved . . . in from one to ten million years . . .' In fact, it was to take rather less time: nine days to be precise. This famous editorial was a classic case of a very serious and reputable newspaper trying to reflect the mood of the times without doing anything so foolish as giving the matter a few seconds of considered thought.

But why did the meticulous and lavishly funded Langley make such a hash of it? Did his Aerodrome really foul the catapult, on either occasion? I can find no evidence to support this idea on either of the two launches. Had it done so, photographs would have shown the impact and local breakage. A second factor is that he made a mistake with his arithmetic that reduced the power needed, and many people have concluded that the machine was underpowered. I do not see any reason for this conclusion, and the full-size Aerodrome had far more horsepower than the early Wright Flyers and many other pioneer aircraft. In my opinion both disasters were due to structural failure, probably caused by omitting to design for the catapult acceleration. On the first launch the front wing can be seen to have adopted a markedly nose-down attitude, giving an incidence of about minus five instead of plus ten degrees. The down-turned forward section of the stick-like fuselage is obvious. On the second launch the sudden loads, accelerative and aerodynamic, caused immediate disintegration. Nothing more need be said.

Had the machine held together it is still questionable whether Manly, with no piloting experience and a highly imperfect control system, could have actually flown it. And he had no chance of returning to earth except by flying into the river, which would certainly have caused structural breakup. But all these considerations are rather academic. What nobody could ever have expected was that 11 years later the Aerodrome would be completely rebuilt, in the light of later knowledge, so that the Smithsonian could exhibit it as 'The first man-carrying aeroplane in the history of the world capable of sustained free flight'. You can't believe such a thing? Read on.

4

17 December 1903

Inform Press

After hundreds, possibly thousands, of would-be aviators had failed to fly, the brothers Wilbur and Orville Wright went ahead and did just that. On the day above they both achieved sustained, fully controlled (some would say, over-controlled) flight, landing at an elevation not lower than the starting point. They did this, incidentally, nine days after the New York editor said such a feat would take 'from one to ten million years'.

The brothers sent a telegram to their father, a bishop, describing their flights and ending INFORM PRESS. The first of the puzzles is how it came about that, starting with a clear but brief account, backed up on 5 January 1904 by a long and detailed statement by Wilbur to Associated Press, practically nothing got published, and what did get published was so garbled as to be almost meaningless. To the world at large the Wrights, and their wonderful—almost unbelievable—achievement, remained unknown. This, coupled with the fact that flying machines remained universally a subject for jeers and derision, made the brothers secretive. Indeed, a year earlier, when they were beginning construction of the first powered Flyer, the brothers showed their (correct) opinion of the media by writing home: 'Please do not mention the fact of our building a power machine to anybody. The newspapers would take great delight in following us in order to record our troubles.'

In 1904 the brothers at last abandoned the gales, sandswept dunes, and vicious mosquitoes of Kitty Hawk and began flying at Huffman Prairie, just outside their home town of Dayton, Ohio. Very gradually, word got round, the first printed account by an eyewitness being in, of all things, a paper concerned with bee-keeping! The managing editor of the Dayton *Journal* later wrote: 'They seemed like well-meaning, decent enough young men. Yet there they were, neglecting their business to waste their time day after day on that ridiculous flying machine. I had an idea that it must worry their father.' He knew they were flying 'all round the field' but never considered this worth putting in the paper. One day he met Orville, and the following conversation ensued: 'Done anything of special interest lately?' 'Oh, nothing much; today one of us flew for nearly five minutes.' 'Where did you go?' 'Around the field.' 'Oh, I see. Well, we'll keep in touch with you.' The mind boggles—well, mine does.

On 23 May 1904 the brothers invited Ohio newspapers to send representatives to witness a flight. A combination of flat calm and engine trouble prevented a flight, and the journalists departed somewhat puzzled at the apparent sincerity of the brothers in thinking they could fly. I have never been able to decide if the brothers deliberately planned it this way. In December 1905 an independent witness wrote to the *Scientific American* about the flights he had seen, including one of 24 miles in 38 minutes. In its review of the year the respected magazine reported that one of the brothers 'made a flight of over half a mile in a power-propelled machine', but commented 'the only successful flying that has been done this year must be credited to the balloon type'. A month later the same magazine, probably the most influential in the United States where technical matters were concerned, published a leading article expressing complete disbelief of the brothers' claims, making the comment that, if they had been true, 'the enterprising American reporter' would have found out all the details!

In 1905 the brothers were approached by Col Capper, CO of the Balloon Factory at Farnborough, England. Before doing any deal with the British the brothers thought they ought first to offer their Flyer to their own government. The response they got bore not the slightest relationship to what they had written, and merely said that the US Government declined to fund 'the experimental development of devices for mechanical flight'. Despite this, the brothers persisted, repeatedly receiving replies identical in tone to the first. The correspondence went on for a long time, a letter from General Crozier at the end of 1906 having the nerve to say the brothers 'know the Government's attitude and have its offer' (there had been no offer). By spring 1907 not even letters from the President of the United States and Secretary of War could move the Ordnance Board to do more than write to the brothers saying 'the Board has before it several propositions for the construction and test of aeroplanes, and if you desire to take any action in the matter, will be glad to hear from you'.

In September 1907 Lt Frank P. Lahm was posted to Washington. He had won a major balloon race in Europe, knew the Wrights, and was fully informed on their flying. His fortuitous presence played a major role in getting the War Department on 23 December 1907 to advertise for tenders for an aeroplane. Newspapers and magazines from coast to coast wrote vitriolic and scathing leaders over such a ridiculous waste of public money. The New York *Globe* said a brief perusal of the conditions and rewards offered showed the whole idea to be a delusion (a flying machine that could fly would be worth millions), while many editors flatly stated that no flying machine existed that could fulfil the conditions. When the bids were in there were 41. Predictably, over a period, 40 dropped out. The Wrights were intrigued to learn that if their Flyer reached 40.999 mph they would not get the promised 10 per cent bonus for each extra 1 mph, but that if it could not exceed 39.999 mph they would be penalized 10 per cent!

On 11 May 1908 a group of senior pressmen, hidden in pinewoods at Kitty Hawk, actually witnessed the brothers make a series of flights, carrying passengers. Despite this, everyone continued to 'know' that man could not fly. On 8 August 1908 Wilbur began a series of public flights in France which caused absolute amazement—one eminent French aviator said 'We are beaten—we do not exist.' Yet still nothing appeared in the world's press, least of all in the United States. At last, on 3 September 1908, Orville made a brief public flight at Fort Myer, just outside Washington. Theodore Roosevelt Jr said afterwards: 'The crowd's gasp of astonishment was not alone at the wonder of it, but because it was so unexpected. I'll never forget the impression the sound from the crowd made on me. It was a sound of complete surprise.' Tough journalists were so overcome at witnessing the impossible that tears streamed down their cheeks. All this after the brothers had been flying *five years*. And still the newspapers either failed to report the event or tucked it away on an inside page and completely failed to consider it of the slightest importance. Bearing in mind the nice natures, open-handed frankness, and transparent honesty of the brothers, it is surely remarkable that almost all the US media, and most of the general public, persisted so long in considering them at the very least ridiculous, if not knavish charlatans.

The brothers never minded anyone using their patents provided the machine was not to be sold for profit. In 1909, very reluctantly, the brothers began a patent action against Glenn H. Curtiss for the latter's use of ailerons in aeroplanes built for sale. The case dragged on until in 1914 the highest federal courts upheld the Wright patents, and at last described the brothers as pioneers. Sadly, worn out by the litigation, Wilbur died of typhoid in 1912. But then yet another amazing thing happened. The Smithsonian absolutely refused to acknowledge the Wrights as the first to fly, and announced its intention of exhibiting the 1903 Langley (which failed to fly) alongside the Wright aeroplane of 1908, or a quarter-scale model of it. The impression to visitors would thus be that Langley was the pioneer, by five years.

Nor was this all. So determined was Curtiss to uphold Langley and downgrade the country boys from Ohio that, with the eager support of the Secretary of the Smithsonian (who did not consult the proud institution's Regents), the wreckage of the Langley machine was brought out and handed over to Curtiss, shortly after the latter had finally been defeated in the courts. Curtiss thereupon completely rebuilt it. He fitted new wings, of totally different structure, aerofoil section, and span. He used knowledge gained by the Wrights in moving the wing-bracing kingposts 30 in to the rear, so that the bracing wires were in the right place and not where they contributed to wing failure. Internal bracing was according to structural principles worked out by the Wrights. The fabric was varnished. The tail was redesigned, and raised 10 in. The engine was given a new inlet manifold, modern carburettor, magneto ignition, and modern radiator. The two propellers were redesigned exactly according to Wright principles. Not least, the Aerodrome was fitted with ailerons, patented by the Wrights. Every one of the changes was based on technology pioneered by the Wrights and unknown to Langley.

In May 1914 Curtiss took the rebuilt machine out to Lake Keuka and, with floats fitted, made two short hops, neither longer in duration than five seconds. In its report of that year the Smithsonian announced that the Aerodrome had been flown 'without modification'. It continued: 'It has demonstrated that with its original structure and power it is capable of flying with a pilot and several hundred pounds of useful load. It is the first aeroplane in the history of the world of which this can truthfully be said.' Similar statements continued to be made in the Smithsonian's reports for many years afterwards. Moreover, the Aerodrome—after being restored as nearly as possible to its original state—was placed in a prominent place at the Smithsonian, with a placard describing it as 'The first man-carrying aeroplane in the history of the world capable of sustained free flight'.

For the next *14 years* Orville Wright tried to get the facts investigated. At first he thought the noble officials of the Smithsonian might have been ignorant of the fraudulent nature of Curtiss's tests of the Aerodrome, but in 1921 Griffith Brewer in England gave a major lecture exposing what had been done, and Dr Walcott, Secretary of the Smithsonian, made a statement in reply (full of half-truths) which showed that the Institution had certainly not been in ignorance and indeed appeared to have planned the tests with Curtiss. Orville failed to get anyone in authority— Chief Justice Taft was also Chancellor of the Smithsonian—to show the slightest interest. It was obvious that the crime was so base, so unfitting for a nation's top scientific body, that everyone wanted to hush it up. As Orville said, 'Silent truth cannot withstand error aided by continued propaganda.' At last, in 1928, Orville gave up and agreed to the request of the Science Museum in London to have the 1903 Flyer exhibited there indefinitely.

Another *14 years* went by, during which Orville continued to try to get history corrected. It was not until 24 October 1942 that the Smithsonian at last published what amounted to a retraction, truthfully describing what had happened, and regretting the claims made. The placard beside the Aerodrome had previously been replaced by one simply saying 'The original S.P. Langley flying machine of 1903, restored'. The 1942 statement hoped the Wright Flyer could be returned to the US National Museum where 'it would be given the highest place of honour, which is its due'. It was shipped back in 1948, and today has that 'highest place of honour' in the NASM, the most visited museum in the world. I hope the brothers know.

5

March 1912

Great Oaks . . .

Everyone knows the old saw 'Great oaks from little acorns grow'. This story is about a little acorn that was planted in 1912 and had an immediate effect on aircraft design at the time. What turned it into a great oak was that, once planted, the idea refused to go away, in Great Britain at least, and exerted an extremely important effect in retarding the national onward march of progress in the British aircraft industry. As a result, when in 1934 a major air race was organized from Britain to Australia, not one firm in Britain had any experience of modern stressed-skin cantilever monoplane structures. We learned just in time! This was of enormous importance, as explained later.

The first aeroplane to fly in Europe was a monoplane. Its full designation was the Santos-Dumont 14*bis*. Like today's Grumman X-29 it looked fairly normal in plan view until you realized that it flew in the opposite direction. To be facetious, there are pictures of the 14*bis* where at first glance it looks as if the pilot is facing backwards while his cap is facing forwards! Several other monoplanes followed, notably a succession of progressively better designs by Frenchman Louis Blériot, who flew his No XI (Mod) across the Channel to Dover on 25 July 1909. This achievement, which ranks alongside that of Lindbergh, was accomplished despite use of an Anzani engine of suspect reliability and a maximum power of only 23 hp.

It brought Blériot worldwide fame, and orders before the end of 1909 for more than 100 aircraft. Further orders followed, so that by 1912 he was by a short head the world's most successful planemaker. Nevertheless, when early in that year he realized that there was an inherent weakness in his aeroplanes, he did not hesitate to broadcast the fact. Around the last week in February 1912 he wrote a rather long-winded report in which he pointed out that, like those of his rivals, his aeroplanes were designed for straight and level flight—what we technically call the 1 g stressing case. In those days methods were very rough and ready, by modern standards. Many aircraft (not those of M. Blériot) were designed purely by eye and supposed common sense, with hardly any calculations at all. Blériot did work out stresses in a rough way, adding a factor of safety to take care of the extra loads imposed in pulling out from a *vol plané* (glide) or *vol piqué* (dive), but hardly anyone ever tested wings to see if they really met the supposed strength requirements.

At least two monoplanes broke their wings downwards whilst taxiing over rough ground. This made Blériot think harder, and he realized from his own experience that even in straight and level flight the natural turbulence of rough air results in endlessly repeated random variations in the stress on the wings. Often, in real turbulence, the loading reaches zero or is even reversed. Blériot had never designed for any downward stress, other than the weight of the wings themselves with the aircraft at rest. The central kingpost was used as the anchor for what were called anti-lift wires, which sloped downwards to attachments at about half the semi-span (ie roughly half-way to the tip) to take the weight of the wing. Blériot was very concerned to realize that rough air could cause much greater downloads than the mere weight of the wings, and that these reversals of stress could even be added to a further and sustained download in pushing over into a dive. He wrote all this into a detailed report, drawing attention to the unsuspected likelihood of wing failure, especially after long flights through rough air.

Far from hurting his business, the report brought him renewed prestige for his honesty in drawing attention to a problem which could hurt him more than his rivals who made biplanes. But it did have the immediate effect of causing the French Minister for War to issue an edict forbidding the purchase or use of monoplanes. Both the report and the ban were quickly brought to the attention of two British monoplane constructors, Robert Blackburn and L. Howard Flanders, who were naturally concerned. But the French ban was quickly rescinded, once it was understood that a properly designed monoplane was as safe as any other aeroplane. (Incidentally, I am quite sure that the reversal of stress that worried Blériot had never been allowed for in the design of biplanes either.) So there were numerous monoplanes in the French army manoeuvres in September 1912.

Thus the French took a critical look at monoplanes, realized there was nothing inherently wrong with such aircraft, and never again looked back. By the outbreak of World War One the Deperdussin company's monoplanes had gained an unbroken string of ten successive world speed records, while the monoplanes of the Blériot and Morane-Saulnier companies also had an unrivalled record in every kind of sporting flying. It is particularly significant that the first sustained inverted flying was demonstrated in 1913 by Adolphe Pégoud in a Blériot, which proved in the most public way that there was no longer any negative-g problem. Indeed, he even demonstrated the inverted loop or bunt, the toughest test of wings possible.

Incidentally, another cause of inflight structural failure was aviators replacing their engines by more powerful ones. This did not affect monoplanes only.

The fact that, once modified for negative-g loads, monoplane wings were as safe as any others was officially communicated to the British War Office in late April 1912. It was possibly filed without the information reaching anyone of importance. As related in the next story, in August 1912 the War Office held a Military Aeroplane Competition. A number of monoplanes took part, most being highly placed. Now the War Office had not been particularly concerned at the occasional fatal crashes that had afflicted aviation, but when the casualties were British officers it sat up and took notice. On Friday 6 September 1912 Capt Patrick Hamilton and Lt Wyness-Stuart were killed in the crash of a Deperdussin monoplane at Graveley, north of Stevenage. It was proved that part of the engine (possibly a complete cylinder) had come off in flight, and it was surmised that this had hit the wing bracing wires, causing immediate failure. On the following Tuesday Lt C. Bettington and 2nd Lt

Hotchkiss were killed in the crash of a Bristol-Coanda monoplane near Wolvercote, Oxford. An eyewitness said the aircraft 'swerved, then made a twanging noise'. There were various explanations, ranging from loss of control in a steep glide and 'failure of a bracing wire quick-release' to 'the shallow, ineffective angle of the upper bracing wires', and even 'the basic weakness of the monoplane type of machine'.

I prefer not to speculate on whether the wires of the Deperdussin were indeed severed in flight, or what happened to the Coanda, and in 1912 the science of accident investigation was primitive and almost non-existent. Suffice to say that, acting apparently on purely emotional grounds, on 15 September 1912 the War Office issued an order with immediate effect forbidding any member of the Royal Flying Corps Military Wing to fly a monoplane (the ban applied even if he owned it). The monoplane was officially described as 'not a good type'. Another document said that the ban was meant to include the RFC Naval Wing; this was never put into effect, but the RN pilots had hardly any monoplanes anyway.

According to the *Daily Telegraph*, 'The ban is intended to be permanent'. But the magazine *Flight*, already a considerable repository of knowledge and with a very good Technical Editor, Algernon E. Berriman, was able to make informed comment. Among other things it observed: 'It is not by any means proved that the monoplane, *per se*, is any more dangerous than the biplane as a type . . . That a permanent prohibition on the use of the monoplane would have a crushing effect is undoubtedly true.' Moreover, while the Deperdussin monoplanes went from strength to strength (at least, until M. Deperdussin was arrested for embezzlement in 1913) the Bristol-Coanda also found customers for use as a school, competition, and (outside Britain) military aircraft, 38 being delivered. One more (No 146) broke up in severe turbulence in Romania, and because of the British ban the Romanians had their remaining Coandas converted to biplanes. It seems to me that the anti-lift wires did indeed have a 'shallow ineffective angle', but that was just a design fault from which no properly designed monoplane need suffer.

This seems to have cut no ice with the 'Colonel Blimps' at the War Office in Whitehall. Though the absolute ban on flying monoplanes was repealed in February 1913, the pilots of the RFC were strongly advised to have nothing to do with such machines. Thus it was a very bold move by British & Colonial's Chief Designer, Capt Frank Barnwell (Story 18), when, to meet the nation's desperate need for a fighter able to have some chance against the Fokker E-series (which were monoplanes!) in July 1916, he designed a monoplane, the Bristol M.1A. This was a splendid little machine, and with its speed, before guns were fitted, of 132 mph it was streets ahead of any other fighting scout in the sky. Nor was it lacking in manoeuvrability; it demonstrated its ability to outmanoeuvre almost all the biplane fighters, only the Sopwith Pup (an exact contemporary in timing) being its equal. But only 125 production M.1Cs were ordered, at a time when this number of aircraft were often lost in a day, and never went where they were needed on the Western Front (they were shipped to the Middle East). The excuse given was that the monoplane landed too fast, but historian Jack Bruce commented that 'this reason was adduced to conceal the lack of skill of a certain senior officer, who misjudged his landing . . .'. Norman Macmillan, one of the best judges of aircraft between the Wars, flew M.1Cs at Turnberry School of Aerial Fighting and liked them very much.

One has to remember that before 1914, despite all the work of the Wrights and a few other methodical or analytical people, the aircraft designer worked on a basis of almost total ignorance. The biplane, which is based on the two-wing cellule called a boxkite, as pioneered by Hargrave in remote Australia in 1890, overcame the ignorance by being a beam of great structural depth (the distance between the two wings). Thus, even when made very light, it was strong in bending and in torsion, provided that the wire bracing was correctly tensioned. In contrast, the monoplane wing was a beam with extremely shallow depth. It therefore needed most careful bracing by struts or wires in order to acquire safe stiffness in bending and in torsion (also see Story 12). But nobody knew how to do this. In the film *Those Magnificent Men in their Flying Machines* the replica Antoinette had to be given additional bracing wires not on the original drawings. The whole science of aeroelasticity, the behaviour of real (ie flexible) aeroplanes, was unknown.

Beverley Shenstone wrote: 'Successful monoplanes could emerge only if the wings were stiff without much aeroelastic knowledge, or flexible with aeroelastic knowledge.' Thus, the only way to make a successful monoplane before, say, 1930 was to brace it until it was stiff. The British ban merely held back the acquisition of the knowledge needed to build safe monoplanes. Shenstone, a Canadian who had designed monoplanes for Junkers in Germany, reached England in 1931, and was asked by a prospective employer how he would design a fighter. He replied: 'First, I would consider whether it would be a monoplane or a biplane.' The manufacturer said, 'Oh no you wouldn't, it would be a biplane!' That might even have been a good choice in 1931, because, thanks to the lack of incentive, nobody in Britain knew how to make cantilever (unbraced) monoplane wings unless they were enormously deep, making the aircraft even slower than a biplane.

Now the most remarkable thing about this story is not that the War Office imposed a precipitate and short-sighted ban on monoplanes in 1912 but that its after-effects lasted right up to World War Two. To some degree the trouble lay in the British designers. They understood biplanes, and traditional structures, and were loath to have to tackle something new where they might produce an inferior design. Another factor was that, in the days of strut-braced, fabric-covered aeroplanes, with high drag and low performance, the monoplane was not necessarily all that much better than the biplane. In 1932 the Air Ministry deliberately ordered, from the Blackburn company, two quite large aircraft as identical as possible apart from the fact that one was a biplane and the other a monoplane. The result showed that there was almost nothing to choose, though on balance the monoplane was slightly superior. This was good news to British industry, which continued to make aircraft to the old formula, though there were disturbing rumours of a species called 'cantilever stressed-skin monoplanes' from the USA, and, increasingly, Germany.

This was ironic because, as is so often the case, Britain had been one of the pioneers of all-metal construction with the Bristol M.R.1 (see Story 18) of 1918 and the Short Silver Streak mentioned later. These were not true stressed-skin aircraft, because the thin metal skin of their wings was used merely as a slightly tougher replacement for fabric, and would have buckled elastically under modest compressive or shear loading. But if the British industry had had some kind of incentive, or appreciation of the advantages, it could have produced aeroplanes of the totally new species in which stressed-skin, all-metal construction made it possible to build aircraft with quite thin cantilever wings. This in turn so increased speeds that it spurred the perfection of long-chord cowlings for air-cooled radial engines, ducted low-drag radiators for liquid-cooled engines, enclosed cockpits, retractable landing gear, variable-pitch propellers, flaps, and streamlined aircraft in general.

I do not know how far anyone in the British industry could foresee these things, in the period immediately following World War One, but if they did their ideas would have been firmly nipped in the bud by the officials. Oswald Short's great experience of Duralumin (light alloy) construction of airships during the war had convinced him this was the way to go. After fruitlessly trying to convince the metallurgists at the Air Ministry and at the Aeronautical Inspection Directorate that such material could be made flawless and reliable, he set about designing an all-Duralumin biplane, the Silver Streak. Knowing what a great advance this would be, he asked the Air Ministry to contribute to the cost. After a long delay he got a refusal. He went ahead and built the Streak with company money, showing it at the Olympia (London) air show on 9 July 1920. Told that Dural would corrode, he exposed test specimens so that they were under water or in the atmosphere as the tides changed twice a day; steel soon rusted away but Dural was no problem. The registration G-EARQ was issued, but the Streak was refused a C of A 'because we have no long-term knowledge of Duralumin primary structure' (only a few thousand hours in many airships!). Later, from June 1921, it was flown by test pilots at Farnborough, getting rave reviews. This so enraged the officials that further flying was forbidden, and Short was denied access to any further information. Over the next 18 months questions were repeatedly asked in Parliament. Not until 1923 did the Air Ministry reluctantly admit that the Streak had stood up wonderfully to every test they could devise, had not corroded, and was a very fine machine. But they did nothing so foolish as to ask anyone to build them any light-alloy aeroplanes.

Instead, when in 1924 the Air Ministry announced it would buy no more wooden aircraft, the various chief designers merely repeated their old wooden structures but in metal, almost always steel. They got very good at making wire-braced fabric-skinned biplanes with metal structures, which the Air Ministry was delighted to keep on buying. Can you believe that not one Gladiator reached the RAF until 1938; and even the Hurricane was fabric-covered! Barnes Wallis's Geodetic construction was a flexible metal basketwork covered with fabric; though mathematically ingenious it was really only a variation on the traditional theme. In 1933 Rolls-Royce realized that all the aircraft they had available in which to test engine installations were so slow that reductions in engine or radiator drag made hardly any difference; a big improvement in one installation in a Horsley increased speed from 123.5 to 124.5 mph, for example. In the absence of any streamlined British aeroplane they bought a German He 70—incidentally incurring criticism from British manufacturers—which on the power of a single Kestrel engine could reach 260 mph with six people on board, 53 mph faster than the RAF's new Fury single-seat fighters powered by the same engine. A year later Bristol engine designer Roy Fedden had a prolonged fight to get the Bristol board to agree to build a modern stressed-skin cantilever monoplane (the first in Britain) for newspaper tycoon Lord Rothermere. The Board were desperately afraid such a machine (called *Britain First*, it reached 307 mph) might gain publicity despite the fact it was contrary to Air Ministry design policy!

The pioneer of stressed-skin construction was Adolf Rohrbach, from 1919 onwards. Had he not been a German, perhaps Britain might have learned from him, as did Northrop in the USA. As it was, 'Haven't we won the war?' (Story 34) seemed to have shut our minds to progress.

6

August 1912

Start The Way You Mean To Go On

Let's forget about hindsight for a moment and just think about common sense. This shows us that the relationship between the British government and the world of aviation has been far too strong, too far-reaching, and almost uniformly disastrous for everyone. I shall return to this theme later, if I can summon up courage to rake over such terrible chapters of imbecility. Many people can remember those days, but they may not know that the relationship was a disaster from the very beginning.

One of the enduring themes in this relationship is that the government has either taken wrong decisions or, more often, failed to take any decisions, and has subsequently blamed the industry for the consequences. We could hardly expect those in the 'corridors of power' to have taken note of what happened at Kitty Hawk in December 1903, but they could hardly have failed to notice all the flying that went on in Europe from 1907. My old paper, *Flight*, came out every week from 2 January 1909, and on 25 July of that year a foreigner—a Frenchie, by Gad—had the audacity to fly across the Channel and land beside Dover Castle. Did the Powers That Be rush off and start creating an air force? Hardly. While the *Daily Mail* announced 'Britain no longer an Island', their lordships at the Admiralty pronounced a weighty conclusion: 'Their Lordships foresee no practical application for flying machines in Naval service', while in 1910 the Secretary of State for War announced: 'We do not consider that aeroplanes will be of any possible use for war purposes.' As for the Top Brass, try this from the Chief of the Imperial General Staff: 'We have done very well without aeroplanes so far, we can do without them today.'

Despite all this, a groundswell of public opinion forced some action to be taken, and on 4 March 1912 Col J.E.B. Seely, then Under-Secretary of State for War, announced a committee (Britain's answer to everything) to set up a Royal Flying Corps. The RFC was constituted by Royal Warrant on 13 May 1912. Today's chaps, who cost me and a few other taxpayers about £3 million each to get them as far as a front-line cockpit, may like to know how their predecessors got into the RFC. They paid for their own flying training, typically £75, and got this refunded only if they were subsequently accepted into the new corps. Anyone care to pay for an *ab initio* course to qualify on the Tornado F.3?

Great, so now we have a Royal Flying Corps. Incidentally, this was meant to be an across the board 'air force', drawing personnel from the Army and Royal Navy who would serve in a Military Wing and a Naval Wing, but of course such an idea was instantly squashed by the Admiralty, which set up the rival Royal Naval Air Service. The RNAS fairly soon began negotiating direct with such proven constructors as Short Brothers, Sopwith, and Handley Page, and even with seemingly talented young men such as Richard Fairey, with uniformly good results. The lumbering War Office, however, considered that there was virtually no British aircraft industry, apparently failing to appreciate that this was its own fault, because it had buried its head in the sand and shown not the slightest inclination to order any aircraft.

In March 1912, when the RFC was announced, Col Seely also revealed that 71 aircraft (why 71?) had been sanctioned. Nobody had the slightest idea what these might be, but the gallant colonel (and I do not blame him, he was merely the political spokesman, and thus the visible part of the decision-making process) said that only a few of these would be bought from British suppliers 'as French aeroplanes have been proved better'. Well the obvious thing to do, surely, would be to lay down the RFC's future requirements for aircraft. Perhaps it would have been too much to expect precise numerical demands, as is done today, though even this should have been possible if the preliminary discussions had involved a few people who knew a few rudimentary things about aeroplanes. At the very least the Government should have issued basic guidelines, giving an indication of the tasks and operating conditions they had in mind. A competitive fly-off should then have been held at least six months later, which would have given everyone interested a chance to build the best aircraft.

Instead the politicians started in the way they have carried on ever since, and made a real old hash of it. They did organize a big military aircraft competition. They offered an attractive first prize of £5,000. They decided to do everything properly, and get everything examined, measured, and checked. But unfortunately the whole thing was a waste of time. First, the competition was announced on 15 May 1912 and stipulated that all competing aircraft had to be ready just two months later, on 15 July. This virtually precluded any competitor designing an aircraft to meet the RFC's requirements. In any case the War Office, who ran the trials, gave not the slightest indication what these requirements might be, apart from general suggestions regarding good pilot view, dual controls, the ability to start the engine and take off without external assistance, and a need for easy maintenance. The aircraft also had to be able to be towed on its own wheels (wings removed or folded) in an army column, and to be submitted to the judges in a rail packing case not more than 32 ft long. Perhaps one could not have expected any more than this.

Forcing entrants to submit existing machines was one grave error. Another was not relaxing the ludicrous rules regarding the operations of the Royal Aircraft Factory at Farnborough. This had grown out of the long-established HM Balloon Factory, which had developed very efficiently under Col J.E. Capper. The factory was permitted to indulge in 'aeroplaning', with a view to 'creating an expert body of airmen'. This makes it sound like a mere flying training establishment, which was not its role at all. At Farnborough there swiftly grew the biggest collection of brilliant physicists, aerodynamicists, structural engineers, mathematicians, metallurgists, and test pilots anywhere in the country, and almost certainly in the world. The factory also had large and growing facilities for aircraft construction and test, but it was expressly *prohibited* from making aircraft.

The factory tried to get round this by repairing or rebuilding unsatisfactory or crashed aircraft. They began in 1911 by rebuilding a crashed Voisin which had been given to the War Office by the Duke of Westminster. The Voisin had been a typical pusher looking like a Wright Flyer. After 'repair' it was a modern tractor machine, the B.E.1. B.E. stood for Blériot experimental, but this just meant that the propeller was at the front. Apart from having the same 60 hp Wolseley engine, the only thing it had in common with the Voisin was the joystick. Later this was changed, and the engine was replaced by a 60 hp Renault. It reminds me of the execution axe on display in the Tower of London, which had had three new heads and four new handles but was otherwise absolutely the true original.

The B.E.1 was designed by Geoffrey de Havilland and F.M. Green. Maj Green later designed the Armstrong Siddeley Jaguar and other famous engines, while the initials 'D.H.' need no introduction. From the B.E.1 they produced various slightly improved aircraft called B.E.2s, all slightly different and all created by the permitted process of repairing or modifying existing machines, and nobody seemed to mind if the modification resulted in replacement of all the parts! But officially, of course, the factory did not make aeroplanes, and so it could not take part in the military trials.

Altogether 25 aircraft took part, eight of them French. Competitors roared and clattered aloft—or, often, failed to—and demonstrated climbing ability, speed, duration, load-carrying, and their ability to take off from a ploughed field and land back on it. They were also required to demonstrate flight in a 25 mph wind, but every flight took off in different weather conditions, and while some unfortunates had to fly in winds of over 30 mph (or declined to) some were never able to find the required wind at all.

It was soon obvious that the famed S.F. Cody, the American who had been flying at Laffan's Plain (Farnborough) since 1907, was pulling further ahead with every test. In the end he was declared the outright winner, and received the cheque for £5,000. This was partly because of his experience as a pilot, but also because of his engine. He swore by his Austro-Daimler, a water-cooled six-in-line designed by Dr Ferdinand Porsche and the prototype for numerous German engines of World War One. While the engines of almost all rivals gave hesitant and erratic powers in the bracket 30 to 80 hp, the Austro-Daimler gave a steady and reliable 120 hp. As a result Cody won, as everyone thought he would. And the irony of it all is that this fine engine was bolted to a vast and ungainly contraption called *Cody's Cathedral*, which was strictly in the style of the ancient pushers of the Wrights and Voisins. By 1912 it was totally outdated, and Cody himself admitted that it was ridiculous to consider it as a standard type for the future RFC.

And, all the time, the factory-built B.E.2, which won the highest marks in almost every section, was of necessity flown *hors concours* by Geoffrey de Havilland because no factory machine could be officially entered. In the end, of course, the RFC adopted the B.E.2 and its successors, and instantly forgot all about the archaic *Cathedral*. But the famous 1912 military trials did have the excellent effect of teaching pilots and manufacturers that aircraft performance should actually be measured, using such things as barographs and stopwatches, and that climbing and gliding could even be recorded photographically against a ruled grid of horizontal and vertical lines. But all these clever techniques were worked out by

Farnborough, which wasn't allowed to take part.

Certainly 1912 was the year that the Establishment in Britain suddenly took notice of aeroplanes, but not a lot happened. The following, dating from some time in 1914, is related by J.D. North, who served the industry for nearly 60 years, many of them as leader of Boulton Paul: 'Joynson Hicks had challenged War Secretary Seely to tell the House of Commons how many aeroplanes the Army had; I think the figure given was 112. Joynson Hicks disputed this, and insisted on counting them. Within a few days the Government purchased any reasonable aeroplane they could get their hands on in order to make up the quantity. It was rumoured that some were given new numbers and new paint so that they could be counted twice.'

7

26 August 1914

Death of the Aces I

Few subjects in aviation are so hedged about with uncertainty and argument as that of aces. Here we are unconcerned about their scores, but take note of the fact that a very high proportion of the most famous suffered mysterious deaths, or at least unconventional ones.

Our first choice hardly had time to become an ace. Lt P.N. Nesterov, of the Tsarist Russian army, must have been the very personification of the dashing young officer, of the type that used to act first and then didn't think afterwards. He already had a reputation for daring when, on 20 August 1913 (some accounts give the date as the 27th), he took off in a Nieuport and performed a loop. This is generally regarded as the first deliberate aerobatic manoeuvre in history. For his pains, he was placed under arrest, for 'risking government property in useless audacity'. Less than a year later his country was at war, and on 26 August 1914 Nesterov's airfield at Sholkiv, Galicia, was strafed by an Austrian two-seater. Unhesitatingly, Nesterov rushed to an unarmed Morane-Saulnier Type M and rammed the enemy. Nesterov and Lt Baron von Rosenthal were killed.

Max Immelmann was a bird of a totally different feather, though no less lacking in courage. As a Prussian officer he had an iron sense of discipline, though that did not preclude reasoned experiment. Immelmann shared with Boelcke the very pioneering of air fighting, being the first to use the Fokker Eindecker in combat and the first to use multiple forward-firing guns. His name is preserved for all time in the half-loop half-roll species of turn, and in the reflection of the blue enamel of the Pour le Mérite decoration on his pale neck and chin that led to the award itself being called 'The Blue Max'. On 18 June 1916 he was engaging RFC FE.2b two-seaters over Douai when he suddenly veered away. Corporal Waller, gunner of an FE of 25 Squadron, was firing at Immelmann and, as the Eindecker broke up in its dive and crashed, he was credited with the kill. At first it seemed obvious that 'The Eagle of Lille' had been shot, but there were no bullet wounds in his body. To this day, nobody knows what happened. One theory is that Immelmann's synchronization gear failed, so that he shot off his propeller, but there is no evidence of bullet holes along the shattered edges of the blades.

The other great pioneer of air fighting, Oswald Boelcke, undoubtedly did more to lay down the basic principles of aerial combat than any other individual. His amazing prowess is best shown by the fact that on 28 October 1916, when practical air combat was little over a year old, his score stood at 40. On that day he was killed because of a quite minor mid-air collision with his wing-man.

Another of the very greatest aces was Albert Ball, from Nottingham. He shot down 'Huns' at a seemingly fantastic rate, until, on 7 May 1917, at the age of 20, he failed to return from a patrol. His body was found by the Germans, who gave him a full military funeral, but to this day nobody knows what happened. No SE.5a was claimed by the enemy in the area. Did he simply fall out of his aircraft during combat?

The most famous, and second most successful, of all France's aces was Georges Guynemer. He racked up a score of 54 despite being chivalrous; on one occasion he realized that his foe's guns had jammed and, instead of shooting him down, gave him a cheery goodbye wave, allowing Udet (see last entry in this story) to live on. On 11 September 1917 he entered a cloud with his wing-man, but the latter emerged alone. From that moment on, no trace of Guynemer has ever been found. Nobody claimed to have shot him down, though a week later, when his absence had been published, the Germans issued a statement to the effect that he had been shot down by a Lt Wissemann (who was embarrassed and refused to be interviewed) and that British shelling had eliminated all evidence. Common sense suggests that Guynemer would have held his course in the cloud and emerged near his partner. No enemy aircraft was seen in the vicinity.

Top-scorer of all the British aces was Edward 'Mick' Mannock. He shot down his first enemy on the day his idol, Albert Ball, was killed. From then on he showed himself not only a dangerous fighter pilot but also a born leader. He became famed for always giving credit for a shared victory to one of his juniors, but despite this by 26 July 1918 his score had reached 73. On that day his SE.5a caught fire at low level and went straight into the ground. It is possible the fire was caused by shots from the ground, but what actually happened remains a mystery.

By far the most famous, and top-scoring, Russian ace was Aleksandr Kazakov. He first gained notoriety at the start of the war by equipping his Morane with a grappling hook! He fought hard until the Revolution, managed to escape being shot, despite being an officer, and then joined the White Russian forces. In the bitter civil war he was given command of a British unit and fought successfully until, on 28 July 1919, he was told that Britain had decided to withdraw its forces. For the next few days Kazakov appeared upset and morbid. Then he clearly came to a decision as to what he would do. He took a Camel out, got it started and (without waiting for the engine to warm up, as would have been proper) took straight off. He held the Camel down to gain speed and then pulled straight up into a vertical climb. Speed bled off to a stall; the Camel then plummeted vertically down into the middle of the airfield, as he clearly intended.

Another ace who hated the situation in which he found himself after the war was Rudolf Berthold. Already a pilot when war broke out, Berthold became known as the Iron Knight, because of his incredible fortitude in going on fighting for nearly a year despite the intense pain of a shattered and suppurating right arm. After the war, his score at 44, he was appalled at the Communist revolts throughout Germany. On 15 March 1920 he was set upon by Communists, beaten, kicked, strangled with his Pour le Mérite ribbon, and finished off with seven bullets in the back.

France's third-highest scorer was Charles Nungesser. As a youth he went to

Argentina, asked permission to fly an aircraft and, when this provoked laughter, calmly climbed into the aircraft, flew it and brought it back in one piece. On the Western Front he suffered an amazing series of injuries, in crashes and in combat, but somehow survived the war with his score at 45. On 8 May 1927 he set out to fly from France to North America, in a Levasseur PL 8 with special long-range tanks. The aircraft vanished without trace.

W.G. 'Billy' Barker gained nearly 50 of his victories in just one of his aircraft, Camel B6313 (stupidly, it was scrapped after the war). He also gained many decorations, including the VC for his incredible last fight in which, fighting single-handed in a Snipe, he attacked a two-seater only to be set upon by about 15 Fokker D.VIIs; though gravely wounded and at least twice falling unconscious he shot down the two-seater and three of the fighters. On 12 March 1930, back in his native Canada, he was testing a new Fairchild at Rockcliffe. Climbing away, engine power faded; it was surmised that the throttle lever closed and that Barker's crippled left elbow prevented him from grabbing it in time. The Fairchild stalled and dived into the Ottawa River, Barker being killed by the impact.

Second-highest scorer on the German side, with 60 confirmed victories, was Ernst Udet. A brilliant and flamboyant pilot, he was, next to Lindbergh, perhaps the world's most famous pilot between the wars. In 1936 he became the Luftwaffe's Inspector of Fighters and Dive Bombers, then the head of the all-powerful Technical Office, and in 1939 Director-General of Equipment. He hated bureaucratic office work, and when this was compounded by being made the scapegoat for deficiencies in both output and aircraft types Udet became depressed and shot himself on 17 November 1941.

Of course, another World War One ace, Hermann Goering, was convicted as a Nazi war criminal. Alone among the defendants at Nuremberg, he never cringed, apologized, blamed Hitler or said he merely obeyed orders. He escaped hanging by taking poison (nobody found out how he got it) in his cell on the night of 15 October 1946.

8

January 1918

Cancel the Others . . .

One of the oft-told stories of World War One is how, in 1917, the British took the momentous decision to base most of their airpower on an engine that proved to be one of the most complete failures in history. I have repeated it here only to draw attention to the surely obvious fact that a vital engine, or any other item of hardware, should not be made virtually standard for a nation's war effort, and put into production on a colossal scale, without first finding out whether or not it worked.

Granville Bradshaw, chief designer of ABC Motors, might fairly be described as a better salesman than engineer. In the early part of World War One he produced several aero engines, one of which, the Wasp 7-cylinder radial of 1917, gave a reliable 170 (later 200) horsepower for a dry weight of 290 lb. This excellent performance made persuasive Bradshaw very important in the eyes of the Air Board, and in particular Sir William (later Lord) Weir, Director of Aeronautical Supplies. In April 1917 Bradshaw was invited to submit one or more engine designs for the 1918 aircraft production programme, and he very quickly came up with drawings and a brochure describing a bigger 9-cylinder radial, the Dragonfly.

The Dragonfly looked like everything an aero engine should be. Air cooled (with copper plating on the steel cooling fins), it seemed to be a model of simple design, and Bradshaw carefully explained how every detail had been planned for easy mass-production. The dry weight was estimated at 600 lb and the maximum power at 340 hp.

At this time British engine supplies were in a state of crisis, which grew to the extent that in January 1918 over 400 SE.5a fighters were waiting for engines, while hundreds of others had French-built Hispano-Suiza engines whose reduction gears were unevenly heat-treated and known to be dangerously unreliable (the official view was that dangerous engines were 'better than none at all'). Imagine the delight when clever Mr Bradshaw arrived with drawings for a brilliant new engine which looked like the solution to all the problems. In August 1917, ABC Motors was given an order for three Dragonflies, and in October the Air Board decided to place an initial contract for 1,000 Dragonflies with Vickers at Crayford. The Air Board was mindful of the fact that the principal cause of the engine crisis had been massive reliance on an untried engine, the Sunbeam Arab V-8 of 200 hp, which proved to suffer from a weak crankcase, faulty cylinder attachment, and severe vibration, which took many months to cure. Accordingly, it did not cancel existing contracts for such engines as the 200 hp Bentley BR.2 rotary.

I have never managed to discover when the Dragonfly first ran, but it was in or close to October 1917. Bradshaw must have given away very little about the results, because in January 1918, and against the advice of his technical staff, Sir William Weir decided to make the Dragonfly virtually the standard engine for all future fighters and bombers. The Nieuport Nighthawk, selected as the standard single-seat fighter, was designed around the Dragonfly, and so were a growing number of other vitally important aircraft. It was planned to phase out production of all other engines except the Rolls-Royce Eagle (made in relatively small numbers) and Siddeley Puma. Orders for the Dragonfly were placed with Vickers (1,000), Beardmore (1,500), Crossley (1,000), Ransome Sims & Jeffries (500), F.W. Berwick (1,000), Belsize Motors (1,000), Maudslay (500), Vulcan (600), Sheffield Simplex (500), Guy (600), Clyno (500), Ruston Proctor (1,500), and Humber (850).

Some programme! These companies tooled-up with all speed, and manufacture of the Dragonfly got going on a vast scale. It is at this point that published accounts say something like: 'After the engine was in full production it was discovered that it was a major disaster.' For a start, it weighed not 600 but 656 lb. It did not give 340 hp but a maximum of 315 hp when overspeeded to 1,800 rpm; at the rated speed of 1,650 rpm (at which 340 hp was promised) the actual power was 295 hp. Much worse than this was that the mechanical design could hardly have been worse. Even running at partial power most of the upper parts of the cylinders glowed dull red. S.D. Heron said the Dragonfly had 'probably the worst example of air cooling ever used on a production aircraft engine'. Even more fundamental was the fact that vibration was appalling, and after only an hour or two in the air engines literally began to break up. Frantic measures were taken to remedy the deficiencies. New pistons were substituted, and then completely new cylinder heads were fitted at Farnborough to the designs of Gibson and Heron. But little could be done about the fact that, by sheer chance, Bradshaw had designed the Dragonfly to run at the critical torsional-vibration frequency of the crankshaft. Little was then known about this mode of vibration, but the results were all too obvious. The crankshafts swiftly broke, but not before the wooden propeller hub had been charred or even ignited by the heat from the friction. The cure would have been to redesign the engine completely.

Of course the vast production programme just fell apart, with over 1,300 engines completed. By amazing good fortune, Britain was spared a second and much worse engine crisis by the fact that the war ended on 11 November 1918. But the point to be made is: all these faults were present on the very first Dragonfly. The AID (Aeronautical Inspection Directorate) had inspectors in the factories. The government had its own test pilots and engine experts whose job it was to test things and find out the answers. The one good result was that it spurred Major B.C. Carter at Farnborough to undertake valuable research into torsional vibration.

9

5 August 1918

'They Taught Us to Navigate . . .'

This little tale will appeal to every pilot, most of whom will think 'it doesn't usually work like this'. So cast your minds back to the days when instruments were primitive and inaccurate and there were absolutely no electronic aids to navigation.

In Europe, at least, aviation buffs and even students of World War One often know very little about the big part played in the final months of the war by the embryonic US Naval Aviation. Its aircrews had their beginning in a nucleus of Yale undergraduates, but very soon pilots and other crewmen were being trained by the thousand. Plans were rushed ahead for the US Navy to fly from bases in many parts of Europe, notably around the coasts of France and England. Equally large-scale efforts went into producing aircraft, though large numbers of European machines were also used, especially at first. Some were land-based bombers, while others were flying boats whose chief mission was to find and destroy U-boats.

In June 1918 a tall Texan, Ensign Ashton W. Hawkins, who had been a member of the first Yale unit, reported for duty to Cdr Kenneth Whiting, CO of NAS Killingholme, on the south shore of the Humber estuary in Lincolnshire. Tex Hawkins was credited by Admiral Sims with having done more war flying than any other pilot operating from USN bases round the North Sea. It was to stand him in good stead.

On 5 August he was assigned to hunt for a Zeppelin reported to be heading towards Killingholme. It was a wild night, with a tempest of wind and rain, but he collected another man from the first Yale unit, Lt jg G. Francklyn Lawrence, as co-pilot/navigator, together with a radio man and a machinist's mate. It was midnight by the time they were able to take off in the big Curtiss H-16 flying boat. Tex flew by the proverbial 'seat of his pants' through cloud and severe turbulence, the H-16 thundering and creaking all around him, until they finally emerged into the clear night air close to the ceiling at 10,000 ft (the published service ceiling was 9,950). There was no moon, but suddenly they noticed a reddish speck near the cloud horizon. It could be the exhausts from a Zeppelin, and they headed towards it with the two Liberty engines at maximum continuous power. After 30 minutes both pilots agreed they were trying to reach Mars.

After several more hours of aimless searching they were getting low on fuel.

Dawn was breaking, and there would be no chance of a Zep. Tex dived the H-16 back into the turbulent clouds. England lay somewhere to the West, but they did not have the slightest idea of their position. By now the cloud went down to the sea, and it was only by careful altimeter reading that they managed to level off just above the wavetops, still in thick fog. The situation was frightening. Suddenly they almost rammed a trawler. They avoided it, and then passed close beside a second. Altogether they encountered seven trawlers in line ahead. Instinctively, Tex had altered course to head directly for wherever the trawlers might have come from. Cautiously, he reduced power. Suddenly a breakwater loomed up in front. Tex lifted the big boat over it and put it down on the smooth water of a harbour. He taxied forward until he found the H-16 running up a seaplane ramp. Willing hands hauled the boat on to the concrete apron. Beyond, through the fog, Tex could just see a huge hangar. The amazed British duty officer asked 'However did you find this place in such weather?' Tex drawled: 'They taught us to navigate in the United States!' They were, in fact, at RNAS South Shields, 80 miles from Killingholme, the only seaplane base for dozens of miles in either direction, and the only place where they could have landed without being dashed against rocky cliffs.

10

4 April 1922

Head-on

The great Sir George Cayley, 'father of the aeroplane', described our wonderful atmosphere as 'an uninterrupted navigable ocean, that comes to the threshold of every man's door'. It is a 3-D ocean; unlike ships and land vehicles, aircraft can avoid each other by going up and down, as well as by altering course to left or right. It seems to me, therefore, that it is not a very impressive record for us to have had so many head-on collisions. I am of course unable to make an exhaustive list, but it was not difficult to find 42 near head-ons that involved commercial transport aircraft. If one adds military aircraft and general aviation the number is certainly in the thousands.

To a very large degree the problem is that we have completely failed to navigate the great ocean sensibly. In pioneer days there was so little traffic there was no serious problem, though there were several collisions over or very near aerodromes. Dogfights in World War One must have resulted in hundreds of collisions. Then in 1919 peace reigned, in Western Europe at least, and a handful of airliners began plying a very small number of air routes. There were so few aircraft that there were very few rules. Pilots could select their own cruising height, usually between 1,000 and 3,000 ft, and reach their destination by any route. They usually favoured known routes passing over fields which looked good for a forced landing. They generally navigated by map reading, following major roads, railways, and towns.

On 2 April 1922 Daimler Hire opened a service between London's Waddon Airport at Croydon and Paris. Its temporary equipment was a D.H.18A, registered G-EAWO. It looked beautiful with new white wings and a fuselage painted bright Daimler red. On 4 April it took off for Paris. One airliner was expected in the reverse direction: Farman Goliath F-GEAD. With nothing else in the sky, they collided head-on.

Visibility had been bad, and both pilots had been intently following the N1 road from Paris to Calais (today this stretch of road is called D901). Daimler pilot R.E. Duke naturally kept to the left, while the French pilot kept to the right. By sheer chance they both picked precisely the same height, despite the fact that one thought in feet and the other in metres. All aboard were killed, and the aircraft burned out on the ground, between Poix and Grandvilliers.

This woke a few people up to the fact that there ought to be tighter Rules of the Air, and additional rules, almost all very necessary, have been added ever since. Today most of the busiest parts of the sky, in all parts of the world, are covered by 3-D radar surveillance, and all traffic is kept separate by controllers who can see impending conflicts. Despite this, there have been plenty of collisions in controlled airspace (several of them head-on), the most tragically inexcusable example being on 10 September 1976 when BEA Trident 3 G-AWZT met Inex Adria DC-9-32 YU-AJR head-on in controlled airspace at 33,000 ft near Zagreb, Yugoslavia. I am cautious about using the word 'obviously' (ever since my maths professor said it instantly made him suspicious), but surely it can be used in the statement that such an event should *never* happen?

Many people, not least airline captains, have commented on the fact that, entirely because of American political pressure, we have taken Cayley's 'uninterrupted navigable ocean' and carved it up into very narrow overcrowded streets along which most of the world's air traffic travels. The rot began to set in with the invention of the Radio Range in the 1920s, which covered most of North America and a few other places by 1940. This led naturally to VOR, which in 1958–9 was bulldozed through a conference at Montreal as the world standard navaid. Ever since, we have been suffering the consequences. The amazing thing is that we have made this highly flawed system work, and most mid-air collisions have not been because of it.

11

9 May 1923

What Were They For?

Today not many official (ie government funded) flying machines can get off the ground within about 10 to 15 years of the requirement for it being agreed. Over 60 years ago things moved faster; 15 weeks might have been nearer the norm. Moreover, though the inter-war period was marked by exceedingly tight budgets for such things as taxpayer-financed aeroplanes, there seems to have been a marked propensity to pay for strange aircraft that served no particular purpose. At one time I compiled a list of 145 types or variants of British aircraft funded by the taxpayer in the period 1920–40 which appeared to serve no useful purpose and accomplished nothing.

If we take just the year 1923 as an example, when funding had for years been very tight indeed, seven types made their first flights in that year whose purpose seems hard to justify. The biggest was the first Fairey N.4 flying boat, named *Atalanta*. When it was flown on 4 July 1923 it was in some respects the largest aeroplane in the world. Two years later a second N.4 was flown, by which time it was realized that 'no requirement existed for such aircraft'. Admittedly, they had been ordered during the war by the Royal Naval Air Service, which in 1918 had been absorbed into the RAF; but that had little bearing on the matter. Having paid for two gigantic flying boats, they might have been put to some use, had a use existed. As it was, the first was dismantled, the second was simply stored for four years, and a third hull was used for 'flotation tests' (whatever that means).

Can you imagine a more exciting name than 'the Westland Dreadnought Postal Monoplane'? Of course, such a machine had to be secret, and secret it was. Only a select team helped build it at the Yeovil factory, to the secret plans of the mysterious Russian refugee, Woyevodski (or Voyevodsky). At a time when most aircraft were fabric-skinned biplanes festooned in struts and wires, the 'postal monoplane' was a strange creation with a tough skin of metal. In fact it was simply seen by the Air Ministry as a possible way of bringing Britain up to date with cantilever monoplanes with corrugated metal skin, without going to the pioneer of such aircraft, Hugo Junkers. In addition, Woyevodski (like Junkers) believed in the all-wing configuration, or at least in a fuselage that merged into a thick wing braced internally. He almost got an earlier version built by Airco at Hendon in 1918.

As actually built by Westland, the monoplane had fabric covering on the outer wings and rear fuselage. It seemed enormous in comparison with the single Napier Lion engine, but on 9 May 1923 Capt A.S. Keep made the first takeoff. Just a few seconds into the flight the Dreadnought appeared to stall, fell off on the right wing and crashed. Poor Keep, who lost both legs, tended to be blamed (in my opinion, without justification). As far as Westland were concerned the disaster prompted them to get a wind tunnel. As for the Air Ministry, I cannot believe they learned anything new about either metal structures or blended wing/body aerodynamics. The name was surely just a cover: who was going to use this underpowered research aircraft to carry mailbags? As a final thought, I believe a major factor in the crash was the wing section, the leading edge of which comprised a big generous curve down to a sharp edge along the junction with the undersurface. This is a pronounced characteristic of today's stealthy Northrop B-2. In fact, a lot about Woyevodski's design had stealth qualities.

Just a month after the demise of the Dreadnought, the Parnall Possum made one of its few (I think six) flights. Designer Harold Bolas loved unconventional features, and the Possum just seemed like a way to spend money, and a way to make a reliable engine unreliable. It looked rather like a triplane bomber, with three sets of wings and three seats—but no apparent engine. The 450 hp Napier Lion was in the fuselage, driving tractor propellers on the middle wings by means of shafting and three sets of bevel gears. These drives predictably proved dangerous; the first Possum stayed mainly on the ground, and No 2 never flew at all. But what was it all for? The idea of a fuselage engine driving wing-mounted propellers had been almost done to death years earlier. How was the Possum described on the Air Ministry contract? Would you believe, as a Postal Aircraft?

A few years later, in 1927, the Air Ministry decided to buy an aeroplane 'to study methods by which range increases could be obtained by all practical means'. It was better known as the 'Fairey long-range monoplane', and one cannot help wondering at the mentality of designers (and customers) who talked of 'all practical means' and then left a huge landing gear from a high wing completely out in the slipstream. Like the Possum it was powered by a Lion, and—perhaps you guessed it—quoting H.A. 'Tony' Taylor's Putnam book on Fairey aircraft, 'to placate the Treasury and Parliament' it was known as the Fairey Postal Aircraft. I wonder if anyone in the Treasury ever checked up to see how much mail was actually being carried by Britain's armadas of 'postal' machines?

One machine so huge it could hardly be called a 'postal monoplane' was the Beardmore Inflexible. This was schemed in 1923 by German Adolf Rohrbach, pioneer of stressed-skin construction. He then fell out with the British constructor, William Beardmore & Co, so that the latter had to do protracted testing and get their W.S. (Bill) Shackleton to do most of the design. As a result this angular beast did not fly until 5 March 1928. It proved free from any vice, but was badly under-powered. It did a fair amount of rather pointless flying, some of it with Sir Alan Cobham's private circus which toured Britain fostering airmindedness. In 1930 the Inflexible was dismantled and some parts used for strength testing and research into atmospheric corrosion. The Inflexible, with a span half as big again as a Lanc or B-17, was probably the most expensive single aircraft built in Britain up to the 1930s. If it was to show that stressed-skin construction worked, why did we continue to build only fabric-covered aircraft?

The British seem to have been consistently good at voting large sums in order to build aircraft to prove that an idea works. Then, having proved that the idea works, forget all about it. One example was the Short-Mayo Composite aircraft of 1937, which did everything it was supposed to do in showing that you could launch an overloaded seaplane from a lightly loaded carrier flying boat. Another was a series of Hillson Bi-Mono aircraft during World War Two which showed that you can take off as a biplane and jettison the upper wing. Why did we do all this if we never intended to use the idea?

12

July 1927

Lateral Control

Earlier, I rather belaboured the point that most of the early would-be aviators not only did not solve the problem of lateral control but appeared never to think about it at all. There is nothing like getting up in the sky for 'concentrating the mind wonderfully'. Once Otto Lilienthal got his feet well off the ground, in 1891, he found he had to learn about control in both pitch and roll, and learn fast. That great German was the first pilot. We all owe him a big debt, even though most of his piloting was done with the crudest of methods: shifting the body relative to the aircraft in order to vary the position of the CG (centre of gravity).

The Wrights, being methodical chaps, addressed the problem of control about all three axes. Thanks to prior testing with gliders, their very first powered Flyer, in 1903, had provision for direct pilot control of pitch, yaw, and roll. It was the first flying machine in history to be thus positively controllable, the only criticism from today's viewpoint being the difficult nature of the pilot input; the pilot lay on a cradle and had to move his hips left or right to apply roll control by warping the wings. Later the Wrights replaced this method by using two control columns, one for pitch and the other for roll, and replaced warping by fitting hinged ailerons.

Ailerons were invented by the Wrights and patented by them. At first they were commonly mounted between the upper and lower wings, pivoted between pairs of the outer interplane struts. By about 1911 it was becoming normal practice to incorporate ailerons as hinged portions of the outer trailing edge of the wing, and this is the way we have provided lateral control in probably more than 98 per cent of the two million or so aeroplanes and gliders built since.

Of course, there have been many refinements to the idea of a simple hinged aileron. One of the first, named for the originator, Leslie Frise of Bristol (Chief Designer from 1938), provided a solution to the problem of asymmetric aileron drag. With simple ailerons the drag of the downgoing aileron is appreciably greater than that of the upgoing surface, which is the opposite of what we want. Frise put the hinge well back from the leading edge so that the nose of the downgoing aileron projected into the slipstream balancing out the drag or even pulling back the downgoing wing (which is what we *do* want). Another simple scheme is differential ailerons; the downgoing aileron moves through a small angle and the upgoing aileron through a much larger one.

Of course, ailerons roll the aircraft by applying upward and downward forces near the wingtips. As these forces are applied near the trailing edge they also inevitably twist the wing, and they twist the wing in the opposite sense to the one we want. Put another way, they tend to warp the wings when we want them to be stiff. Even before World War One it was not uncommon for pilots to notice that their ailerons were twisting the wing, and occasionally the wing's torsional stiffness was so poor that something had to be done about it, usually by adding tight internal or external bracing wires. As might be expected, this problem was seldom encountered except on monoplanes.

Beyond doubt, lateral control was a real problem in many early aeroplanes, and in very large ones the problems were seldom fully solved. The result was that, with the giant bombers and flying boats designed prior to the 1930s, you could have got a reasonable rate of roll if you were either the strongest man in the world or else had three or four other pilots to help! Today's technology of powered flight controls did not exist, so various ideas were tried out to put more power into the huge ailerons. Major Arthur 'Queenie' Cooper, at Felixstowe, patented an interesting scheme powered by a slipstream-driven windmill. When the tension in the aileron control wires exceeded a certain value (near the limit that a pilot could be expected to apply) the windmill power was engaged via a sprocket and chains. This scheme, called a servo motor system, was never really satisfactory. Later ailerons were improved out of all recognition, with various forms of aerodynamic balance and either 'park bench' auxiliary surfaces or trailing servo tabs to make the slipstream assist the pilot's input. Neverthless, really satisfactory roll control was seldom achieved before about 1935, and even then the achievable rate of roll on some of the most important fighters was totally inadequate when diving at high speed.

As related in Story 5, Britain built few monoplanes prior to 1935, but two were built in the 1920s at Bristol and both suffered from completely insufficient wing torsional stiffness. The first was the Type 72 Racer, a stumpy (and in my opinion incorrectly shaped) little beast, built around a Jupiter engine in 1922. Test pilot Cyril Uwins found lateral control was reversed! He managed a quick glance sideways and saw that the full-span ailerons were twisting the stubby wings. He told the present author: 'I was never so scared in my life. I knew the Racer would be a hot little bus, but never expected complete reversal of lateral control.' Accordingly, the wings were braced by wires, attached just ahead of the ailerons. Later still a special cam linkage was added to increase aileron gear ratio as stick deflection increased—in other words, to give very small aileron deflection for small pilot inputs, but progressively larger deflection as stick angle increased. This worked on the ground, but in flight the linkage distorted out of contact and ceased to function, so Uwins again made a hairy circuit with no lateral control.

After all this, one might have expected the Bristol designers to get it right, but Uwins had to suffer similar problems with the much bigger and more sedate Type 95 Bagshot. This was a rather pedestrian fighter—intended mainly for shooting down even slower bombers at night—powered by two Jupiters. The crew comprised a pilot and two gunners each with a 37-mm COW gun. On the first flight, on 15 July 1927, everything seemed satisfactory. On the second, a few days later, Uwins tried a run at full throttle. As speed climbed above about 120 mph violent aileron reversal was encountered. It was obvious that the designers had contrived to build a wing with almost zero torsional stiffness. Lateral control returned as speed bled off, so

Uwins had no difficulty in getting back in one piece, but it eliminated the Bagshot as a practical fighter. What to do? I'm afraid, when I talked with Uwins about it he had become Bristol Aircraft's Chairman, so he didn't appreciate my facetious suggestion: 'Why not just swap over the control wires?' What actually happened is that Chief Designer Barnwell (him again, Story 18) came to the conclusion that the only solution was to redesign the Bagshot as a biplane (I did say we were better at biplanes!)

The Air Ministry got Bristol to keep the Bagshot in solitary state in a special hangar while they played with the wing, loading it in various ways and then trying to strengthen the structure to improve its ability to resist twisting. After all, it seemed quite important to be able to make a monoplane wing, even if we didn't actually make any monoplanes. In the end all this work led to quite ludicrous answers, so that Bristol's next monoplane wing, for the Type 130 Bombay, was a stressed-skin structure with *seven* spars!

Once designers had learned how to design stressed-skin structures severe torsional instability was seldom encountered, though some designers pushed their luck. Reginald Mitchell designed the Spitfire with a wing that was very thin by the standards of the day, and yet had almost all its torsional stiffness provided by the heavy D-nose section ahead of the main spar at 25 per cent chord (one-quarter of the way back from the leading edge). In fact this wing did not suffer from severe torsional flexure, but lateral control in early Spitfires was poor above 300 mph and almost non-existent at 400 mph, which could easily be reached in steep dives. Test pilot Jeffrey Quill blamed himself for 'not having made more of a song and dance about this before the war'. When he joined RAF No 65 Squadron to get combat experience during the Battle of Britain the importance of good lateral control was thumped home to him several times a day. As a result by 1941 Spits had metal-skinned ailerons, which made things a lot better. Laborious development eventually led to the Spitfire 21, with a totally new wing, with thicker skins, modified structure and redesigned long-span ailerons, which gave absolutely superb lateral control just as the Spit was about to be replaced by jets.

The tremendous expansion in flight envelope that jet propulsion made possible often caused problems with lateral control. Chuck Yeager would say that roll control on the original Bell XS-1 was not exactly brilliant above Mach 1, though this was mainly not because of wing flexure. When North American Aviation came to design the F-100 Super Sabre they were so afraid of aileron reversal with such a thin wing (7 per cent) that they chickened out and put the ailerons inboard. This meant that there could not be any flaps, so even with full-span slats the low-speed properties of this wing were unimpressive. Someone, I believe from the 20th TFW, said that each landing by an F-100 was 'a controlled crash'. Five years into the programme, in 1955, NAA rolled out the first F-100D, which at last moved the ailerons some way towards the tips to make room for little flaps. Today thin wings are less of a problem.

Gradually over the past 30 years lateral control systems have diversified in a way that designers in World War Two never suspected. Today we have the choice of ailerons, elevons, tailerons (or ailevators), spoilers, and even a few other odd methods. One of the first of the odd methods was seen on the North American YA3J-1, predecessor of the RA-5C Vigilante, first flown on 31 August 1958. This brought wing thickness down to a challenging 3.5 per cent. It had no ailerons, roll

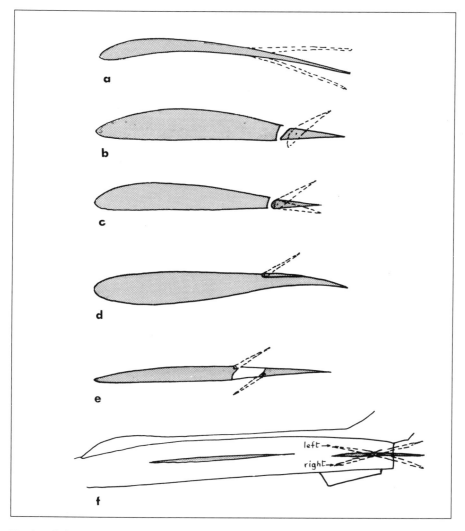

Freehand sketches by the author: (a) warping; (b) Frise ailerons; (c) differential ailerons; (d) spoilers (on a modern supercritical wing); (e) Vigilante; (f) tailerons (angular movement exaggerated).

control being by means of three sections of most odd spoilers in each wing. Each outer section comprised a spoiler hinged in the normal way but underneath the wing, and a deflector hinged at its trailing edge above the wing. The upper and lower surfaces were so arranged that, when they were open, there was a huge duct right through the wing from above to below. In contrast, the middle and inboard sections were the other way round, the deflector being in the underside and the spoiler being on top, to form a duct taking air from below the wing to above. To roll the aircraft, the outer unit would open on one side and the middle and inboard units on the other side. It sounds complex and it was, besides filling a lot of the wing with high-speed air instead of fuel. What was even stranger was that the Vigilante had huge slab tailplanes which, as well as serving as the primary control in pitch, could also be driven in opposition to apply a rolling moment. But these tailplanes were used for roll *trimming* only. I never did prise out of NAA the reason why they did not use the tails as the primary roll control, eliminating the mass of trickery in the wings.

Today tailerons are fast becoming the preferred method of roll control, especially on fighters. Also called by the much less attractive name of ailevators, and even as 'rolling tailplanes', these are one-piece 'slab' horizontal tails capable of being driven by power units either in exact unison, to control the aircraft in pitch as elevators, or differentially in opposition, to control the aircraft in roll. In combat their movements are complex, because pitch and roll demands occur simultaneously. They have numerous good features, not least being the fact that they do away with the problems of lateral control imparted through the wings. If the tailerons roll the back end of the aircraft there is every chance the rest will follow, and without any problems of torsional flexure.

Even with tailerons there is plenty of scope for interesting answers. The SEPECAT Jaguar supersonic attack aircraft uses inboard upper-surface spoilers as the primary lateral control, supplemented at low speeds by tailerons. The Panavia Tornado, also a supersonic attack aircraft, works exactly the other way round. The tailerons are at all times the primary roll control; but at low speeds, with the wings spread, they are supplemented by upper-surface wing spoilers. Early Airbus A300Bs had conventional ailerons, but today's A300-600 and A310 use only a small 'all-speed' aileron between the flap sections to augment the primary roll control surfaces which are electrically signalled spoilers. Surprisingly, the A320, 330, and 340 have traditional ailerons, as well as a row of spoilers. So far nobody has put a taileron on a widebody, which would seem a good idea.

We shall have to see in due course how far future fighters will use their canard foreplanes for roll control. Meanwhile, having been spellbound by Evgenye Frolov's display in the Su-27A at Paris in 1989, I was intrigued to see that it had the most powerful pair of tailerons in the business, but absolutely no ailerons.

The arrow indicates the conventional outboard aileron of the Airbus A300B, not fitted to today's A300-600.

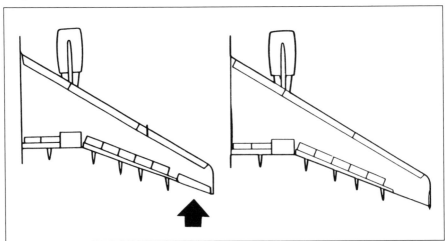

13

25 May 1928

Lost in the Arctic

In the mid-1920s courageous aviators were turning their eyes towards the North Pole, and several reached it, by aeroplane and by airship. The first airship to do so was the *Norge*, thus named because the commander of the expedition was the famous Norwegian, Roald Amundsen. The commander of the airship was its designer, the Italian Col Umberto Nobile.

Sadly, these two brave and experienced leaders then quarrelled bitterly for two years (1926-8), partly because of a clash of personalities but mainly because of childish fighting over who did what, and who should get the limelight. Nobile became No 1 public hero in his own country, but this made him very unpopular with Mussolini, the Italian dictator, who permitted only one person to be adulated in Italy. So when Nobile announced he wished to organize an all-Italian airship expedition to the Pole, the Fascist dictator, fearing how even more popular Nobile might become afterwards, curtly refused to help. But the people of Milan put up the money, and in March 1928 Nobile's excellent airship *Italia* made its maiden flight. She duly left for the Pole, reaching it on 24 May. But on the following day something catastrophic happened. It was as if all the gas had gone from the bags towards the rear. Weather was (at last) good, and the crew were in high spirits, and there has never been the slightest explanation of what happened. At first the symptom was merely stern-heaviness, but soon it was obvious that the airship was dropping like the proverbial brick. Nobody could do anything to arrest the fall, and the underside of the ship crashed with terrible force into a field of jagged ice. Almost everyone and everything in the shattered control car was thrown out on to the ice. Thus lightened, the silver-grey ship shot back into the sky and disappeared. It left behind nine men and Nobile's dog (the only uninjured member of the party). Fortunately, the wreckage strewn across the ice included a tent, sleeping bags, food and a workable radio.

Despite this, it was almost a month before they were found by Umberto Maddalena, flying a Savoia-Marchetti S.55 flying boat. Three members of the expedition had sought help by walking across the ice; one died and the other two were rescued nearly two months later by a Soviet icebreaker. The men who stayed at the crash site were all rescued over a period by no fewer than ten aircraft, of which a DH Moth was left with engine failure, a Fokker was left after a crash landing, and a Latham 47.02 twin-engined flying boat took off on its last leg from Tromsö on 18 June 1928 and was never seen again. On board the Latham, eager to rescue the stranded Italians, was Amundsen, all thought of conflict forgotten.

Now it may seem strange that the Latham could vanish without trace (it is thought that one float was found), but if it plunged into the sea one can imagine little remaining. But what about the enormous *Italia*? That too vanished without trace. I wonder where it is.

14

16 January 1930

'The Invention of F/O Whittle . . .'

Hindsight is handicapped by the difficulty of imagining how people thought many years previously. Having said that, I have still been puzzled for much of my life why Frank Whittle's invention of the turbojet was not grasped with both hands by everyone he told about it.

Let me make one point clear at the outset. Many writers today seem to be so unsure of their facts that they cannot bring themselves to say that Whittle 'invented' the turbojet. Plenty of people, especially in the United States, are eager to give equal credit to H.P. von Ohain. This young German had the benefit of working for an autocratic aircraft constructor who gave him almost *carte blanche* to build an engine and then fly it in an aircraft, long before any jet engine flew in Britain. But when von Ohain hit on the idea of a turbojet Whittle had spent *six years* trying to get someone interested. Moreover—though von Ohain did not copy them— Whittle's initial patent drawings had been openly published in Germany.

This is all by the way. The basic facts are that Hero of Alexandria is credited with the basic concept of reaction jet propulsion, in around AD 60. In 1791 John Barber of Nuneaton patented a gas turbine, but it was a primitive stationary plant looking rather like a Watt beam engine; had it been built it would probably have developed no useful power. In the 1860s we find a steam tip-jet-drive helicopter, and in the first years of this century a wealth of ideas for gas turbines and for propulsive jets. What you will never find is a turbojet, which is a gas turbine used to provide a propulsive jet. This is such a blindingly obvious synthesis of two known ideas that it seems amazing that nobody thought of it.

The man who thought of it was Flying Officer Frank Whittle, RAF. He thought of it in October 1929, whilst he was a flying instructor at RAF Wittering.

By sheer chance Wittering not only still exists but is one of the RAF's most important operational stations. Obviously (there's that word again) there ought to be a plaque, in the entrance to the Officers' Mess, recording that it was right here that the turbojet was invented. So, you aviation writers: do not shrink from daring to claim that Whittle *invented* the turbojet. (He also invented the turbofan, afterburning and a lot more besides.)

The date above, 16 January 1930, is that of his provisional patent. Some time before this, Whittle had done the natural thing and tried to get people interested. As a serving officer—and, incidentally, not only a brilliant test pilot but also one of the greatest aerobatic display pilots of his generation—he began with his employer. All his life he has loved the RAF, but this feeling of affinity tended to be confined to people in uniform. The technical Civil Service caused him little but aggravation and ulcers, and this started with his very first meeting with the eminent Dr A.A. Griffith. Griffith was probably the world's No 1 expert on aircraft gas turbines, but his thinking was fixed on complex axial machines with many hundreds of compressor and turbine blades, and reduction gears to drive a propeller. Suddenly he was asked to pronounce on something invented by a very junior officer, a breed who are not supposed to invent things. His invention was clearly technically sound. There were no flaws in his reasoning. His engine would be light and simple, burn any reasonable liquid hydrocarbon fuel, and give smooth vibrationless propulsion up to speeds and heights far beyond anything possible with piston engines and propellers. All it needed was applied research into high-intensity combustion and high-temperature materials.

It was all entirely possible. Such an engine clearly had enormous implications for both military and civil aviation, and here it was waiting for Britain to pick it up. Yet Griffith showed only a very negative interest, poured cold water on it and, though he could not fault it, he pretty well made sure it went no further. Even eight years later, after Whittle had overcome appalling difficulties and run an engine, Griffith wrote a very cool report damning Whittle's work with an almost sarcastic faint praise. This truly great gas-turbine man was, like Whittle, a visionary, who loved to invent ever more complex engines. Some looked very like the engines of today, but in the context of the 1930s such schemes were totally incapable of realization. Unlike Whittle, Griffith was no engineer. He did not have the slightest interest in the intractable problems that confront people who try to develop real engines. In 1939 he joined Rolls-Royce, and from then until after World War Two he tied up large numbers of the company's engineers trying to build his ever more fantastic schemes. Eventually, the famous firm got the message and went into production with Whittle-type engines, which Griffith despised as being far too simple.

Having drawn a blank with Griffith, Whittle next received permission to try to interest firms in the industry. All turned him down flat. Their reasons varied. The most understandable was that of the firm that later built his first engine (as a paid job), BTH. They simply said that to develop a turbojet would cost £60,000, and they did not have that kind of research budget. The established engine companies showed no interest. Armstrong Siddeley merely said such an engine could not be built, because it needed high-temperature materials, which is rather like saying an aeroplane cannot be built because it needs light materials. It really does seem to me strange that nobody said, 'This is something of the very first importance, and all it needs is a big development programme.'

While writing this book I was also proud to be one of a team of four creating a rather special book to sell at £1,600 per copy, to raise money for the RAF Benevolent Fund. It contains a valuable contribution from Sir Frank. He regrets the fact that his jet engine made no contribution to the Battle of Britain, but points out that it could have done. Indeed, he says, 'The RAF could have been equipped with Meteors and Vampires, or the like, by about 1937, and bombers with turbofan engines, based on our LR.1 turbofan, by about 1939.' He adds that his German rival

Hans von Ohain, is convinced that, had the Whittle engine not been held up for seven years, there probably would have been no World War Two. Von Ohain insists that, 'Having heard Hitler claim repeatedly that the Luftwaffe would be certain to bring Britain to her knees, then if he could not have been certain about this, he would not have dared to do what he did.'

Today the LR.1 is almost forgotten, yet this was an even more outrageous example of government myopia and incompetence. It was the world's first turbofan, designed in the winter of 1943–4. As the diagram shows, it had a high-pressure core with axial and centrifugal compressors, with a reduction gear to a two-stage fan. The bypass ratio was 3, just about what we use today and far more sensible than the timid 0.3 of the first turbofan to go into production (the Conway for the Victor, 15 years later). Moreover it had a full-length bypass duct and single nozzle. By 1944 everyone knew that jet engines worked. As with Whittle's original engine, there was no way the LR.1 could be faulted, and it was the obvious next major step forward. So, on the grounds of 'Ministry policy' it was cancelled before it could run. In the 1950s I asked why, and was informed: 'The LR.1 was intended to power long-range bombers to attack Japan. When Japan was defeated there was no longer any need for long-range bombers, so the engine was cancelled.' The idea of a long-range civil aeroplane never occurred to anyone; the workings of the ministerial mind will forever elude me!

Whittle had originally patented the basic concept of the turbofan back in 1936, and a little later he added patents for various forms of front fan, aft fan, and afterburning. The power plant for the 1,000-mph Miles M.52 was to be a W.2/700 turbojet with an aft-fan and afterburning (Story 35). This too would have been ahead of the rest of the world, so we cancelled that as well. It all makes me wonder: has Britain lost any desire to be ahead in technology? If another Whittle were to emerge, would we do any better?

Postscript: After writing this I sent a draft to Sir Frank, because his memory is

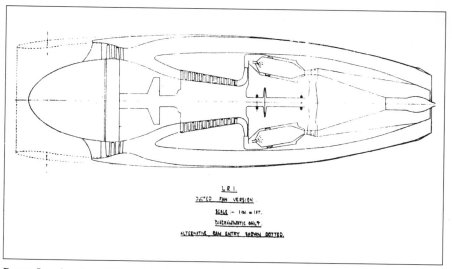

Power Jets drawing of the LR.1, the world's first turbofan, shortsightedly cancelled by the Government at the end of World War Two.

razor-sharp and he would pick up any error. He told me he had no important comments, but added:

1. Don't you think you ought to give rockets a mention, including Opel's rocket 'plane of the late twenties?

2. As I often stress, making the damn thing *work* was many times more important than the invention.

3. Hero of Alexandria's project was not for propulsion. It certainly used reaction, but to rotate an elementary turbine. No one seems to know whether he actually made it.

4. Don't you think you ought to make some reference to Stern's report?

5. I think Newton's 'steam carriage' deserves a mention; it was a jet-propulsion proposal.

6. When Admiral Lord Fisher pressed the great Sir Charles Parsons (about 1911) to develop an internal combusion engine, Parsons replied that the IC engine 'could not be Parsonized'.

I am grateful to Sir Frank for these suggestions. Item 4 refers to the only document relating to gas turbines on file at the Air Ministry in the inter-war years. It was written in 1920 by Dr W.J. Stern, of the Air Ministry Laboratory at South Kensington. Because it made incredibly conservative, and indeed pessimistic, assumptions it said, in effect, that you might as well forget about gas turbines entirely. Incidentally, when in 1945 Sir Roy Fedden was picking a team to accompany him on his official technical-intelligence mission to the shattered aircraft industry of Germany one of those he selected was Stern. I did not put this in my biography of Fedden, but he told me he did not have the slightest doubt that Stern was either a British agent or a double-agent . . .

15

5 October 1930

The Bad Ship

One of my earliest memories is of seeing the great airship R.101. About four months later, like thousands of others, I heard her humming and thundering past in the gloom on her way to India, but in fact did not then catch a glimpse of her (it was a stormy night). At eight minutes past two next morning she crunched against a hillside south of Beauvais, in northern France. Within seconds she caught fire, and 48 of the 54 on board were incinerated. It marked the end of a wonderful imperial dream.

The dream had begun in 1922 and been properly launched in 1924. The idea was that, at a cost of £1.35 million, two huge new airships should be built to operate commercial services throughout the Empire, and especially to India and Canada. If the services prospered, more ships might be built. Nobody explained why one airship, the R.100, was to be a 'capitalist' project, designed and built by Vickers, while the other, the R.101, should be a 'socialist' creation, designed and built by the Royal Airship Works at Cardington. Again, for no obvious reason, the R.100 was completely straightforward, built with no frills at minimum cost, while the 'government ship' incorporated every conceivable new device and refinement.

Inevitably, in the circumstances, the Vickers ship was finished first. She soon proved to be not only fully satisfactory but the fastest airship ever built (I believe she has not yet been surpassed in this regard) at over 81 mph. The more beautiful R.101, on the other hand, seemed to be riddled with problems from stem to stern. In July 1930, while her 'capitalist rival' was making a return trip to Canada, R.101 went back into the vast Cardington hangar to have an extra bay 45 ft long spliced in amidships. Still she suffered from problems and deficiencies, some very serious.

It so happened that the Air Minister, Lord Thomson (who had aspirations to be the next Viceroy of India), was due to be a key participant in a big Imperial Conference in London beginning on 20 October 1930. He was determined to fly to India and back by airship before the conference in order with more authority to outline the plans for Empire communications. Nobody explained why he had to travel in the R.101 when the R.100 was ready and waiting, but it put the harrassed Cardington team under impossible pressure. The whole idea should have been seen to be exceedingly foolish, but the noble lord—usually the most cautious and thoughtful of men—obviously fell victim to his Civil Service propaganda, when he described the R.101 as 'safe as houses—except for the millionth chance'. This was despite the visibly obvious state of rushed chaos and last-minute patching up at Cardington, and the fact that a fellow-passenger, Sir Sefton Brancker, Director of Civil Aviation, actually called on Lord Thomson to express his grave concern at the great airship's state of airworthiness (both were among those killed). In fact, R.101 never did have a Certificate of Airworthiness. So that she could leave for India, a completely illegal 'temporary certificate' was put on board just before departure. The captain, Flt Lt Carmichael Irwin, was told to perform the outstanding trials during the voyage!

Well, that seems to be that. I shall never forget the shock of hearing about the disaster, and seeing aerial pictures of the burned-out wreck in the newspapers. For the next half-century I knew, like everyone else, that the R.101 was simply a bad ship, riddled with problems and pretty well doomed from the start. Then Sir Peter Masefield produced a book, *To Ride the Storm*, which tells the story of the fated airship, and incidentally the very moving personal story of Lord Thomson. Peter would never do as I do and merely cobble together a story from what has been published already. He does endless painstaking research—heaven knows how, with his incredible list of time-consuming appointments and high offices—and his considered conclusion is that, basically, the R.101 was a sound airship which could, and should, have had a long career. The cause of her crash was loss of gas at the bows. This could have been countered by running the engines at maximum continuous power and raising the elevators, to raise the nose. What actually happened was that the engines were reduced in power (they were almost idling when she hit). Once the throttles were closed, said Sir Peter, the R.101 was doomed. Of course, the flight to India would have had to be abandoned, but the R.101 and its passengers and crew would have lived to make the trip a little later.

So we scrapped a probably sound idea of imperial airships. We also—presumably out of sheer spite—scrapped the R.100, which never had a black mark put against it. And research done half a century later found out the cause of the disaster, which is more than hordes of officials did at the time, *and* showed it was avoidable.

16

26 January 1932

'Prepare to Dive!'

I hope the spirit of designer Harold Bolas will not think I am getting at him. I have already criticized the shaft-drive Parnall Possum, and now I am about to tell what happened to the Parnall Peto. But in fact I do not intend to criticize this neat little seaplane, which was merely one of the victims.

During World War One the British Admiralty laid down the K-class of large submarines, driven by steam turbines and fast enough to keep up with the surface fleet. The idea was foolish on at least six counts, and the last four Ks were built to a totally different specification, and renumbered M1 to M4. The last boat was never finished, but M1 to M3 were commissioned in 1918-20 as submersible monitors, each with a 12-in gun. In the 1920s M2 was rebuilt as an aircraft carrier and M3 as a minelayer.

M2 had her big gun replaced by a watertight hangar forward of the conning tower. The hangar crew of ten, plus the pilot and observer, entered the hangar through a large floor hatch. Electrical, oil, and engine heaters were started, so that, as soon as the order to launch was given, the Peto would be ready. The huge slab of steel forming the front door of the hangar was then opened, and rails quickly laid over it so that the Peto could run forward on to the submarine's catapult. The wings would be unfolded, the already hot engine started and the catapult fired. The purpose, of course, was reconnaissance, though with an endurance of two hours at about 70 knots the Peto could not venture far out of sight! The aircraft's crew, incidentally, received double 'danger money', since they qualified as both submariners and as airmen.

In the inter-war years life was hard for naval ratings. Discipline was strict in the Royal Navy—the cat o'nine tails did not seem so very far in the past—and orders were obeyed instantly. In any case, a crew like that of M2 tended to have a lot of pride in their work as a team, and it would be unthinkable for a single member of that team to be grossly careless or fail to obey an order. Having said that, on 26 January 1932 HM Submarine M2 dived into the Channel, off Portland, with both the outer and inner hangar doors open!

The mind boggles. Of course, hindsight suggests that the hatch giving access to the hangar from inside the hull did not need to be there. The hangar crew and aircrew could just as well have got to the aircraft via the existing hatch at the top of the conning tower and thence through a hatch in the top of the hangar. As it was, 60 men were drowned. The submarine was soon found, but attempts—rather bungling attempts, which at one time got M2 within 18 ft of the surface—at salvaging her were eventually abandoned. The little seaplane was recovered, though battered. With no home, the Peto was scrapped.

17

6 September 1933

Sky Louse

Anyone who lived through the 1930s will remember the way the Flying Flea took Europe, and then a lot of other countries, by storm. It was the best thing that ever happened to aviation, except that perhaps it was the worst.

It was entirely due to a Frenchman, Henri Mignet (pronounced 'Meenyay'). He was totally 'air minded', but he found learning to fly in the orthodox fashion—dual in a conventional aeroplane—almost impossible. Like many before him, and since, he could not co-ordinate his hands and feet, perpetually got 'crossed controls', and frightened his instructors. He eventually decided the whole thing was unnecessarily complicated, and suddenly hit on the idea that he could invent an aeroplane that was much simpler to design, construct, and fly. In France in the 1930s this was actually against the law, but that merely added to the appeal of the idea.

Mignet was well versed in aerodynamics, structures, and general light engineering. One realizes that this was pure divine providence, and he would probably have gone ahead anyway, even if he had known nothing about aircraft design. In fact from this time onwards he, perhaps to some degree unconsciously, acted the part of the ignorant amateur. His whole objective was to broadcast the good news to the population of the world: 'If you can make a packing case, you can build your own aeroplane and fly it.'

Mignet did just that. First, he did the drawings. He created an odd little machine. Superficially, it looked more or less conventional, but actually it had no horizontal tail. Instead there were two wings in tandem. The rear one was mounted on the fuselage and fixed; and of course it gave lift, whereas a conventional tailplane gives downthrust. The front wing was larger, mounted on a pylon above the fuselage and arranged so that its incidence could be varied. His cockpit controls comprised a throttle and stick. Moving the stick left or right worked the rudder (there was no fin). Moving it to the front or rear pivoted the front wing. There was no lateral control, Mignet relying on wing dihedral and the pendulum effect of the underslung fuselage to give adequate stability, whilst making turns on the rudder only.

This was actually Mignet's fourteenth design, so it was designated HM.14. He built it in his bedroom, and when all the bits were finished he took them out of the front door, tied them together with string, fastened the package behind his motorbike and put his long-suffering wife, tools, and a tent into the sidecar. A great adventure was about to begin. It was an adventure almost like a rerun of the 'golden age' of aviation in 1907-10, when aviators learned a little from each crash. The date above is that of the first flight, and first crash. Gradually, the flying got better and the crashes less serious, and by early 1934 Mignet reckoned he had accomplished his twin objectives of creating a flying machine anyone could make, and of learning to fly it. He called it *Pou du Ciel,* the English translation being the title above.

Next he had to spread the good news, so he wrote a new edition of his book, *Le Sport de l'Air,* first published in 1928. At first it seemed to sink without trace. A few weeks later the message got through. First hundreds, then thousands, and then hundreds of thousands bought the book, and learned that they could become a pilot, in their own aircraft, provided they had a saw, plane, hammer, screwdriver, a few bits of wood and wire, the wheels from a child's scooter, and an old motorcycle engine. This is slightly overstating the case: the propeller was a bit of a challenge, and there were also such things as the fuel tank and contents gauge, Bowden-cable throttle, and plenty of metal fittings. Today we would say that any fair DIY person could do the whole job.

Mignet's book was translated—wrote Major Oliver Stewart—'into almost every language under the Sun'. In Britain the HM.14's title was rendered by the Air League as 'Flying Flea' (a flea is *pouce* in French, not the more acceptable *pou*). Most countries stuck with the original French, and this was the case even in the Soviet Union, where Mignet's book triggered off no fewer than 34 different types of *bloxhi* (Fleas) as well as at least 30 examples of Mignet's original. In Britain the number comprised 1 in 1935—made by Stephen Appleby—133 in 1936, and threatened to be several hundred in 1937. Unfortunately, by 1936 Europe was becoming pockmarked by Fleas diving fatally into the ground. RAE Farnborough tested one in a tunnel and found that, if the pilot let the front wing get to $-15°$ (ie leading edge down) incidence, he could never recover. The Flea would go into an ever-steeper dive.

The Flea, which had from the start been an *enfant terrible* of the kind that officials (such as licensing authorities) simply hate, was promptly banned. Most other countries followed suit. It was estimated that in 1936-8 more than 2,000 finished or part-finished Fleas were dismantled in Europe alone. Things that burst on an excited world like a nova often tend to be extinguished just as quickly. If you think that letting everyone, and the man next door, build and fly his own aeroplane was a good idea, then it was tragic that Mignet should have let his creation loose on a receptive world when, in the opinion of any competent licensing authority, it was undeveloped and downright dangerous.

This is doubly sad when it is realized that there was nothing about a Flea that a little thoughtful development would not cure. Various examples of such improvements were made in the USA before and after World War Two, and Mignet himself perfected the Flea, and indeed in France and Brazil produced a series of extremely safe and virtually unstallable lightplanes in 1953-62. As late as 1971 W.H. Cole in Britain startled the Popular Flying Association's rally by arriving in a brand-new and completely safe Flea. But even the homebuilder today seems to be looking beyond packing cases and moving towards carbonfibre and advanced avionics.

18

September 1933

How It Used To Be

Have you ever visited a US aircraft factory? Most of them are impressive. As a visitor you can probably park somewhere near the front door; indeed the cop on the main gate may tap a keyboard to a computer terminal and tell you which numbered space is yours. As a mere employee you may have a ten-minute walk past 20,000 other cars to get to your entrance. The plant is probably a mile long, windowless, surrounded by immaculate manicured lawns, and without the slightest blemish anywhere on its appearance or efficiency. The British disease of an illuminated sign with a letter that doesn't work would be unthinkable. Inside, it's air-conditioned, with every colour, light intensity, and noise selected for the best low-stress environment. Often interiors put sci-fi 21st-Century movies to shame. The McDonnell Douglas Apache plant at Mesa, Arizona, has an atrium—a kind of central courtyard—which I assure you has nothing in common with ancient Rome except grandeur of scale.

If we go back 40 years to the immediate post-war period, US plants were still impressive, but things were on a more human level. Visiting Grumman at Bethpage I noticed fine pictures of the F4F, TBF, and other types, but there was a blank frame where the F6F might have been. I was told: 'We gave it to a bar-keeper down in Farmingdale, and don't seem to have gotten a fresh enlargement to replace it.' On a later visit the cop on the gate said: 'Who are you visiting?' I showed him my letter from Jack Retalliata. 'Not today, Bud,' said the friendly policeman, 'didn't you look at the date of your appointment? July the fourth is our Independence Day!' On my first visit to Douglas's plant at 3000 Ocean Park Boulevard in Santa Monica, in 1955, I was met in the foyer by Chief Engineer Ed Burton. I drew him over to the huge map of the world on the left-hand wall and asked 'How long has that been misspelt SIDNEY?' Ed scratched his head: 'Since 1929 I guess . . .'

In those days British aircraft factories, with three exceptions, did not go in for big wall maps, or even foyers. Most employees worked either in hangars and primitive machine shops or in soggy wooden huts where, if they were lucky, there might be a coke-burning stove. Design staff often did better, especially those who in 1940 had been evacuated to such stately homes as Claremont and Hursley Park. Unlike the glorious houses wrecked by billeted troops, these bits of our heritage were lovingly cared for. One day a delegation from Rolls-Royce visited Sydney

Camm at Claremont, Esher. It was all part of Camm's act to pretend to despise engines and their designers. At the end of his vitriolic greeting (which anyone not 'in the know' would have taken seriously) A.G. Elliott, the eminent R-R Chief Engineer, quietly replied, 'Such a beautiful fireplace, Sydney; so convenient for burning all those mistakes.'

By 1945 the British industry had expanded perhaps twenty-fold. The oldies who had been in at the beginning thought it was much more fun in the 1920s and 1930s. Everyone knew everyone else, and the whole industry had about it an aura of delightfully simple inefficiency that today we jokingly associate with the Irish.

Later (Story 27) I comment on how the man who designed the Martin B-26 Marauder also took it off on its first flight. Chief designers surely ought also to be pilots; but such have been a rare species since the very earliest days of aviation when the chief designer was also the chief test pilot, chief ground engineer, and chief certification authority. One of the best-known in Britain was Capt Frank Barnwell of the Bristol Aeroplane Company. He had trained as a marine engineer in Fairfield's shipyard at Glasgow, but this did not result in his structures being overweight. His background did, however, make him coat the unique monocoque duralumin fuselage of his M.R.1 Metal Biplane with good quality marine varnish. I reckon this fuselage would have lasted 100 years. The result was quite a good-looking aircraft, until Barnwell flew it to Farnborough. He collided with a pine tree near the RAE North Gate.

In 1924 he designed the little Brownie ultralight monoplane. It was indeed an ultralight. Barnwell designed the fuselage on the basis of welded steel tubing, and this was of so thin a gauge that, when someone knocked out the ashes of his pipe against it, the tubing buckled! Seeing this, the Air Council refused to let the Brownie compete in the Light Aeroplane Trials at Lympne until Barnwell had flown it with two on board, looped it, and demonstrated that it would not fold up. Later Barnwell used a Brownie as his own personal hack. He ought to have avoided Farnborough, because on 21 March 1928 he took off from there into what was thought to have been downwash over trees and, despite firewalling the throttle, crashed onto Farnborough Road within a few feet of his crash in the M.R.1. He had a few more scrapes, and eventually the company considered him uninsurable, and so instructed him not to fly any more Bristol aircraft. But in 1938 he and a small group of helpers designed and built a tiny single-seater, the BSW.1, for use by Civil Air Guard pupils. The designation came from Barnwell, Scott (28 hp engine), and Whitchurch (airfield). On 2 August 1938 the engine failed on the second takeoff and Barnwell was killed.

There is no reason why a gifted designer should also be a capable pilot; the skills are in general unrelated. In the same way, a brilliant pilot can be a menace behind the wheel of a car. I have known several pilots, two of them truly famous, who on the road seemed to have no judgement whatever. Rod Banks, in his autobiography *I Kept no Diary*, comments: 'It has often surprised me that a number of first-class pilots were such bad car drivers.' In sharp contrast, Ernest Hives, later Lord Hives of Duffield and probably the most inspiring leader British industry has ever had, joined Rolls-Royce initially as a mechanic and car tester; in 1911 he drove a Model 40/50 from London to Edinburgh with three passengers without ever changing out of top gear. Many have attested to his ability to cruise at 80 mph along narrow winding roads using a sixth sense to tell him if an oncoming car was round the next bend. Sir Stanley Hooker believes he only once had a minor shunt, and that was with a crowd of bookies going to the Derby. They were obviously going to thump him, but drew back when they heard he was the General Manager of Rolls-Royce. 'In that case,' said one, 'we won't hit him, we'll sue him.'

Of all the great 'characters' of the early British industry, I suppose HP (Sir Frederick Handley Page) was the greatest. I first met him when, having left the RAF, I went to read engineering at NEC, Northampton Engineering College (which is not in Northampton but in the City of London, and is today the giant City University). 'Sir Fred' had been a pioneer lecturer there from 1906, and about once a year we 'full-time day students' would gather in Room 102 to be addressed by the great man. His ability as a speaker was legendary. His giant character showed strange contrasts. For example, his disarming generosity was coupled with strict Plymouth Brethren upbringing which led him to save pennies. After World War One he was a wealthy man, yet John Yoxall told me how, in 1921, he came into the *Flight* offices and begged to be given extra time to pay an advertising bill of ten shillings (50p).

This story is about his factory. This had been a riding school, address 110 Cricklewood Lane. If you look at the map today it seems to be in the centre of London, but in 1912, when young HP bought it, the urban sprawl had not quite reached there. Next door was a farm, and HP had no difficulty in establishing an aerodrome next to the factory.

When war broke out in August 1914 HP was asked by the Navy to build a big bomber, 'a bloody paralyser—not a toy'. The result was the O/100, which incidentally was completed with a box-like cabin for the pilots, with bullet-proof glass, making it look like an Ilya Mourometz; it also had sheets of armour all over the cabin and engines. No 1455 was completed on 9 December 1915. That night, its great wings folded, it was pulled by an army of sailors from the factory to the aerodrome at Hendon. The procession travelled down (or up) the Edgware Road, today called the A5, and anyone who knows today's traffic (24 hours a day) would find it hard to believe that the huge bomber several times stopped while overhanging branches were sawn off trees. People in pyjamas came out to watch. No 1455 flew at 1.51 pm on the following Saturday, 18 December. Before long the glass cabin collapsed in flight, so the nose was redesigned and we have very few pictures of the original configuration.

Later, while the houses engulfed Cricklewood and for 15 miles beyond, swallowing up the airfield in the process, Sir Fred determined to rearrange his now large factory so that it had a perfectly efficient 'flow scheme'. Over the years the factory had grown in a haphazard manner. Around 1934 HP tore everything apart and put in an ideal arrangement in which raw material came in at one end, passed through all the various processes in logical sequence and emerged at the far end as finished parts of aircraft, sent for final erection to Radlett, the new assembly and test airfield.

There was just one small snag. Raw material didn't actually follow the ideal sequence, so carefully worked out by HP, at all. Instead it kept making giant hiccups, being carted off at frequent intervals to the far end of the factory. 'Why on Earth?', the visitor might ask. It was all because of their damned neighbour, who had started up a small business in a shed alongside. He had complained that HP's solution heat-treatment and cadmium-plating were polluting the atmosphere and

damaging his product, so HP had to move these departments to a totally wrong
location. The neighbour's name was Smith, and he had invented a product called
potato crisps.

An equally great character was Noel Pemberton-Billing. Extremely tall and well-
dressed, P-B was one of those 'larger than life' people who abounded in the early
years of this century, and in 1913–17 he designed 23 different aircraft, founded
Pemberton-Billing Ltd in a factory at Woolston, Southampton, was commissioned
in the RNAS, planned the pioneer Avro 504 bombing raid on the Zeppelin sheds
at Friedrichshafen, wrote powerful political books, became an MP, told almost
everyone how to build aircraft and conduct the complete war in the air, and among
other things got the entire management of the Royal Aircraft Factory at
Farnborough sacked and the 'Factory' turned into the 'Establishment'. He also
learned to fly in a single day, taking £500 off HP in a bet (both being unheard-of
achievements!). I don't know what he did with his spare time.

You'll have got the general idea that P-B didn't hang about. Eventually the
Woolston works was to become the famous Supermarine factory; previously the
name had merely been P-B's choice of telegraphic address. It made various aircraft,
experimental floats, engines and various other things, but on 4 August 1914 P-B
called the workforce together and said: 'We're at war. We must build a small fighting
scout. Nobody goes home until it's done.' Straight away P-B and a draughtsman
(Romanian Vasilesco) did the drawings; a side elevation, dated 4 August, survives
to this day. On the same day he drew the full-scale lofting drawings on the factory
wall, so that on the second day manufacture of parts could begin. The scout, called
the P.B.9, was designed for an 80 hp Gnome rotary, but P-B could not get hold of
one in time and so he re-used an old '50 Gnome' which he had already flogged round
the sky in the P.B.1 flying boat until it was reckoned to give only about 33 hp. While
various groups stitched and varnished fabric, another finished carving the
propeller. At last, after a week, the P.B.9 was finished. It was towed about three
miles to a field near Netley, where the maiden flight was made by Victor Mahl.
Despite its very low power the P.B.9 handled beautifully. Indeed, it had quite a long
career, mainly at Brooklands and at RNAS Chingford, though the hoped-for
thousands did not materialize.

For obvious reasons, it was called the Seven-Day Bus. But with all our computers
we could do just as well today. One of today's bosses could say 'Nobody goes home
until we've finished the feasibility study, which shouldn't take more than ten years.
Nobody's son goes home until we've finished full-scale development. Nobody's
grandson goes home until we've finished flight test and begun production. And
nobody's great-grandson goes home until we've got into service.'

So what happened in September 1933? The very first aircraft firm in the world,
Short Brothers, was registered in 1898. Eustace, Horace, and Oswald Short came
from Derbyshire, but began making balloons near Hove. They moved in succession
to a mews off Tottenham Court Road, in the heart of London, then to the arches
of the London, Brighton & South Coast Railway at Battersea Bridge, then to the
Isle of Sheppey (first Leysdown and then Eastchurch), at the start of World War One
to Rochester, and from 1947 to Belfast. In the 1950s I was privileged often to chat
with Oswald, the last surviving brother, who had become a stationmaster on British
Rail's Southern Region after his firm had been rather summarily nationalized in
1942 by Sir Stafford Cripps. After he had retired yet again he moved very near me

in Haslemere, but this little story does not come from him but from another near-neighbour, Robert Page, to whom I am indebted.

In 1932 the company completed the S.14 Sarafand. This extremely large biplane flying boat had been built to Reconnaissance specification R.6/28, but I think this was just an excuse to get the thing funded. A similar contract was placed with Supermarine, but they were told to make their mighty boat a monoplane. Both were to have six of the most powerful engines available, and several people who were involved consider that this was just a research effort to see if a very large monoplane would be better than a very large biplane. The Supermarine aircraft might have been quite significant, with six 825 hp Buzzard engines, 4,000 sq ft of wing and a maximum weight of 75,600 lb. It was to have been registered as a civil aircraft, and I wish Reginald Mitchell had been allowed to complete it—in the same works where they made the Seven-Day Bus—but sadly it was axed by the economy-minded Labour government in 1931 (poor chaps, they always get blamed for trying to deny Britain the Schneider Trophy as well). This left just the Sarafand, with military serial S1589. It was first flown on 30 June 1932, and once one accepts the idea of a traditional British biplane, it was a very fine machine. So far as I know, it never carried any kind of military load and never accomplished anything, and, with the Supermarine monoplane axed, its original comparative purpose had disappeared. Anyway, as the public had paid for it, it could hardly just be scrapped, so like all other Service flying boats it went to the Marine Aircraft Experimental Establishment at Felixstowe. It arrived just after one of MAEE's most gifted test pilots had left; his name, Frank Whittle.

In those days aircraft were refuelled by hand, pouring ordinary motor spirit (the Air Ministry specification was equivalent to about 74 octane) into each tank using cans and funnels. You were supposed to strain the fuel through a thin chamois leather inside the funnel. and, to avoid dangerous sparks caused by static electricity, the can had to be earthed (grounded) to the funnel and to the airframe. Well, of course, when about 200 cans were needed, as in the case of the Sarafand, occasionally the earthing might be overlooked and a spark occur. Anyway, for whatever reason, they were fuelling the giant boat (must have been rather like trimming a lawn with scissors) in 1933 when a fire started. The boat was saved, but the outer panel of the lower port (left) wing was burned out. The spars were stainless steel, and appeared to be airworthy, but the aluminium lattice ribs were severely damaged, so it was decided to unbolt this wing panel and send it back in component form to the maker. Short Brothers duly made up a new set of ribs, threaded them on to the spars and then completed the wing and reskinned it with fabric. When it was all finished it was decided to send it back by barge to Felixstowe.

This is where the problems started. Even though it was only part of a wing, the S.14 was so big that the panel measured about 45 ft by 20 ft. The shop in which it had been repaired was on the steep bank of the Medway, and to reach the barge the wing had to come out of the end of the shop facing the river, where there was a 15-ft drop. It was soon established that there was no way the works mobile crane could do any good. There was only one answer, and it had been used by Short Brothers many times: manpower. About 200 men were gathered—in those days every aircraft works had about 200 spare labourers, with massive boots and cloth caps—and told to get the wing out. There was nowhere to fasten ropes, so when the wing teetered on the edge and began to overbalance, some men were holding ropes just looped round the end inside the shop, some were trying to lift it clear of the sill to avoid damage, and some were down below apprehensively waiting to catch it.

About two hours and numerous frantic shouts later the wing was outside the shop, with surprisingly little damage. Then it began to move off down the road to the barge quay, looking like a giant millipede. The men were in random order, so the tallest were bent almost double, while the youngest or shortest could barely touch the silver skin with their fingertips. Eventually they came to a large gate. It was obvious that the 20-ft chord of the wing would not go through the 3 ft (or so) width of the gate, and there was no way the wing could be tilted upright, so a discussion was held, while the straining team wondered how long they would have to stand there. Eventually there came the cry, 'Fetch trestles, we must put it down.' In about ten minute numerous trestles had been laid out—all of different heights. and standing on uneven ground—and the team was gingerly shuffled backwards, and the trestles rearranged, until at last the wing could be put down. Then 'Back to your jobs, come back here in an hour when we've dug up the gatepost.'

The wing did eventually get bolted back on the Sarafand, and it probably even flew a few times before someone decided to scrap it, new wing and all. I am reminded of Sir George Edwards's description of his first wander round the Vickers works at Weybridge: 'The first thing I saw was an enormous man stripped to the waist (whom I subsequently found out was the Works Manager) with a very large hammer breaking up what looked to me to be an absolutely new Viastra transport . . . It dawned upon me that this was no ordinary industry that I had strayed into, and I must say that nothing has happened since to make me change my view.'

19

12 February 1935

The New Idea of 'Stealth'

People who dare to trespass into the highly classified region of LO (low observables) or stealth aircraft take it for granted that it is the very newest of new ideas. Certainly, the objective first identified in the United States in 1974 of making a combat aircraft invisible at all pertinent EM (electromagnetic) wavelengths, which include radars, visible light, and IR (infra-red, or heat), as well as completely silent, is fairly new—well, new since 1974! But the broad concept goes back much earlier. In May 1912 Hauptmann (captain) Petrocz von Petroczy, an Austro-Hungarian officer, had a Lohner-built Taube covered not with the usual doped fabric but with Emaillit (there were several similar proprietary materials, all variations on Cellophane). The result is said to have been very successful; *Flight* reported a witness as saying that, even when the engine sound gave away the aircraft's position, it was usually almost impossible to see. Subsequently, mainly in 1914-16, at least 14 and possibly over a hundred aircraft of the Central Powers were subjected to similar 'invisibility' experiments.

The idea was picked up again in the Soviet Union in 1935, when S.G. Kozlov, professor at the VVA (air force academy), received permission to conduct experiments with a Yak AIR-4 cabin monoplane. The covering used was Rodoid, a French flexible glass-like material. Great care was taken to minimize the visual signature of the engine, fuel, pilot, tyres, and other 'impossible' parts, and the results during flight testing in 1936 were said to have had 'a measure of importance'.

But these ideas were set virtually at nought by the invention of radar. Many groups had ideas about radio detection, in different countries including Germany and the United States, but the first man clearly to outline the design of an air-defence radar system was a Scotsman, Robert (later Sir Robert) Watson Watt. On the date given above he outlined how a pulsed radar should be used to detect the presence of aircraft, indicate range, azimuth (bearing), and height, and with suitable coding give automatic IFF (identification friend or foe). Prior to this date none of these things existed.

As an afterthought he added that it would seem logical for future bombers to be designed for minimal radar reflectivity (today we would say 'minimum radar signature' or RCS, radar cross-section). Of course, at the time this was not published, and as the officials began to comprehend the enormous importance of radar it became highly secret. I learned about radar signatures, and the far-seeing comment of 'Wattie', in the 1950s. Clearly, it was of immense importance. The designer of the Lancaster, Roy Chadwick, had unfortunately been killed in 1947, but I managed to ask his chief assistant, S.D. 'Cock' Davies, about it. He assured me that, during the whole of World War Two he did not recall radar signatures or cross-sections being mentioned, let alone used as a basis for aircraft design. (Of course, the 'Lanc' began life as the Manchester III, a new version of an aircraft designed in 1937, but that does not invalidate the surprising situation.)

Some time in the 1950s I asked Noah Showalter of Boeing if radar signatures had played any part in the design of the B-29. His reply was 'Definitely not; at least that was one problem which we did not have.' Several later Boeing engineers said the same about the B-47 and B-52, though with the latter aircraft radar signature did have to be measured, from different directions. When I went to Chadderton to do the first permitted description of the Avro Vulcan I asked the same question, and after a lot of persistence got J.R. Ewans to give a negative answer (so I guess the same goes for the other V-bombers). It just so happens that, except for the giant engine inlets, the Vulcan must have had an extremely good (ie very small) radar cross-section; but that was purely fortuitous. In any case, in mid-1956 the Ministry of Supply came up with an anti-flash white paint with which the V-bombers were sprayed all over. It was some time afterwards that it was realized this approximately doubled the radar cross-section!

Usually, in things that really matter, countries like Britain and the USA get it right. So how is it that 'Wattie's' timely suggestion in February 1935 went totally unheeded? Even today we seem to make a point of designing aircraft along traditional lines and then tinkering with them cosmetically so that a word or two about 'stealth' can be put into the brochures. I am emphatically referring to Britain, not the United States.

One other point: when people, especially in the media, talk about stealth they concentrate almost entirely on radar. You only have to think for a moment to see that even reducing RCS to zero is pointless if the aircraft pumps out IR (heat) and deafening noise, and eliminating these is *far* more difficult.

20

1936-43

The Treason of Tupolev

The Soviet Union—which so many people today insist on calling Russia, which is just one of its 15 republics—was born in 1917 in an atmosphere of discord and inhuman brutality. This naturally coloured the years that followed, which by any standard were horrific, with many millions dying unnatural deaths (I include starvation among unnatural causes). By the 1930s one might have expected things to be settling down, though perhaps one could understand the continuing wish of Stalin, an absolute dictator, to eliminate anyone who might be considered a threat to him. Such things happen in most dictatorships.

What actually happened was, to a naïve and simple Briton, much more dreadful and wholly puzzling. The 1930s are remembered as the period of 'the Terror'. Many thousands—possibly three million—of ordinary citizens were arrested and, by any and every means, forced to sign wholly fictitious admissions of various kinds of political guilt. Thereafter they spent up to 35 years in Siberian forced-labour camps, and if they survived to become 'free' again they still remained marked men (or women) as 'political prisoners'. For the armed forces it was if anything worse. Vast numbers of officers, from marshals down to majors (sometimes even as junior as captains), were simply arrested and shot. These killings very seriously retarded the modernization of the Red Army, and deprived it of valuable leaders who were to be desperately needed after 22 June 1941.

As for the aircraft industry, someone thought it would be a good time if the designers could be arrested, grouped into special prisons, and kept under close surveillance. I have never been able to discover why it was thought this would be good for the Soviet Union. In view of the prolific output of the relevant design and experimental construction bureaux the men concerned could hardly have been accused of slacking! Of course, it was a time when any fault tended to result in charges of 'crimes against the State', and poor Konstantin Alekseyevich Kalinin was arrested in 1938, charged with spying and conspiracy, and put to death. Maybe the inflight structural failure of his huge K-7 bomber in 1933 had a bearing on his execution, but of course the whole thing was trumped-up nonsense. Several design teams chose not to fly their prototypes for fear of the consequences of a crash. From 1936 to late 1938 anybody who was anybody in the Soviet Union cannot have had much time to do their proper job because, so the courts proclaimed, they worked day and night conspiring with 'reactionaries', hostile countries and baddies of all kinds in order to harm their own country. Simply written down like this it can be seen to be the utter nonsense that it was, but at the time it was real enough and it meant a bullet or being behind bars at the end of it. Nobody was ever known to have been 'acquitted'; that wasn't the idea!

Back in the 1920s the leading Soviet aircraft designer was Nikolai Nikolayevich Polikarpov. Inevitably, because of his position, he was the first of his profession to be arrested, and this happened as early as September 1929. He was kept under armed guard in Hangar 7 at GAZ-39, the factory named for V.R. Menzhinskii, head of OGPU (which became the NKVD and then the KGB). A few months later he was joined by the most important designer who had begun under the Tsar and gone on to head a brigade after the Revolution: D.P. Grigorovich. These two famous designers were the guinea pigs who pioneered the idea of a VT (*Vnutrenniya Tyurma*, internal prison).

The great Andrei Nikolayevich Tupolev was thus perhaps fortunate to be left alone until 1936, especially in view of the success and fame of his huge monoplanes such as the ANT-6 family and the ANT-20, largest aeroplane (by far) in the world. When the blow fell, in October 1936, he asked what the charge was. He was told he had committed treason by secretly giving the design of the Messerschmitt Bf 110 to the Germans! The charge was so ludicrous he knew there was not much point in arguing, or in trying to point out its numerous impossibilities. He spent the next 18 months in the Lubyanka and Butyrkii prisons, generally wasting his time and fretting about the numerous important programmes that were hanging fire in his absence. Then, in 1937, he was given a vague command to 'design an aeroplane to beat the Ju 88', which he could have done infinitely faster and more efficiently back at his design bureau. Even in 1937 you needed a bit more than paper and pencil. He accordingly began the design of the ANT-58, whose number by chance was the same as that of his cell in Butyrkii.

In 1938 the NKVD belatedly realized they had wasted a good many vital man-years of top designer time, and began to organize their captives into proper design bureaux. These were given numbers beginning with 100. Tupolev was assigned No 103, so the ANT-58 became Samolyet (Aircraft) No 103. The work went ahead a bit more purposefully, the design was approved on 1 March 1940, and the first aircraft was completed, except for engines, on 3 October of that year. Eventually the big AM-37 engines arrived, but various snags delayed the first flight until 29 January 1941. The design went through several further stages of development, but proved to be a real winner. Unfortunately, Tupolev's absence behind bars caused endless delays to both development and the organization of series production. At last on 15 April 1943 he was released, and Aeroplane 103 went into mass production as the Tu-2, Tupolev receiving a Stalin Prize.

I once asked Tupolev about those seven years. Clearly, he did not wish to discuss the matter, and merely said 'I was just required to breathe purified air.' But what an outrageous waste of time and talent! Anybody got any ideas what the Soviet leaders thought they were playing at?

21

Late 1938

Comrade Silvanskii is Banned!

Back in the 1920s London had lots of bus companies, but the two giants were the London General Omnibus Co and Thomas Tilling. Both bought buses to their own design, hundreds at a time. One day a driver, taking the first of a new design out on the road, found it difficult to change gear. In fact it was impossible, because the gear lever would have had to pass through the steering column. This was a bit of a setback, because a large number of identical buses were either completed or on the assembly line.

Of course, such things could never happen in the aircraft industry. Everything is done with much more care, and mock-ups are made to ensure that everything will fit together in 3-D space to perfection. At least, so we would all like to think, though even in very recent times I have heard of odd little quirks which show that there were a few afterthoughts, or—in at least one case—that no mock-up was thought necessary. But my favourite story concerns the Soviet Union in the late 1930s.

Is it not strange that in this strict totalitarian state, at a time when sheer terror reigned against anyone who was in any way important, all sorts of people could get money and materials to build aeroplanes? Mostly these were lightplanes, or even what we today call ultralights, but A.V. Silvanskii, who was already working in an aircraft factory, went one better. He thought it would be nice to build a high-performance fighter! He must have had permission to open his own OKB (experimental construction bureau), and we know his partners were V.D. Yarovitskii and Yu. B. Sturtsel. In early 1938 the IS (*Istrebitel,* ie fighter, Silvanskii) was fast taking shape. It looked very like other fighters of the day, such as the Polikarpov I-180 and 185, though it was clearly much more crude. The sliding canopy looked amateurish, it had a tailskid, and several other parts looked what they were: home made. One is reminded of one of Sir Sydney Camm's favourite sayings, on passing the drawing board of one of his 'young gentlemen': 'H'm, looks like muvver done it.'

Probably any of those young gents at Kingston would have made a better job of the IS than Silvanskii did. On the first landing-gear retraction test it was found that the legs were too long, and the wheels came up beyond their recesses. When the legs had been made to fit, the wheels did go fully into the recesses but stuck out underneath, because there was not enough depth for them. When they put the propeller on, partly because of the shortened legs, it fouled the ground if the tail was raised at all off the ground. Silvanskii just cut 10 cm (4 in) off each blade. There were numerous other faults, most of them of a scarcely believable character (for example the ailerons were difficult to move, as the hinges were not dead in line).

The GAZ (factory) manager could hardly fail to form his own opinion, and he refused permission for the IS to be flown anywhere on his premises. Somehow Silvanskii managed to get the IS brought to Moscow, where he talked the LII (State Flight Research Institute) into providing a test pilot and carrying out preliminary flight trials. According to historian V.B. Shavrov, simple calculations could show that, with its cropped propeller, the IS could hardly take off and could not climb. The unfortunate pilot did manage to get airborne, but found himself at 300 m (1,000 ft) on the point of stalling, with the engine at full power. He managed to get the creation back to the airfield, and in shaken tones pronounced the IS as 'incapable of flight'. It was rather like the 1907 era. Silvanskii was bankrupted, and an industry commission banned him from designing any more aeroplanes.

Anyone think they've got a Silvanskii Special? Seriously, it's amazing what a large effect small changes in shape can have to an established aircraft type. I can personally remember a Spitfire, an Oxford, and even a Harvard that must have been modified by Silvanskii.

22

1937-9

The Luftwaffe That Was

A nation's secret service is normally rather secret itself. In recent years the United Kingdom has sadly made rather a point of turning its secret service into a prolonged story for the world's news media, but back in the 1930s things were quite different. One took it for granted that our unknown agents were feeding back from around the world valuable information on every topic of national interest, virtually as it happened. In 1930 one of the countries regarded as a potential enemy was France. Germany was an unknown quantity, but one precluded by the Treaty of Versailles from posing the slightest military threat.

Then in 1933 the situation changed dramatically. Adolf Hitler, leader of the NSDAP (Nazi party) and previously regarded merely as a loud-mouth rabble rouser, was summoned by President Hindenberg and appointed Chancellor (which was quickly interpreted as absolute dictator) of Germany. The subsequent changes were enormous. Among many other things, colossal emphasis was put on building up industry, and especially the armaments industry. As early as 24 October 1933 farsighted Winston Churchill stood up in the House of Commons and said: 'Germany is already well on the way to become, and must become, incomparably the most heavily armed nation in the world, and the nation most completely ready for war.' He was shouted down, and gained a reputation as a very dangerous warmonger.

On 9 March 1935 it was announced that a German air force, called the Luftwaffe, had been formed. Subsequently this was to become the propaganda spearhead of all the resurrected German armed forces. Under its impressively large and flamboyant leader, Reichsmarschall Hermann Goering, the Luftwaffe became with incredible swiftness the most formidable aerial armada in the world, just as Churchill predicted. On 3 April 1936 Hitler told British ministers that the Luftwaffe had reached 'parity with the RAF'. Its expansion was, moreover, accelerating. Hitler was, in fact, most anxious to avoid war. Instead, he aimed to achieve his objectives by cowing his opponents, and his biggest single propaganda weapon was the mighty and growing Luftwaffe. Far from keeping it secret, he invited aviation experts to come and visit not only the Luftwaffe but also the powerful aircraft industry that supported it.

One such visitor was Roy Fedden, famed engine designer from Bristol and a man selected because of his great international stature. Fedden told the Air Ministry of his invitation, but received no instructions (can you believe it?). He left for Berlin on 7 June 1937, and wrote up this visit in 110 densely packed pages. The Junkers plant at Dessau alone rated about 20,000 words. From Krupps at Essen to a secret magnesium plant deep in the Harz mountains, every door was open, every question answered. He made a second tour in September 1937, during which he visited nine gigantic 'shadow factories', each built within the previous two years and until then unknown in Britain. He again wrote long and detailed reports, but he need not have bothered. There is evidence to suggest that nobody in authority in Britain even read these reports, though—prodded by the Air Staff, which wanted to know what the Germans were doing—the Air Minister, Sir Kingsley Wood, almost a year later (3 August 1938), asked Fedden for 'a short precis'! On 11–14 October 1938 Fedden made yet a third official visit, again to a host of interesting places.

Thus, far from keeping everything secret, the Germans were eager to broadcast their new armed might to the world, and especially to their neighbours. To show how highly un-secret it all was, in 1937 (shortly before the Coronation of King George VI on 12 May) I was thrilled to accompany my Uncle Charles on a visit to Germany. He was a bigwig in the Bank of England, and spoke several European languages fluently. I revered him, not least because he was the only person I knew who flew in airliners. One day he told me we would pay a visit to the 'aircraft works' outside Augsburg, purely because he knew of my interest in aircraft. We went in a humble tram. We were received by Willy Messerschmitt himself, who among many other things showed us the prototype Bf 110. There were lots of 109s. He patted me on the head and said I asked highly intelligent questions. My uncle told me he said 'Bring your nephew back when he is grown up and I will give him a good job here.'

Yet to read the British aeronautical press one would think everything in Germany was highly secret. More than a year later, after the Munich crisis, *Flight* thought it ought to break its near-total silence on the Luftwaffe by trying to put something together. It said there was great difficulty in getting information, but that 'a certain amount of data . . . have filtered through by devious means'. There followed a load of half-truths, liberally sprinkled with errors. They obviously did not take any of the excellent German aviation magazines, nor see the lavish annual produced by the German aircraft industry each year (it weighed about a kilo and was a work of art, besides being crammed with information) which illustrated not only aircraft available for export but also some of the latest prototypes.

So let's look at a few specific aircraft. The Fw 189 twin-boom army co-operation aircraft first flew in July 1938. An excellent photograph appeared in *der Flieger* just over a month later, and an accurate and detailed three-view was in that year's industry yearbook. In England no illustration appeared until rather poor pictures and a demonstrably 'provisional'—ie inaccurate—silhouette appeared in *The Aeroplane Spotter* in May 1941.

What might we have expected to be the best-known Luftwaffe aircraft? Certainly one would have been the Heinkel He 111 bomber, hundreds of which, in several versions, had fought in Spain and been publicized with all the power of propaganda minister Josef Goebbels and the German industry. Yet not only did we fail to read what the different versions were called but we didn't even look at the detailed and accurate drawings that had been published, with the result that as late as February

1940, with several almost intact 111Ps and Hs on our soil, we were publishing grossly inaccurate drawings, with a symmetric nose, totally incorrect shape of wing, and a length of 60 feet instead of 54!

So what did we think the various He 111 versions were called? They say 'a little learning is a dangerous thing'. Someone in Britain had managed to find out that *Krieg* is German for war, and so it became the instinctive and automatic reaction to stick K after a German type number to show that it was a military version and not a civil one. The British-invented designations were quite arbitrary. The 'K Mk IIa' was meant to apply to all the pre-war versions with elliptical wings and a conventional cockpit windscreen. The 'K Mk Va' were the later versions with incredibly broad straight-tapered wings and an asymmetric all-glass nose. A little later a torpedo version appeared, and somebody in London decided to call this the 'He 111HaE', or 'HaE Mk Va'. Then in 1943 a German magazine published a comprehensive feature on the He 111, and British publications sheepishly admitted that all the silly designations were simply British concoctions. They were exactly like the NATO reporting names for Soviet aircraft, which made sense when we didn't know the correct designations.

The Dornier Do 217 bomber first flew in August 1938, not at a secret establishment but at the very place where anyone might have expected to see it, the company's main works at Friedrichshafen. Before war broke out five further Do 217s had gone on test there, and had been repeatedly illustrated in magazines, the pictures including the radial-engined V7 (seventh prototype). Not a word appeared in Britain. That at last in January 1942 a poor picture appeared in British magazines, showing the Do 217 with crudely retouched nacelles bulging above the wing and extending far to the rear. By this time 217s were being shot down over Britain, and in February it was realized that the original 'cat out of the bag' picture had been deliberately distorted in an amazingly childish attempt to mislead. As over 300 Do 217E-1, E-2, and E-3 bombers had been delivered before the end of 1941, and a substantial number (from KG2) had been shot down and investigated, this seemed little more than a joke. But the British aviation press, and the official Air Publication 1480, acted throughout as if the 217 had never been heard of until examples began to be shot down over Britain.

Unquestionably, the most important single type of aeroplane in Germany in 1935–45 was the Messerschmitt Bf 109. I am simply at a loss to explain how it could come about that in World War Two we in Britain believed 'the prototype first flew in 1936', while in 1949–86 we thought it 'first flew in late September 1935'. In fact Hans-Dietrich 'Bubi' Knoetzsch made the first flight on either 29 or 30 *May* 1935! By the outbreak of war hundreds existed, in five main sub-types, and they had fought in Spain and been seen in many public places (and, as I noted earlier, small boy Bill Gunston had crawled all over one). Two of the official visitors to the German Air Ministry had been Major Al Williams and Charles Lindbergh. Both had been invited to fly several aircraft, including a 109. They raved about it, thinking it superior to the Spitfire I, the only other fighter they considered in the same class. A 109 prototype fitted with the DB 600 engine did brilliantly at the 1937 Zurich meeting, and a little later, with a specially boosted engine, gained a world landplane speed record at 379.38 mph. Thus, the Luftwaffe's standard fighter must have been an absolutely known quantity for years before the war.

So what was the problem? First, Messerschmitt really put Ernst Heinkel's nose out of joint in having his upstart fighter selected over the He 112 (which had naturally started out favourite). So Heinkel did his utmost to spread all sorts of malicious propaganda about the 109. Its handling was bad to the point of being dangerous, the slats kept flicking open in manoeuvres (there was a grain of truth in this), and the wings simply came off in high-speed dives. The amazing thing is, these rumours were given a lot of credibility in England. As late as March 1940 the British technical press was repeating these assertions as if they were fact. Even more incredible, we appear to have fallen for the lunatic suggestion that a modified 109 could set a speed record of not far short of 500 mph.

In 1938 Willy Messerschmitt, eager to beat his rival Heinkel, decided to build a small racing aircraft purely to take the world absolute speed record. The result was the Me 209, one of the trickiest and most dangerous aeroplanes ever devised— as far as handling was concerned, right in the class of a previous landplane speed record holder, the Gee Bee Super Sportster. It was this little beast which gained the record on 26 April 1939, and having in later years learned (from that expert on German aircraft Bill Green) something about the 209 I congratulate the skill of Flugkapitän Fritz Wendel on getting it back on the ground in one piece. But the equally tricky Nazis said the record had been gained by something called the 'Me 109R'. They were naturally eager to make the world think the record-breaker was a version of the Luftwaffe's standard fighter. This caused a shock in Britain, though we had already given up hope of getting the record with the N.17 Speed Spitfire when the record was pushed to 464 mph by what we thought was an He 112.

There is no doubt we fell for the '109R' report, though we somehow thought the speed was 481.4 mph instead of 469.22. This unfortunately had the effect of subsequently making the Air Ministry, and everyone else in Britain, think that the Bf 109 had become the 'Me 109'. The error persists to this day, and isn't helped by the fact that no less an outfit than MBB, the giant German aircraft company which succeeded Messerschmitt, is perpetuating the myth of the designation 'Me 109'. But why did we fall for the '109R' in the first place? Any aircraft designer would tell you no Bf 109 could do it. And Augsburg Haunstetten airfield was hardly a secret place. Like I said, you get there on a tram, and could walk past any time of the day. The 209 was so totally different from the 109 I'm amazed nobody noticed it. Wendel said it sounded different, too. Incidentally, four were flown there before the end of May 1939, brightly painted and with civil registration.

The impressive factory of the Henschel company in the Berlin suburb of Schönefeld was the venue for a secret conference on the very latest weapons in late 1936, but the airfield was another example of a place where schoolboys and any other enthusiasts could watch what was happening. In 1937 such observers would have seen the Hs 127 twin-engined high-speed bomber, but this remained unknown in Britain (though featured in the company's advertising). In the spring and summer of 1939 they would have seen the first three Hs 129 anti-tank and ground attack aircraft. But nobody told the British, so when we encountered Hs 129Bs in Tunisia in the closing weeks of 1942 they were hailed as a previously unknown type!

But for my money the most serious and almost unbelievable example of poor intelligence concerns that outstanding fighter the Fw 190. It was an aircraft of extraordinary qualities, with a big and very powerful engine in a small but almost unbreakable airframe, and with everything apart from the propeller worked by electric power. It had such an effect on the RAF in the mid-war years that everyone treated it with the greatest respect. After the war I did my best to get to fly one, but only got as far as starting the mighty BMW 801 engine when a pistol-toting RAF policeman hopped on the wing and asked who had authorized the flight.

As a young cadet, about three years earlier, I was able to visit the acres of rubble that were the main Focke-Wulf design offices at Bremen in May 1945. Those were days when to pick something off the rubble and walk off with it was not thought of as stealing, and I still have notebooks, graph paper and other kinds of stationery collected from the empty Fw offices. I remember seeing projected performance curves, engineering drawings and much else on a version of the Fw 190 that never got built. Instead of a piston engine it had a turbojet in the nose, I believe a BMW 003B. The speed curve had none of the kinks associated with changing supercharger gear and was instead a smooth curve peaking at 800 km/h (497 mph). As I rummaged, I could hardly help thinking about those days, a short five years or so before, when in this same factory everyone had been enthusiastically getting ready to fly the first Fw 190 prototype, the V1.

Eventually I found big albums of photos that none of the Allied tech-intell staff had bothered to grab. They showed the Fw 190 V1 under construction. There were stacks of similar albums; indeed I pinched a few empty ones to put my own photos in, and still have them. To my amazement the 190 V1 album began on 30 July 1938! There were various detail parts at that date, closely followed, in August and September, by landing-gear legs and the complete main spar. By the first weeks of 1939 the first Fw 190 was in final erection, and in another album I found pictures of ground running of the engine on 3 May 1939.

Subsequently, and again thanks to Bill Green, I learned that this aircraft had been taxiing around the Bremen airport in May 1939, and was flown on 1 June. Bremen is a big city, like Augsburg. Its airport was hardly a secure establishment. Again, you could get there by tram, and in any case several thousand people a year passed through as airline passengers. Moreover, there were other more direct clues to the Fw 190. For example, Bruno Bruckmann of BMW told Roy Fedden about his BMW 139 engine and commented that, as well as the Do 217, it had been selected for 'the new Fw 190 fighter'. Later this engine was dropped and replaced by the BMW 801. Of course, all this went into Fedden's meticulous report of his third German visit in October 1938.

Yet somehow we seem to have contrived to remain in total ignorance of the 190. In cities such as Berne and Lisbon, where we had legations or embassies, one could go to news-stands and buy German aviation magazines, which from April 1941 featured the 190 in Focke-Wulf advertisements, with the slogan *die schnellster Jäger der Welt* (the fastest fighter in the world). The artwork showed a 190A diving, guns blazing, accurately showing the disposition of the six guns. Apparently we missed these ads as well.

In early September 1941 three Spitfires were shot down by Fw 190s of 6/JG 26, but the four Focke-Wulfs attacked out of the sun and the luckless Spits (of a much larger force) never knew what hit them. But on 18 September the RAF shot down a 190, and another was claimed on the 27th. This seems to have at last made someone notice the 190, and on 3 October *The Aeroplane* reported '. . . an enemy fighter with a radial engine. One had been shot down the week before, and been identified, a little doubtfully, as a Curtiss Hawk. In reporting the second, the Air Ministry made no attempt to name the type. Nor was it stated whether the machine was operating with a squadron or whether it was an odd one.'

Only gradually we realized that the RAF was meeting Fw 190s. For some reason we invented the designation 'Fw 190H'; but then, as explained in the next story, we made a habit of inventing designations when we didn't know the real ones. Having at first reported that the 190 bore a 'close resemblance to the Curtiss Hawk', we then concocted various drawings showing something that resembled neither the Hawk nor the 190. For good measure we put a pale ring round the German insignia and a vertical white stripe up the fin, over the swastika, in the curious belief that it was Luftwaffe practice to try to look like their enemies. All of this was pure invention. At last, on 23 June 1942, helpful Arnim Faber landed his Fw 190A-3 by mistake in England. This was one of the biggest windfalls the RAF ever had. What the British public did not know was that, in nearly a year of sporadic fighting over northern France, the 190 had established such an ascendancy over the Spitfire VB that the scale of fighter sweeps was considerably curtailed, because such missions were accomplishing almost nothing and becoming very costly. I shall never forget hearing Peter Masefield on the radio broadcast the first public details of the 190, and the shock I felt when he revealed that it was armed with four cannon and two machine guns.

By sheer chance Rolls-Royce had a marvellous new Merlin up its sleeve which, even though of not much more than half the capacity of the BMW 801, was to put the Spitfire right back in the running. Ultimately, despite our seemingly non-existent intelligence, we won the war. But how ever could we have been so ignorant; couldn't we have sent a few plane-mad schoolboys to Germany?

23

1938-42

The Luftwaffe That Wasn't

Whereas in the final years of peace we totally failed to notice the new German fighters and bombers that *were* to become important, we did take note of types that never entered Luftwaffe service at all, as well as of some which were never built and one most interesting fighter which never even existed at all! Even bearing in mind how simple it is to be wise after the event, the efforts of British intelligence, or the British aviation press, to find out about Hitler's Luftwaffe really do not stand up to much scrutiny. (Of course, maybe we didn't *have* anyone charged with Luftwaffe intelligence; perhaps it was just overlooked entirely!)

We have already seen how the publication of the designation 'Me 109R' caused the Bf 109 henceforth to be called the 'Me 109'. The 109R was a pure invention of Goebbels' propaganda machine. The aircraft that set a world record, as noted earlier, was the Me 209, and it was 'Me' rather than 'Bf' because on 11 July 1938 the directors of BFW (Bayerische Flugzeugwerke) voted to change the name of the company to Messerschmitt AG in honour of the man who had designed the Luftwaffe's standard fighter. All *subsequent* designs were prefixed 'Me', while those previously in existence continued to be prefixed 'Bf'. Oddly, the 'Me' craze took Britain by storm, and it has gone on to this day. Not only did we rechristen the 109 and 110 but we also rechristened even the Bf 108B four-seat communications aircraft as the 'Me 108', despite the fact that we had four right here in Britain, with Bf written both on the aircraft and on the flight manual (we also gave it a name, Aldon, from H.J. Aldington, BFW's British agent). And, of course, every one of the thousands of 109s we inspected, either shot down or captured intact, had Bf 109 written in at least three places, and a few other Bf prefixes to part numbers. Of course, if you repeat a lie often enough, people come to believe it. For this reason, chaps who lived for seven tough years facing the threat of 'Me 109s', and who were used to writing the designation repeatedly in their log books, find it difficult to accept that no such aircraft existed. One veteran wrote to *Air International* and said he would never believe it unless someone could show him the designation written on a nameplate, so Bill Green showed him just that!

Of course, the powerful propaganda machine of Josef Goebbels was only doing its job in trying to make the world think that the Luftwaffe's standard fighter could set a startling new world absolute speed record. It was a time when Nazi Germany was exploring every route by which its prowess, and especially that of the Luftwaffe, could be extolled around the world. Sometimes—as in suggesting that any 109 could nudge 500 mph—these efforts went to absurd lengths. On 22 November 1937 the technically very interesting Heinkel He 119 V4, powered by one of the first DB 606 double engines, set a 1,000-km closed-circuit record with a payload of 1,000 kg at 504.98 km/h. In fact, Heinkel had been looking for a speed close to 600 km/h, so later the same aircraft tried again but was written off in a crash landing. The former record was immediately picked up by the propaganda ministry and broadcast to the world as having been set by 'a twin-engined He 111U bomber'. As the Germans had intended, this made the air staffs in London and Paris reassess the He 111. I wonder what they would have done had the figure been near 600 km/h? As it was, the figure equated to about 314 mph, and a fully loaded 111 could never get within about 100 mph of this; I flew one once, and speed was the last thing you looked for (but a nice aeroplane, nevertheless). But when I was a boy and collected cigarette cards the data on the card for the He 111 in the fine Players 'Aircraft' set quoted the figure set by the He 119. I wonder if the Air Ministry believed it?

What is more interesting is that in World War Two we repeatedly frightened ourselves with awesome German warplanes that either never got into service or never existed at all. One of the first to appear was the Dornier Do 29. It was included in a set of 'Four of the newest aeroplanes in service with the German Air Force' in *The Aeroplane* for 9 February 1940. Accompanying artwork was by Harold E. Bubb. Often his perspective was wildly out, but his rendering of the Do 29 looked fine. It showed a 'two-motor fighter' very like the Bf 110 but with annular frontal radiators (if Bubb had put these engines on his Ju 88 it would have been a big improvement). We learned 'The Do 29 is a smaller aeroplane than the Me 110 and thus has not the same long range. Yet . . . its speed is probably in the neighbourhood of 380 mph or even more.' The Do 29 made a few repeat appearances, but gradually faded. In fact it never existed. The whole idea was a complete fabrication, but why and by whom? Back in 1934 the German air ministry had issued a challenging *Kampfzerstörer* specification for a multi-role fighter/attack aircraft. Seven projects were submitted, one being the Do 29. The finalists were the Fw 57 and Hs 124 and, though it became a pure fighter, the Bf 110. The Do 29 was never more than a drawing, never published in 1934 and in no way resembling the 'Do 29' unearthed by the British magazine six years later! (The post-war Dornier company did make a Do 29, a piston-engined STOL of 1958.)

As a teenager I bought that outstanding weekly *The Aeroplane Spotter* from its first issue of 2 January 1941. It is nostalgic to thumb through them. The first issue contained comparative silhouettes of some confusing fighters with V-12 engines, one being the Heinkel He 113. From April 1940 onwards this was known to be one of the Luftwaffe's principal types of fighter. Dozens, if not hundreds, of RAF pilots reported meeting it in combat. It continued to be an important type in the syllabus for the various Allied recognition tests, though late in the war pictures of it tended to be accompanied by the comment that not much had been heard of it lately. Hardly surprising, because it never went into production, far less into service.

Indeed, as many readers will know, it was not the He 113 at all but the He 100. This rakish and outstandingly fast fighter was designed by Heinkel in 1937 as a final fling to try to supplant the Bf 109 as the standard single-seat fighter of the Luftwaffe. It first flew on 22 January 1938, and by this time the reader will not be surprised that, though both Roy Fedden and Charles Lindbergh were shown He 100s, not a word of the former's detailed report seems to have been read by the British Air Ministry. Soon more than a dozen of these beautiful little fighter prototypes were thundering round north Germany, and Ernst Udet used one on 6 June 1938 to set a new world 100 km record at 634.8 km/h. About two months later the Chief of the French Air Staff visited Germany and Udet put on a great show in the fifth He 100. Milch asked 'How's the series production coming?' and—this was apparently completely unrehearsed—Udet, climbing from the cockpit, replied 'The second production line is ready, and the third will be in action in a fortnight'!

Actually the He 100, for all its speed, got nowhere. Heinkel was therefore permitted to seek export orders, and three were soon sold (for study purposes) to the Soviet Union. The first He 100D-0 bore civil registration D-ITLR, and I never discovered if the pun on the Führer's name was deliberate (I doubt it). Japan bought three of the 12 He 100D-1 fighters, and a manufacturing licence, but the outbreak of war prevented the shipment of jigs and tooling (odd, because later such items were common cargo aboard submarines). Hungary also intended to build He 100Ds, but the contract was never signed. So this left nine He 100D-1 fighters with nothing to do. Probably as little more than a joke they were painted with various supposed 'Luftwaffe unit insignia', one lot on one side and another on the other side, and large white numbers—which bore not the slightest resemblance to real Luftwaffe codes. Then they were photographed in flight and on the ground in what looked like convincing front-line situations, with uniformed ground crew holding starter handles, helping intrepid pilots on with their parachutes and kneeling by the chocks. We fell for it hook, line and sinker—largely, I suppose, because we had completely failed to notice the He 100s two years previously.

We can't get rid of the thing even today. Wanting a picture of a Bf 109, the Editor of the beautiful *Rolls-Royce Magazine* put in an He 100D, fictitious markings and all!

The second issue of the *Spotter* announced that it was now possible to refer to the Westland Whirlwind, but that photographs of the British fighter, lots of which had been flying round Yeovil since October 1938, were forbidden. The magazine commented that this was a great pity because 'there seems a great likelihood of confusion between it and the new German Focke-Wulf Fw 187 Zerstörer two-motor fighter, upon which the enemy are pinning great hopes for the coming offensive'. I'm not sure which offensive was referred to—Balkans, Crete, Soviet Union?—but the Fw 187 certainly played no part in it, because again the type concerned never went into production. The prototype 187 flew in May 1937, and displayed outstanding performance. Like the Whirlwind it had only low-powered engines, in this case 700 hp Jumo 210s. The sixth prototype was fitted with DB 600s, and reached 635 km/h (395 mph), making this particular prototype unquestionably the fastest fighter in the world at that time. Despite its good qualities and excellent performance, the Fw 187 was rejected by the Luftwaffe.

Three Fw 187A-1s were painted with large white numbers and used to form an *Industrie-schutzstaffel* to defend the Bremen factory. Inevitably, the propaganda ministry seized on this unit as another perfect subject for global misinformation. Hundreds of pictures were issued of *'die neue Zerstörer* [destroyer] *der Luftwaffe'.* Equally inevitably, we took it all on board.

Also in the second *Spotter* was the solution to the recognition test from issue No

1. One of the tough photos was a Spitfire, the other being the (very similar in plan view) Heinkel He 118 V1 (first prototype). We were told 'The He 118 was used in the Polish campaign, but little has been heard of it recently.' Again, not surprising, because far from fighting in Poland the He 118 never went into production. Its failure was ensured on 27 June 1936 when top procurement boss Ernst Udet forgot to select coarse pitch before making a steep test dive; the engine blew up and the tail came off. As that was three years before the war, whatever made us think 118s had served in Poland? In fact the 118 did have one claim to fame: in the spring of 1939 (we don't know the date) it was the first aircraft ever to take a turbojet into the air, even though it was just slung underneath for test purposes.

Another aircraft said to have served in Poland was the 'Messerschmitt Jaguar'. This again was a case of Britain falling completely for that same old propaganda ministry. The Jaguar was a fine looking twin-engined bomber, superficially very like a Bf 110 but with a glazed nose and a few other differences. It was featured in various British publications. Vol 1 of *Aircraft of the Fighting Powers* stated that the Jaguar was 'serving in many squadrons of the Luftwaffe', described the camouflage schemes, and quoted an example of the unit code lettering, to assist model-makers. All rather silly, because the 'Jaguar' was actually the Messerschmitt Bf 162 V2, flown in September 1937 as civilian aircraft D-AOBE. Its resemblance to the Bf 110 was superficial, and only three prototypes were ever constructed, all different. Even at the time none of my schoolfriends believed that the Jaguar was a real service type, partly because—as far as we knew—it had a name only, yet it took years to fade from British recognition tests!

Issue 3 of the *Spotter* had a set of head-on views of fighters which included not only the He 113 but also the He 112 (which did serve very briefly with the Luftwaffe, but only because 12 bought by Japan were temporarily held back and given to III/JG 132 during the Munich crisis!). The same issue contained a list of Luftwaffe types which had been observed over the British Isles. The list included the Ha 139, Ha 140, Do 24, Do 26, Go 149, He 49, He 111K Mk IIa, He 113, He 114, Ju 86K, Ju 90, and Me Jaguar. Not one of these had been operated by the Luftwaffe over Britain by January 1941, and most never served with the Luftwaffe at all. The Do 24 did serve with the Luftwaffe, but not until two years later. The three Do 26s went to Norway only, and were withdrawn from operational use after April 1940. The Go 149 was a civil aerobatic trainer of which three prototypes were built. The He 49 was not a 'float seaplane' but a biplane fighter, again restricted to three prototypes. I know the Luftwaffe sang '*Wir marschen gegen England',* but I don't think they marsched in the He 49 because it dated from 1932. The He 114 served briefly before the war, and again in 1941 but only on the Soviet front. One or two of the others on the list seem doubtful; He 59, yes, but on rescue missions well away from our coast; Ar 196, very possibly; Fw 200K (well, 200C), doubtful; Hs 126, why should that come to our prickly shores?

Issue No 5 contained a description of the Fw 187, the engines being given as 1,150 hp DB 601As, resulting in a speed quoted precisely as 362 mph. I don't know where this came from, as full descriptions of the 187 had appeared before the war. As noted earlier, one prototype did have DB 600 engines, but of 950 hp, and nudged 400 mph. Issue 9 contained the first picture of the Fw 200C Condor, but it was called the 'Fw 200K Kurier' and was said to have 1,320 hp BMW 801 engines. This notion that the Condors had these engines persisted to the end of the war, only the power was raised to 1,600 hp. The designations Fw 200K-1 and K-2 were invented, the K-2 having 801s. (In fact the engines were 1,000/1,200 hp Fafnirs.) It was also stated that the 801 was the Twin Wasp built under licence; the Ju 88G and Fw 190 wouldn't have been quite the same if this had been true! Many years earlier the Bayerische Motorenwerke had indeed purchased a licence for the Pratt & Whitney Hornet, and the P&W cylinder design had certainly influenced their subsequent engines, but with such a brilliant team of engineers headed by Sachse and Loehner (later joined by Bruckmann and Oestrich from Bramo) they had no need to copy anyone. But the World War Two period was a time when, in Britain at least, even quite intelligent people automatically assumed that each new German, Russian, or Japanese aircraft or engine was either made under licence (usually from the USA) or else a flagrant copy.

This leads to the most incredible tale of all the 'non-Luftwaffe' aircraft. The Focke-Wulf Fw 198 started its life in 1939, and it endured throughout the war. From time to time RAF aircrew would report encountering this very distinctive fighter, but towards the end of the war it began to fade from the scene. Not surprisingly really, as it never existed!

I believe it first emerged into the public gaze in a French magazine in November 1939. I have never tracked down the article, but it showed an impressive twin-boom machine, 'powered by a pusher DB 601 engine of 1,360 hp' (at that time the same engine in the Bf 109E was rated at 1,175 hp, but for this super fighter someone thought they'd up it a bit). On top of the nacelle was a remarkably big canopy giving perfect all-round view, and in the nose was a battery of cannon and machine guns. Altogether the Fw 198 looked uncannily like the D.H.100 Spider Crab, prototype of the Vampire, but of course with a pusher propeller instead of a jet.

It was stated that this interesting new fighter 'appeared at Nürnberg' (British magazines said Nuremberg) in September 1938. This was the occasion of a giant Nazi rally, and the only way the Fw 198 could have 'appeared' there would have been to take part in the big fly-past. As about 100,000 people were present it should not have been too difficult to discover if such an aircraft really did fly over, and as the Fw 198 never existed I'm surprised that this purely dreamed-up report was never questioned. Having once been created, apparently in Paris, this fighter had to be described as a copy of something else, and the French magazine naturally picked on a French aircraft, the Hanriot H 110. This was designed by Jean Biche in 1931, so it was hardly a suitable basis for a new fighter of 1938.

Well, the 198 went from strength to strength. In *The Aeroplane* of 9 February 1940 it was illustrated and described as 'now in service with the German Air Force'. Peter (now Sir Peter) Masefield was at that time the journal's Technical Editor. Unlike most British aviation writers 50 years ago he travelled widely and, a few weeks before the factory was destroyed by the Luftwaffe, he visited the Koolhoven company at Waalhaven, in the Netherlands. Fritz Koolhoven, known to everyone as 'Cully', was a large and expansive man who loved to entertain. He told Peter about a Dutch twin-boom pusher fighter and then produced drawings of the 'Fw 198', saying 'Now see what the Germans have built'. I asked Sir Peter about this recently, and he said, 'It was a long time ago, but I remember the occasion clearly. What I do not know is whether he believed in the Fw 198 or whether for some reason he wished to mislead.'

Their rival, *Flight,* published their own drawing six days later, and were rather

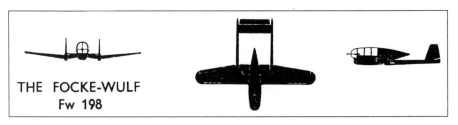

THE FOCKE-WULF
Fw 198

In the mid-war years the Fw 198 looked different, as in this silhouette from *The Aeroplane Spotter* of 24 April 1941.

upset that 'the disposition of the radiator is not known'. But by March 1940 the elusive 198 had begun to change its appearance, and soon it took on a completely distinctive form, quite unlike the original idea but much more convincing. Now the pilot sat in a completely glazed nose, rather like some of the German bombers, but a giant cannon projected ahead and there were clearly other guns in the fuselage or wings. Issue 17 of the *Spotter* included a detailed silhouette showing the retracted landing gear and the four fixed slots in each wing leading edge. But a 1943 USAAF recognition manual, which I found on board a B-17F, reverted to the original 1939 appearance (but included precise specifications).

In Issue 122 of the *Spotter,* dated 2 November 1944, a correspondent asked about the Fw 198, and correctly pointed out that the number had been assigned to the Arado Ar 198 observation aircraft. The Editor's astounding reply was 'No irrefutable proof of the existence of the Fw 198 has ever come to light, and the drawings of such a type are believed to have been mistaken impressions of an Fw 189 . . .' This seemed arrant nonsense. The Fw 189 and Fw 198 were as alike as chalk and cheese.

Some time later I met Dipl-Ing Kurt Tank and asked if he could tell me about the Fw 198. He said: 'I was shown pictures of it in an English magazine during the war. Of course, I was at a loss to understand it. How could there be such an aircraft without my knowledge!!' A little later an ex-USAAF recognition expert told me they had picked up the 198 from the British (and clearly introduced their own modifications) but that it had been discovered that the whole thing stemmed from the Czech Praga E.51. It was not until I saw *Air International* for February 1974 that the puzzle was solved at last. Here was a description of the Dutch de Schelde S.21 fighter, designed in 1938 and almost complete when the factory was occupied by the Germans in May 1940. It never flew, but here at last was the 'Fw 198'. So what I have been trying to discover is: who sent the description of this Dutch fighter to Britain at the beginning of 1940, calling it the 'Focke-Wulf Fw 198', which we were already convinced existed? There are a host of minor puzzles, such as 'Didn't the British already know about the S.21', and 'What did the escaped Dutch chaps who knew the S.21 think when they read about the Fw 198?'

After this, everything else is surely anti-climax! By mid-1941 we were beginning to get a bit more 'clued up' and less naïve. The inventions tended to be fairly minor, such as the Do 18K-2 flying boat, which burst on the scene in September 1941. The original Jumo 205 diesels were replaced by BMW 132N radials. It was explained that severe cooling problems with the rear engine had to be overcome, but that now the installation worked well, and that the new Do 18K-2 was the standard Luftwaffe version. The famed J.H. Clark did detailed drawings of it. All a bit odd, because only one radial-engined Do 18 ever flew, and that was the civil Do 18L, in November 1939! The 'K-2' never existed.

One minor puzzle endured almost to the present day. Many authoritative works of reference state that in 1944 the Luftwaffe began receiving three improved Ju 88 night fighters, the Ju 88G-7a, -7b, and -7c. These are usually described as being similar to the G-6 series but fitted with Jumo 213 engines and new radars. In fact, these aircraft (built at Bernburg, with Werknummer beginning with 62) were all G-6cs. This was the standard production night fighter to the end of the war. Only 12 G-7s were ever built, with the pointed and extended wingtips of the 188 and 388. They were found to offer no advantage, and the G-7 never went into production. There was also a plan for a G-10, with the stretched fuselage of the Ju 88H to give 'all-night' endurance (14 hours), but this never got off the drawing board.

Today we are probably much more cautious or sophisticated, but in World War Two there was a vast amount of rather naïve enthusiasm. As we have seen, this resulted in people being eager to believe almost anything, such as invented German aircraft. Having taken it aboard, it would then grow firmer by the hour. One chap would produce artwork, another would make a model, and another would report he had encountered it on an operational mission. All with the best intentions.

24

25 February 1938

Sources of Trouble

By judicious selection of one's facts, I suppose it is possible to prove almost anything. Nevertheless, I have been struck throughout my life by the way, whenever a new aircraft has appeared bristling with radical or even seemingly dangerous features, it has seldom been these that have caused the serious trouble. Invariably, the problems have been posed by the conventional parts. Here are a few examples from the past 50 years.

On 25 February 1938 Blohm und Voss in Germany flew the first prototype BV 141 (totally unknown in Britain, of course). Visually, this was perhaps the most unbelievable aircraft ever designed, because it was grossly asymmetric. On one side of the centreline was a completely glazed crew nacelle. On the other side was an engine, behind which was a slim tail boom and asymmetric tail! It was such an extraordinary creation that the German air ministry at first refused to provide any support or funding. One might have thought it would be impossible to fly. What actually happened was that the BV 141A was a delight to fly, but suffered interminable problems with the hydraulics and landing gear.

On about 30 March 1940 the Blackburn B.20 made its first flight. This was again an extraordinary machine, a reconnaissance flying boat with the speed of a fighter, powered by two Sabre engines. The key to its speed lay in the unique retractable planing bottom; the entire aircraft was supported above the lower part of the hull, which was called a pontoon, on groups of hinged powered struts. The stabilizing floats could also retract to form the wingtips. The whole thing looked most unlikely, but what actually happened was that there was severe trouble with the ailerons. On 7 April 1940 the B.20 crashed into the sea at high speed. The extraordinary retractable hull was no problem.

On 5 March 1943 Britain's first jet fighter, the Gloster F.9/40 (Meteor), at last got into the air. Many officials and experts had predicted all sorts of dire trouble, mainly concerned with the jets blasting past the tail. What actually happened was that the test pilots spent months sorting out difficulties with the ailerons, rudder, nose gear, and wheel brakes. They also spent weeks searching for a suitable airfield from which to do the test flying (can you believe it?). The revolutionary jet propulsion was forgotten beside all these other difficulties.

On 6 December 1944 the first Heinkel He 162 made its first flight, after the most incredibly fast jet design and development programme. This was a last-ditch 'panic' programme for an aircraft to be built at the rate of 4,000 per month and flown by hastily 'trained' Hitler Youths. One might have expected all manner of problems, but the only serious one to raise its head was defective wood bonding caused by British bombing of a distant chemical works!

On 27 July 1949 the civil jet age opened with the first flight of the Comet I. Its radical features included jet propulsion, massive fuel capacity in integral tanks, fully powered flight controls served by triplex hydraulic systems, slightly swept wings, bogie landing gears (not on the first prototype), and engines buried inside the wing roots; but what killed the programme was structural failure of the fuselage skin caused by too sharp a corner in a small cut-out!

On 20 July 1951 Neville Duke made the first flight in the beautiful Hawker P.1067, later named Hunter. This was at last the first British swept-wing jet fighter, but its troubles had nothing to do with sweepback, but with unacceptable airbrakes, engine surge when the guns were fired, the need for an 'all flying' tail, damage caused by spent shell cases, dangerous accumulations of gun gas in the nose, severe misting of the windscreen and canopy, and chronic shortage of fuel capacity!

On 7 August 1951 the flight test programme of the McDonnell XF3H-1 Demon was opened. This aircraft really looked futuristic, and certainly a generation later than the Hunter. Who would have thought that, while the advanced highly swept wing, full-span droops, sharply swept tail with slab horizontal surface, and many other advanced features would work as planned, the entire programme would grind to a prolonged and costly halt because of the terrible engine? Five years later the Navy got a redesigned Demon with a different engine.

On 24 October 1953 the first Convair YF-102 flew at Edwards. Designed as a supersonic all-weather interceptor, this featured a bold tailless delta layout, with a very thin wing of pure triangular form, and a large triangular vertical tail. It was the world's first supersonic delta, and some aerodynamicists were apprehensive, fearing uncontrollable pitch-up and various other hazards. What actually happened was that the YF-102 proved to have drag far beyond estimate and to be incapable of exceeding the speed of sound! Convair had to redesign it according to a newly discovered 'area rule', resulting in severe delays and massive escalation in costs. But the radical delta configuration had nothing to do with it.

On 6 October 1954 Peter Twiss made the first flight of the Fairey FD.2. This was Britain's first supersonic delta, combining a tailless layout with a very thin wing, fully powered flight controls (with no feedback, so the pilot would not feel any flutter), and a droop-snoot hinged nose. So what troubles were encountered? On the fourteenth flight an internal pressure build-up collapsed the fuel collector tank. The engine, starved of fuel, ran down and stopped, which also eliminated hydraulic pressure except what was in the accumulator. Twiss did a masterly dead-stick landing at 265 mph with nothing extended except the nose gear. All the radical features gave no problems.

On 25 March 1955 John Konrad made the first flight of the XF8U-1, prototype of the F-8 Crusader. This was packed with unconventional features, such as integrally machined wing panels, powered leading and trailing variable camber, slab tails, spot-welded titanium rear fuselage, and a huge ventral airbrake hinged to a tray, itself hinged in the opposite sense, containing launch tubes for 32 rockets. The most unconventional feature of all was that the entire wing was pivoted above the fuselage, so that its incidence could be varied for carrier landings and takeoffs, keeping the fuselage level. Many engineers were worried about this bold feature. Subsequently the F8U suffered from a few minor development troubles, including main-gear weakness, but the bold features never gave a moment's anxiety. And one Navy pilot took off and then landed again with the wings folded!

On 16 May 1957 John Booth made the first flight of the Saunders-Roe SR.53. This brilliant little supersonic interceptor was the first fruit of years of effort on mixed-power fighters, with a small turbojet for cruise and a powerful but fully controllable rocket engine for maximum performance. It was planned as a stepping stone to the more advanced SR.177, but many people were apprehensive about the mix of an afterburning turbojet and a rocket fed with kerosene and concentrated HTP (high test peroxide), especially in a densely packed supersonic fighter. In fact everything worked perfectly until, taking off on the short crossing runway at Boscombe in the No 2 aircraft on 5 June 1958, Booth called 'panic stations, come and get me!' He shut down the engines and abandoned the takeoff, but did not open the airbrakes nor stream the drag chute. The white jet carried on down the grassy slope beyond the runway until it hit a giant approach-light pole. The tall concrete pole broke into three and the top portion fell on the canopy, killing Booth instantly. Nobody was ever sure what had happened, but several Saro engineers confided to me that, in their view, the blind-flying panel had become unlatched and fallen back during takeoff. Nothing to do with all the new features!

On 21 December 1964 Dick Johnson and Val Prahl made the first flight in the TFX, the General Dynamics F-111. This was absolutely stuffed with new and radical features, including fully augmented turbofan engines, advanced structure of titanium alloy, a unique ejectable crew capsule (which could serve as a survival shelter on land or water), very comprehensive avionics, built-in electronic-warfare systems, gigantic fuel capacity (turning this aircraft from a tactical fighter into, in one version, a strategic bomber) and, most remarkable of all, pivoted 'swing wings' which could be spread out to a wide span for takeoff and landing and folded right back beside the body for dashes at Mach 2.5. Various critics predicted all kinds of trouble, and they were right. The unfortunate 'One-Eleven' was to endure not only a bad press but years of desperate technical problems. But none of the problems had anything to do with the new features. They centred on escalation in weight (so serious the Navy gave up their version entirely), mismatching between the engine inlets and the engines so severe the TF30 engine installation was called 'a hazard to safe flight', mechanical failures of the taileron power units, and fractures of the steel bridge joining the wing pivots together. According to Johnson, 'The swing wing gave no trouble at all; the one thing we argued about endlessly was which way to move the handle.'

This is surely one of the more outstanding examples where the troubles were not those expected. Others include the P.1127, where nearly all the problems had nothing to do with VTOL or (with the exception of one incident) vectored thrust; the amazing H.P.115, the personification of a paper-dart aeroplane, which suffered various snags connected with systems but flew like a dream; the even more extraordinary Bell X-22A, which had four giant propellers in swivelling ducts instead of wings, but which was destroyed by a hydraulic failure in a perfectly ordinary part of the system; the Tornado, where many people predicted problems caused by trying to fit together parts made in so many factories throughout Europe;

and the exceedingly tricky and totally unstable X-29A, with a forward-swept wing, whose test pilot loved it and then was killed in a restored Grumman Avenger!

Perhaps I ought to make the point that most of today's aircraft suffer from few technical problems, and overcome these swiftly. The lethal problems are the political ones.

25

6 April 1939

The P-400

The scene is a couple of Yanks ('sad sack' GIs) on a Pacific island about 1942. One says: 'Whaddya mean, P-400? There ain't no such airplane!' The other retorts: 'There sure is . . . it's a P-40 with a Zero on its tail.' Well, I hate to be clever-clever, but there was also a *real* P-400. It was the ex-British version of the Bell P-39 Airacobra, one of the most unconventional fighters of its day. And the funny thing is, the Americans thought it had some pretty useful qualities (though not enough perhaps to make up for the shortcomings), the British thought it was a complete disaster and couldn't get rid of it quickly enough, and the Soviet Union thought it was just about the greatest bit of kit supplied by any of their Allies!

Larry Bell—like Jack Northrop, small in stature but a giant in character—had been a vice-president of Consolidated at Buffalo. In 1935 the company moved to San Diego. For some reason Bell preferred the fog and snow of Buffalo to the nicest city in the United States, and so did 56 of his colleagues, so they stayed behind and started Bell Aircraft. Among other things they began designing fighters. This would have been challenging enough, but Bell's engineers, led by Robert J. Woods, O.L. Woodson, and Harland M. Poyer, seemed to take a delight in thinking up as many extraordinary new ideas as they could. Their first offering, the Airacuda, had two pusher engines and a gunner with a 37-mm blunderbuss in the front of each nacelle. This was followed by the Model 4, a prototype being ordered in October 1937 as the XP-39 Airacobra.

As it was a single-engined tractor aircraft there might not have seemed much scope for unconventionality, and in flight the P-39 looked fairly normal. In fact it had: tricycle landing gear, then a novelty; an engine behind the pilot; a massive 37-mm Oldsmobile cannon firing through the propeller hub; and a cockpit with a car-type door on each side. There were also many minor unconventional features, most of them seemingly adopted merely in order to be different. From the start the Airacobra was the subject of flamboyant advertising, and in fact the original XP-39 did have an excellent performance. The 1,150-hp Allison V-1710 engine was fitted with a turbosupercharger. It first flew on the date above, and not only demonstrated a level speed of 390 mph at 20,000 ft but it could reach that height in five minutes. Small wonder that the US Army Air Corps soon placed orders; and this was followed in March 1940 by 200 for France's Armée de l'Air and, a month later, for

475 for Britain, the export versions being designated P-400. Britain took over the French order, so by the summer of 1940 the RAF was looking forward to receiving 675 of the unusual fighters, which were given the British name Bell Caribou I.

It still seems to me almost unbelievable that whereas today we want to test-fly new RAF aircraft before they have been built, in 1940 no British pilot flew an Airacobra until eight months after the British order had been signed. In fact, while the impressive performance referred to a highly polished aircraft with a turbosupercharger and carrying no armament or equipment, the production aircraft had no turbo and weighed at least a ton more. On test in England at the Air Fighting Development Unit in July 1941 the Airacobra I (the name Caribou was dropped) was found to have a maximum speed '33 mph lower than anticipated'. As the British specification always gave the speed as 358 mph, this suggests the RAF was looking for 391. What's more, the rate of climb was not much more than half that predicted, and while performance was quite good at low levels it fell off very rapidly above 15,000 ft. For example, at 13,000 ft the Airacobra was 18 mph faster than a Spitfire VB, but at 15,000 ft they were equal and at 24,000 ft the Spitfire was no less than 55 mph faster. Moreover, range was about 600 miles, instead of the claimed 1,000. On the other hand the US fighter was extremely nice to fly, easy to taxi, take off and land, and had many other attractive qualities. In fact, at low level it was excellent.

In September the unusual fighter re-equipped a famous Auxiliary squadron, No 601 County of London. Received 'with great enthusiasm'—which, as I comment elsewhere, is unusual for new equipment—the Airacobra was soon found to be a mixed blessing. In addition to its other shortcomings, its long takeoff run posed problems on many of the RAF's small grass airfields. Armament comprised a 20-mm Hispano with a 60-round drum, which worked well; two 0.5-in Brownings above the nose which fed lethal concentrations of gas into the cockpit and blinded the pilot at night; and four 0.300-in (not 0.303-in) Brownings in the wings. Accessibility to all guns was poor, the 0.300 magazines (which extended almost to the wingtips) distorted and jammed the belts, and a particularly serious fault was that firing the guns upset the compass to the point where it was usually useless. These were surely all obvious faults which could have been cured very quickly? As it was, 601 made only one combat operation, re-equipping with Spitfires in December.

Subsequently, Bell kept on improving the Airacobra and delivered 9,585. Large numbers went to the US Army, especially in North Africa and the Pacific. I never flew one, but sat in a few. They were very cosy (well, cramped), and I marvelled that anyone could become familiar with so many dials in such a totally haphazard arrangement, unlike the ordered logic of RAF cockpits. But by far the biggest operator, with 4,773 supplied, was the Soviet Union. Here there was a tough war going on mainly at low level, and fighters had to operate from strips paved with boards and trunks of fir trees. Not many aircraft could survive in such an environment—to say nothing of action by the Luftwaffe—but one of the types that made it was the Airacobra. Admittedly most of those on the Eastern Front were of the final P-39Q version (the suffix letter reveals how often modifications were introduced), but the point is that all Soviet Airacobras had a good reputation, from the very first batch received in December 1941.

One of the other stories (No 27) begins with 'Give a dog a bad name . . .' In other words, at least in the rather hectic environment of World War Two when there were lots of aircraft to choose from, first impressions tended to be given undue weight. The Airacobra was to some extent justifiably rated by the RAF as 'a great disappointment', but the only incurable shortcoming was poor high-altitude performance. We had exactly the same problem with the Typhoon, but thanks mainly to Bee Beamont this aircraft was not cancelled and instead did tremendous work at heights mostly below 2,000 ft. In the same way, if the Airacobra I had been given a few simple modifications, such as properly sealed 0.5-in guns with flash eliminators, flame dampers on the exhausts (these were in fact fitted), and a distant-reading master compass, it might have become a valued ground-attack aircraft. At low levels its performance was good, in almost all respects better than that of the Spitfire VB.

When the P-39 got to the Soviet Union nobody had any preconceived ideas. The NII (State aircraft test institute) merely checked it out and recorded all the figures, meanwhile seeing how it handled and which bits fell off. Nothing fell off, and pilots said they liked it. When it got to the front line it quickly built up a reputation that nobody in the RAF had thought of: toughness (I won't use the word 'rugged', which has nothing to do with strength but means 'rough, hairy and uneven'). Time after time Airacobras slammed on to bumpy treetrunk strips without suffering any damage. Time after time they got shot to pieces and flew home, the pilot sometimes protected by the engine behind him.

I grew up in World War Two knowing that the Airacobra was one of those much-vaunted American creations that simply failed to live up to the advertising. Back in the early 1950s not many of the more thoughtful and penetrating analyses of wartime aircraft had been published, so I was rather surprised when the Soviet Air Attaché in London—I cannot remember which, it may have been Col Marakazov or Konobeyev—mentioned that he had been an Airacobra pilot. 'Sorry,' I said, 'but we did send the Soviet Union Spitfires as well.' The colonel expressed astonishment. 'What was so special about the Spitfire?' he asked. 'All along our sector of the front regiments equipped with Spitfires or Hurricanes were converting to the Airacobra as fast as they could. My own unit, the 57th Guards IAP, was almost completely Airacobra equipped when I joined them, and it was only then that we really made our presence felt. In 1944 we changed again, to the Kingcobra, which carried more guns and bombs. I have never understood why all these aircraft were so underrated by the British and Americans.'

So there you have it. The RAF couldn't wait to junk the Airacobra and get Spitfires, while the front-line Soviet regiments couldn't wait to junk their Spitfires and get Airacobras. Perhaps a lot depends on whether you match the mission to the aircraft.

John Blake recalls yet another Soviet Air Attaché, Feodor Rumyantsyev. Extremely tall, and with a booming voice, he personified those tiresome Russians who have absolutely no sense of humour but have a proverb for every occasion. One day his frame loomed over us as we discussed the Airacobra. 'In Soviet Union we have proverb about Airacobra; we never let any pilot over 35 fly one.' This seemed odd, so we asked why. Without the slightest trace of a smile he replied 'Too dangerous, get balls caught in prop shaft.'

Above Sir Hiram Maxim shows the amazingly light weight of one of his two-cylinder compound steam engines. But what about the boiler, fuel, and water? There were easier ways of getting a few seconds of thrust.

Below The author guestimates that in 1935–50 not less than 72,000 aircraft were written off following a swing on takeoff or on landing — all because of having a tailwheel! This Mosquito PR.34 swung to disaster at Asmara, Eritrea, coming to rest 50 yards from a sister aircraft which had done exactly the same thing two days earlier. Both were write-offs. *Fred Adkin via Aeroplane Monthly.*

Above Early retractable undercarriages were often cumbersome monstrosities, while early 'tricycle' gears, even fixed ones, were often even worse. In the author's view the worst was Tolstikh's 1940 gear tested on an SB-2, in comparison with which the first British example, seen here, was commendably neat. The sole ST.25U built for the Air Ministry (many other Monospars were later impressed) is seen here landing at Hanworth on 31 May 1938. In 1940 it went to 93 Squadron to help Havoc crews learn the technique.

Below The Aerodrome prior to its first launch from the complicated catapult structure erected above the houseboat in autumn 1903.

Above On Monday 14 December 1903 Wilbur Wright won the toss of a coin and set off on the first aeroplane flight. He did what countless pilots have done since: let speed bleed off to the stall. The Flyer graunched into the sand, and repairs took until Thursday. Then it was Orville's turn.

Below This closeup of a Bristol Coanda cockpit area (actually of one of the participants in the 1912 Military Trials) shows the dangerously horizontal angle of the upper anti-lift bracing wires. Any student of trigonometry could quickly get a rough idea of the multiplying factor on the wire tensions.

Above far left In contrast, a Russian pioneer, A. V. Shiukov, gave the anti-lift wires almost as good an angle as those under the wing. Note that his 1912 Utka (Duck) had the propeller behind the 50 hp Gnome; it also had winglets.

Left The trim Short Silver Streak, completed in 1920 in the teeth of opposition from Air Ministry experts, was one of the first aircraft to be constructed entirely from Duralumin light alloy. The engine was a 240 hp Siddeley Puma.

Below left Cody's much-rebuilt machine tempted fate during the 1912 Military Trials by flying the Union Jack upside-down!

Above left This cutaway ABC Dragonfly is in London's Science Museum.

Above right The dorsal gunner of this Curtiss H-16 is sitting on the edge of his gun ring, outside the aircraft (perhaps it was a hot day?).

Below The first Airco D.H.18 in the first hangar to be completed at Waddon Airport (later called Croydon), according to a manuscript note on the back of the original print. The pilot sat behind the passengers, like the driver of a Hansom cab. The date is 29 March 1920.

Above left The 'Westland Dreadnought Postal Monoplane' would probably have benefited from tunnel testing.

Left The Parnall Possum was one of several 1923 aircraft whose cost seems hard to justify. The concept of a central engine room driving via gears and shafting had been amply explored with many other aircraft before 1923.

Below left The Bristol Type 72 Racer was the smallest aeroplane that could be bolted on behind a fully cowled Jupiter engine. The retractable undercarriage worked, but the ailerons didn't. Uwins in cockpit.

Above The original WU (Whittle Unit), the world's first turbojet.

Below R.101 riding at the mast at Cardington shortly after her completion, and before being made 45 ft longer.

Above Running the Peto seaplane out of its hangar aboard HM Submarine M2.

Below Mignet himself in one of the first of the Pou tribe.

Two photographs showing the premises of Donald W. Douglas: the original design office was behind a barber shop (haircut 35 cents) on LA's Pico Boulevard; then came the first factory, on Wilshire Boulevard; then came the enormous plant on Ocean Park Boulevard in Santa Monica, seen in the photograph below in 1936. Douglas left Santa Monica in stages in the 1970s.

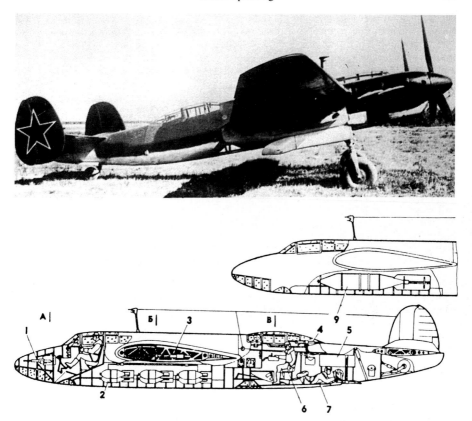

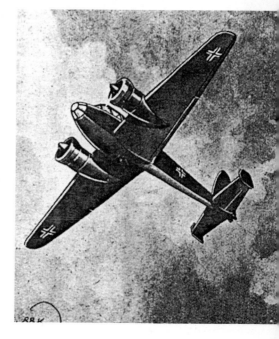

Top left Running up the already very tired Gnome in the 'Seven-day Bus' in the field at Netley a week after the start of World War 1. Mahl in cockpit, Howard Pixton (winner of the 1914 Schneider Trophy) in trilby, and designer Carol Vasilesco far right.

Middle left Taken from the September 1986 issue of *Air International*, this shows two Fokker E III (Eindecker) fighters in May 1916, the nearer machine being No 358/16 covered with transparent 'Cellon'.

Left The only known photograph of Silvanskii's fighter. *Via Nigel Eastaway.*

Above Aeroplane No 103, the ANT-58, was designed in prison. Despite this it led to the extremely successful Tu-2.

Right Would you recognize this February 1940 artwork by *The Aeroplane* as a 'Ju 88K'?

Two photographs of the Me 209, showing it to be a tiny racer totally unrelated to the Bf 109 fighter. Test pilot Dr-Ing Hermann Wurster is shown with the unpainted first prototype; in the other picture Messerschmitt is congratulating Fritz Wendel after setting the record in the same aircraft, painted and with registration INJR. This picture appeared in German newspapers. Try standing behind the wing of a Bf 109 and shaking hands with the pilot!

Right One of the first illustrations of the Dornier Do 29, in *The Aeroplane*, 9 February 1940. The type was wholly fictitious.

Below When we at last discovered the 190, three years late, the 'boffins from the Ministry' couldn't wait to find out how it worked. By the way, this 190A-3 arrived at RAF Pembrey on 23 June 1942, but not a word was permitted to be published about the aircraft until the morning of Monday 10 August. In the first week of August totally inaccurate silhouettes, artist's impressions and descriptions were still being issued!

Left This Heinkel photograph shows the He 100 V8 (eighth prototype), with specially streamlined canopy, which briefly held the world speed record. It was a civil aircraft, D-IDGH, but here has been given phoney 'Luftwaffe' markings.

Below left This aeroplane, the second Messerschmitt Bf 162, competed unsuccessfully against the Ju 88 in 1937. Three years later it was suddenly resurrected by the propaganda ministry as the formidable 'Messerschmitt Jaguar'. Such a ploy could never have worked against enemies who were not totally ignorant.

Above right The first artist's impression of the Fw 198 to be published in Britain, on 9 February 1940.

Below The amazing BV 141 flew beautifully, but suffered from problems with the completely ordinary landing gear! This was the first to be built, flown in February 1938.

Above left The sleek Fairey FD.2 was full of advanced design innovations, including a 'droop snoot' nose, but its career was almost terminated by a fault in the fuel system.

Left The variable-incidence wing, the very bold innovation flown on the XF8U-1 (here seen in the raised position), was one of the items that gave no trouble. Incidentally, this Navy fighter, with the same engine and guns as the Air Force F-100, carried an extra battery of rockets, more than 50 per cent more fuel and had a much higher top speed, despite the penalties of carrier equipment!

Below left Ground running the awesome de Havilland Spectre rocket engine of the first SR.53 supersonic interceptor development aircraft. The ground is drenched to avoid problems from HTP spillage. *Bob Stratton.*

Above A poor reproduction of a unique snapshot since destroyed taken in September 1940 of the first A6M to fall into Allied hands. Most of the damage was caused by angry Chinese fishermen who did not appreciate the significance of the capture.

Below The A6M2-21 parked at Kunming amongst P-40s and P-43s on 20 July 1941, after the abortive attempt to ship it to the United States.

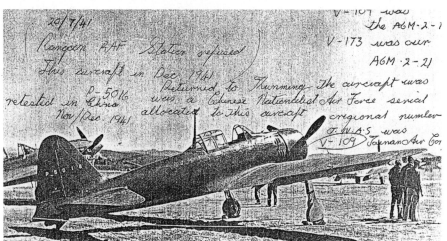

The A6M2-21 at Orlando, Florida, in 1943.
How come it has non-standard exit louvres
for cooling air? Mr Neumann put them
there *two years earlier*.

Dated June 1944, this photo shows a
B-26G-5 prior to delivery to the USAAF.
By this time the Marauder was a mature
aircraft.

Below left Back in the 1930s boys used to read pulp novels with such titles as 'Air Pirates of the China Sea'. Such pirates could well have used the 'Aichi Navy KT-98', had such a machine existed.

Below Among the impressive features of the 'Kawasaki Army OB-97' was a 20 mm cannon in the nose and another 'fixed in front of the cockpit', but the fuel capacity seemed a bit low at 510 gal. Kawasaki must have been puzzled to read about it.

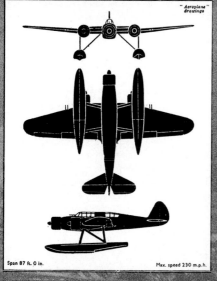

"Aeroplane" drawings

Span 87 ft. 0 in. Max. speed 230 m.p.h.

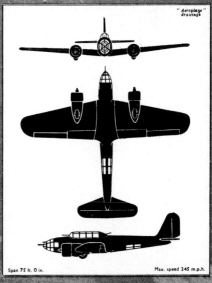

"Aeroplane" drawings

Span 75 ft. 0 in. Max. speed 245 m.p.h.

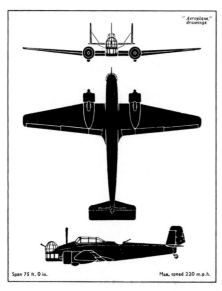

"Aeroplane" drawings

Span 75 ft. 0 in.　　　Max. speed 220 m.p.h.

Left We were told quite a lot about the 'Mitsubishi Army OB-98', such as the wing area of 685 sq ft and fuel capacity of only 480 gal. Better not tell Mitsubishi or they'll send in a bill for making it!

Below When the Fw 190 burst on the scene in 1941 the choice of what in those days was called 'a radial motor' was thought extraordinary in Britain. One contemporary account explained that the 190 was a 'second-rate aircraft', the liquid-cooled engines being reserved for better machines. How wrong this notion was would soon be dispelled by the 190 itself, and by the fact that Hawker's fighters switched to such engines. Here a Tempest II flies over what was to become London Heathrow.

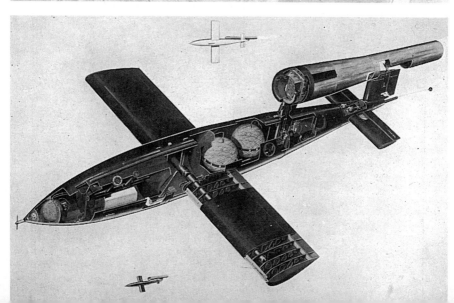

Below left A beautiful drawing of an Fi 103, probably by H. Redmill, prepared for an August 1944 issue of AMWIS (Air Ministry Weekly Intelligence Summary). Some bombs carried a radio transmitter with a trailing antenna (shown here) so the track could be followed to impact.

Above A frame from a ciné film taken on 5 July 1942 showing the third He 280 orbiting Marienehe. In the author's view there can be no question but that the 280 was the first jet fighter, but it is unknown to today's quizmasters.

Below Impression by a British Air Ministry artist of the Me 262 in September 1944, based entirely on interrogation of aircrew and air reconnaissance photographs.

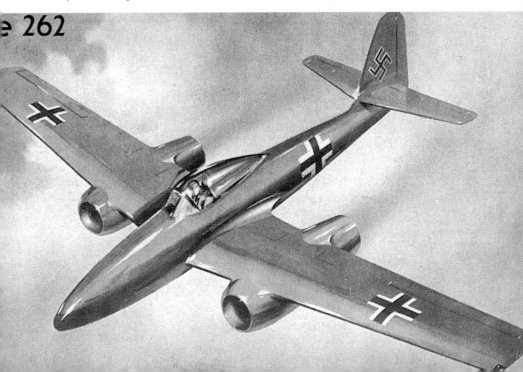

Above The Rolls-Royce Welland, first turbojet in regular squadron service, about seven and a half years later than it might have been.

Below DG202, the very first prototype Meteor (but not the first to fly), photographed in the late 1950s when a gate guardian at RAF Yatesbury. *Mike Hooks*.

Top Full-scale mock-up of the M.52 at Woodley, mid-1944. *Via Richard Almond.*

Above The first Nene-Vampires were slower than the original version with the lower-powered Goblin engine. Boulton Paul used Hawker N.7/46 technology in modifying the inlet ducts of TG276, and this in turn was the basis of the mass-produced Sud-Est Mistral, prototype 02 of which is seen here.

Below The Spey-engined RAF Phantom FGR.2, seen here with the costly but never-used EMI reconnaissance pod, could not be anything but a great aeroplane. But nobody expected it to be slower than the regular version.

Above left The RAF did get something from the years of effort on the Swift. A few F.7s were used to play with a missile that never entered service, while this FR.5 was a reconnaissance version that served with Nos 2 and 79 Squadrons.

Left One factor causing irritation in the USA was the wholly justified belief that US taxpayers were being made to help European industry catch up. In 1952, when offshore procurement started, the USAF had hundreds of B-47s and F-86s, while European counterparts were still years away from service.

Below left One had only to glance at the third Gloster GA.5 (Javelin) to see that it did not remotely resemble an operational aircraft. Superpriority, and even offshore procurement, was intended to hurry up the protracted development of such types.

Above By autumn 1954 the Royal Aircraft Establishment had painstakingly put together all the bits of Yoke Peter which had been equally painstakingly retrieved by the Royal Navy.

Below Models, to the same scale, of the Valiant bomber and V.1000 transport. The V.1000 would have had a much bigger wing and better engines than either the 707-120 or the DC-8-10.

Above One of the chief reasons given by the Government for cancelling the V.1000 was that its weight had grown to 248,000 lb. Nobody seemed to comprehend that jetliners are designed to grow in weight. The DC-8, for example, was launched at 265,000 lb, but this DC-8-73 is flying today at 355,000 lb. I suppose if it had been British it would have been cancelled?

Below The only general-arrangement drawing of the proposed Comet 5, dated 13 July 1956. Had it been built, this aircraft would have been a reinvention of the V.1000, with the same engines but a smaller wing, narrower fuselage, less potential for development and more than four years later.

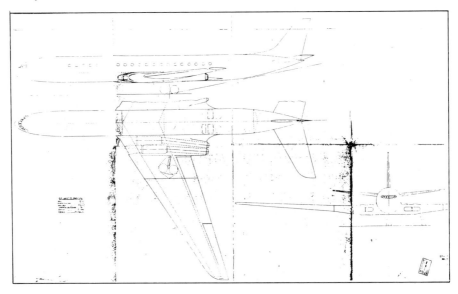

Above Soviet aircrew often say they fly 'a Bear Delta'. Asked what they mean they tell you 'Every time we get intercepted by F-15s they greet us "Hi there, Bear Delta" '. Here a Bear Delta (Bear-D) is escorted by two F-15Cs from Iceland's 57th TFW. Just how missiles could perform this role Mr Sandys's famed treatise did not explain!

Below XA847, the first P.1B, made its maiden flight on the day the White Paper was published. It was said this programme had 'unfortunately, already gone too far to cancel'; so the Government just made sure no money was spent on further development. Subsequently the Lightning had to fight for every penny.

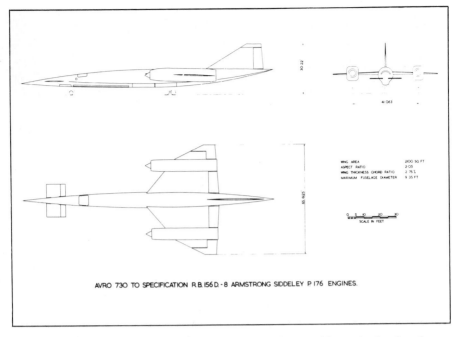

WING AREA   2100 SQ FT
ASPECT RATIO   2·05
WING THICKNESS CHORD RATIO   2·75%
MAXIMUM FUSELAGE DIAMETER   9·35 FT

SCALE IN FEET

AVRO 730 TO SPECIFICATION R.B.156D.-8 ARMSTRONG SIDDELEY P.176 ENGINES.

FARNBOROUGH, 1957

Above At the time it was the cancellation of the Avro 730 that caused just a slight stir in the media. Powered by eight Armstrong Siddeley P.176 engines, it would have had a span of 65 ft 7 in, length of 159 ft and cruising speed of Mach 2.5.

Left This cartoon, by Illingworth, was one of 14 in the magazine *Punch* for 4 September 1957 featuring aviation topics, virtually all harping on the same theme (for example, 'Shall we mention it's scrapped before he flight-tests it?', and a chap in a flying suit carrying a sandwich board UNFAIR TO PILOTS). Nobody appeared to question the basic policy.

Above An official British report dated 7 September 1945 told us 'There is no point in the further development of high-power piston aircraft engines . . .' This CL-215, powered by two R-2800 Double Wasps, was one of a batch for the Royal Thai Navy more than forty years later.

Below Standing in a residential street near London's Heathrow Airport in 1970 a photographer snapped a Vanguard turboprop and a DC-9 jet. One was quiet, economical, and (except for the just-visible white contrails behind the tips of the flaps) left no visible trail. The other was deafeningly noisy, guzzled fuel, and left a trail of smoke. Yet at that time airlines were queueing up to buy DC-9s, and absolutely nobody wanted the Vanguard.

Above In 1958 everyone knew the centrifugal compressor was being replaced by the axial, so that's how Allison designed the Model 250. This later version is rated at about 450 horsepower.

Left Thirty years later Turbomeca knew that the centrifugal compressor was not obsolete at all. That's the only kind of compressor used in today's new TP319, also of 450 horsepower.

Above right No engineering team in history, on any project, had worked harder than that which created TSR.2. For a start, two teams and two aircraft had to be merged into one. Second, the work was done against a background of not just criticism but blind hatred — by the media, the incoming government, and (because they knew only what the media told them) the British public.

Right XR219 was the only TSR.2 permitted to fly. Even today no treetop bomber has been created with the same speed, range, and 'penetrability'. As Sir George Edwards said, 'If you don't have a war, a military cancellation doesn't show.'

Top This is a YF-l7; it is a Northrop product.

Above This is an F/A-18A; it is a McDonnell Douglas/Northrop product.

Below This is an F/A-18C; it is a McDonnell Douglas product.

26

18 September 1940

Discovering the 'Zero'

Everybody knows what a terrible shock it was for Allied pilots to come up against the 'Zero'. We didn't know anything about Soviet aircraft, but thought they might be pretty tough, if primitive. We didn't know anything about Japanese aircraft, but thought they were outdated and flimsy—perhaps almost literally bamboo and rice paper. Then suddenly we came up against a fighter that could overtake us, climb faster and more steeply than we could, turn inside any of our turns, blast us out of the sky with cannon and machine guns and then, amazingly, fly home maybe 1,000 miles.

We never expected anything like this. Indeed, so great was the shock that the 'Zero' became imbued with seemingly magical powers. Some—I mean on the Allied side— said it was invincible. All of this was disastrous for the morale of the desperately harried and overworked fighter pilots whose job it was to fight a rearguard action across a quarter of the globe. To say that the Allies were eager to learn all about the 'Zero' is an understatement. While in Britain the RAF was being outfought by the Fw 190, and overwhelmingly anxious to find out about this formidable opponent, on the other side of the globe a motley collection of British, American, Chinese, Dutch, Australian, and NZ pilots were being shot to pieces by this other formidable opponent, whose very existence had not been known of previously.

Deadly combats involving 'Zeros' took place from 7 December 1941 onwards. Yet *The Aeroplane Spotter*, whose job it was to bring the latest news on Allied and (especially) enemy aircraft, and which it did in a highly professional manner, did not even *mention* the 'Zero' until 26 March 1942! The first very brief details appeared in the issue of 7 May, and the first silhouette (provisional) and illustration (artwork) not until 24 September 1942! On the latter date brief numerical details were given which corrected most of those published on 7 May. So the 'Zero' remained pretty much an enigma. So important did Jiro Horikoshi's great creation loom that a popular song of US origin was 'Johnny got a Zero' (a play on words, our hero Johnny having been used to getting zero marks in class).

At first it was thought the correct Japanese designation was Mitsubishi Navy S-00, the 00 coming from the Japanese year 2600 (our 1940). Because many Japanese designations were uncertain, or unknown, the Americans hit on the idea of allocating invented reporting names. I believe this had never been done before. Fighters were given boys' names, most other types getting girls' names. At first there was some confusion. The S-00 became Ray in the China-Burma-India theatre and Ben in the SW Pacific. These names were replaced by Zeke. Then a fighter was discovered like a Zeke but with square wingtips, and it was named Hap in honour of Hap Arnold, Chief of Staff of the USAAF. Then it was decided the general might not appreciate having a nasty Jap fighter named after him, so Hap was changed to Hamp, which is a new boy's name as far as I'm concerned. At last, in December 1942, it was discovered the square-wing fighter was just a Zeke with the tips removed. Indeed, by this time we were at last getting to grips with what the Japanese aircraft were really called. This fighter, for example, was the Mitsubishi A6M Model 32, so in the Allied system it became Zeke 32. Incidentally, details of these code names were not published in London until November 1943, a year after Capt McCoy, USAAF, had begun to assign them in Melbourne!

In June 1942 US forces in the Aleutians discovered a Zeke upside-down on Akutan Island. It was found to be only slightly damaged. The pilot had broken his neck in a forced landing. In his classic masterwork on Japanese aircraft, Dr René Francillon calls this 'an invaluable prize for Allied technical intelligence'. At last the secrets of the Zeke, Zero or S-00 were about to be unlocked. About time. This fighter had actually entered service in China in August 1940, but—wrote Bill Green in *Famous Fighters of the Second World War*—in almost two years of operational use 'not one Zero-Sen was captured or inspected by the Chinese or American observers'.

This I have always believed. So have we all. We knew that the formidable Mitsubishi Navy fighter remained almost unknown until we picked that example off Akutan Island, shipped it to San Diego, got it airworthy, and at last began flying it in the late autumn of 1942. Pictures and details were at last published in November of that year. This seemed to clear the matter up, leaving one small puzzle: why was no notice taken of the repeated warnings sent to Washington by Claire L. Chennault, later the CO of the 'Flying Tigers', from China back in the summer of 1940?

Of course, I have repeated all this many times, in all sorts of books, magazine articles, video scripts, and talks. It is all known, and taken for granted by the Japanese aircraft buffs. So imagine my surprise when in February 1989, from far off Auckland (NZ), I got a very indignant letter from a man who told me 'Your claims . . . regarding the A6M are grossly incorrect . . .' At first I thought he was a nut case. Then I found he had had a long career in aviation. For example, at the 1936 SBAC Show he was part of the servicing team for the Gloster G.38 (F.5/34), which incidentally had a great deal in common with our friend the 'Zero'. Over some weeks we corresponded at length, and I satisfied myself that he was not a nut case, and that his memory was sharp and reliable.

He was rather scathing about the RAF wanting 'Super SE.5As' in the form of Gladiators. He could see that war was coming, and that tough, well-armed machines (not the Fairey Battle, another of his hates) would be essential. Accordingly, when he was offered a job as a production and armament engineer in China he accepted. He arrived in China in January 1937 and did not leave until October 1945. He told me much that I did not know about the aircraft used by the Chinese, of more than 30 different types including several developed in China, notably at the Flushing Aircraft Works. It was a tough war where what counted was the ability to keep going despite kicks, knocks, lack of maintenance and an open-air life, and then blast the enemy with firepower. In general, out of over 700 combat aircraft wearing Chinese insignia, only those of US or Soviet origin were considered of much use.

My correspondent writes:

In late 1938 the Japanese eased off on us. We were gradually getting on top, mainly with our modified I-16s which used cannon effectively. Their aircraft could not stand up to cannon fire, and their 7.7-mm bullets had little effect on tough metal airframes . . . But they learned, and in August 1940 they came back with the A6M2-11. This had range, manoeuvrability and firepower, but the battle was by no means one-sided. On 18 September 1940 we got word to retrieve a fighter off a beach. We found it was one of the new A6M2s, which had belly landed opposite Fainan Island. It had been vandalized by local fishermen, but it was complete enough for us to write an extremely detailed report on it. I never knew where our many reports went; I imagined President Roosevelt.

This particular aircraft was the 12th of 15 pre-production aircraft. It served with the Tainan Naval Air Corps as part of the 12th Combined Fleet. Most of it was unpainted, and we thought the workmanship excellent. The cowling was black, a diagonal dark blue band encircled the rear fuselage, and the tail carried the black number V-110. We had a big team examining it at Flushing factory, but we knew we could never fly it (for example, the port wing was almost broken into two parts).

We wanted a flyable A6M, and eventually we got one. On 17 February 1941 another Tainan Air Corps machine suffered a fuel-system failure and force-landed near Teitsan airfield. Our troops shot the pilot before he could destroy the aircraft. It was a full production A6M2-21, tail number V-173. We were really pleased about this. Quite soon we got V-173 airworthy, painted in Chinese colours and with serial P-5016. Flight testing and technical examinations were carried out mainly by Mr Fazarahoff and Mr Neumann [that's the great Gerhard Neumann, later 'Herman the German' of General Electric—BG] and they took until May 1941 to complete them and finish writing the massive fully illustrated report. It was, like other reports, sent by courier to Washington.

Then we flew P-5016 down from Kunming to Rangoon in order to get it crated and shipped across to India for a thorough professional investigation. I can only describe the reaction of the people at RAF Rangoon as panic. They simply did not want our 'foreign' 'captured' aeroplane anywhere on their station. After some discussion we uncrated it, put it back together and flew it back to Kunming. We were told that the US State Department did not want it anywhere near the United States, so we just kept flying it ourselves.

In November 1941 the American Volunteer Group started operating, and soon US Army Air Corps engineers arrived to retest 'our' A6M2-21. Between March and June 1942 they pulled it apart and shipped it to the US. Later I saw a photo of it at Maxwell AFB in August 1943. Incidentally, the A6M2-21 was a far better aircraft to fly than the subsequent US report (Air Materiel Command, 20 February 1943) suggests. Part of the trouble was that we flew it on the regular 85-octane fuel we used in our I-16s, P-40s and P-43s, not knowing that the Sakae 12 14-cylinder engine was designed to be run on 100-octane.

Why did the A6M come as a terrible surprise to the Allies? Simple. In 1940-1 the US State Department found our captures embarrassing, and hushed everything up to avoid diplomatic repercussions. After Pearl Harbor they concealed it all to save their own faces.

Well, how about that? As a parting shot, on the very page of Bill Green's book on which he says no A6M was captured or inspected in the first year in China there appears a picture of 'P-5016'!

27

25 November 1940

The Widow-Maker

An ancient Scottish proverb runs: 'Give a dog a bad name and hang him.' I suppose you could translate this as 'It isn't what you are that counts, but what people say you are.' This certainly applies to aircraft. There are numerous examples of aircraft which, usually early in their career, were damned by being thought difficult to learn, tricky to fly, or just plain dangerous. Such types have invariably been military. Chaps up at 'the sharp end', on the receiving end of both enemy flak and what the government bought them in which to face it, have traditionally bitched and griped, because there wasn't much else they could do about either hazard.

Incidentally—and this is a digression—the Royal Air Force has always seemed to me to have a long tradition of running down its new equipment. When I was not quite ten I saw my first Hurricane, newly delivered to 111 Sqn just down the road at Northolt. Soon, on Empire Air Day, I was able to speak to a real live Hurricane pilot. Wasn't he thrilled with his marvellous new fighter, one of which had just been flown by his boss, Sqn Ldr Gillan, from Edinburgh to London at 408 mph (the papers didn't say too much about the 75 mph tailwind)? To my surprise the young flying officer thought the Hurricane too big, too sluggish (compared with the Gauntlet), and even too expensive (maybe he was bothered about bending it); and he hated being cooped up inside a sliding hood. Ever since, I have repeatedly been reminded that any totally new type is derided by chaps who wish they could have the old stuff back. For example, No 11 Sqn at Wunstorf around 1952: 'The Venom? Load of old rubbish, the wings come off. Wish we could have our Vampires back.' No 98 at Jever, 1955, 'The Hunter? Load of old rubbish, can't go above 25,000 feet, can't fire its guns—wish we could have our Venoms back.' Coltishall, 1960, No 74: 'The Lightning? Load of old rubbish. Now we could actually have gone to war with our Hunters.' Back to famous No 11, this time at Binbrook/Coningsby, 1988: 'The Tornado F.3? Load of old rubbish. Now if only we could have our Lightnings back . . .' I can hear them now, in 2007: 'EFA? Load of old rubbish. Wish we could have our Tornados back . . .'

Of course, if you think a bit harder you will realize that at the start of its service career a new type is liable to be prone to all sorts of shortcomings, missing equipment, faults (often dangerous), endemic unreliability, shortages of spares and any other adversity you can think of. Often the manufacturer's harassed test pilots have concentrated so hard eradicating one group of faults that they have overlooked many others (which they don't even notice because they're used to them). In the early 1950s you couldn't have found a better or more professional group of test pilots anywhere in the world than those of the Supermarine company, yet they could not understand the RAF's repeated dissatisfaction with the Swift (a story I relate briefly later on).

Towards the end of its career, which in World War Two might mean three years later and today means about 30 years later, the unpopular menace has miraculously turned into a fine bit of kit, beloved by everyone and operated round the clock with outstanding safety and efficiency. Naturally, everyone in close contact with it hates to see it go. Almost inevitably, the new replacement type doesn't have a chance. The only people who extol the newcomer, apart from the maker, are politicians and air marshals who are far removed from the feelings 'at the coalface'.

Of course, it has been known for a newcomer to arrive with a good reputation, and by a combination of good qualities, good PR, and luck sustain this throughout its career. One example is the F-15. Everyone knows that in 1972–7 the only way a USAF 'lootenant' could make it to captain was by swearing total allegiance to the F-15. One reason for this was that in this timeframe the smaller F-16 LWF (lightweight fighter) was almost universally regarded as 'cheap' and therefore 'inferior', and the USAF took some care to let it be known that the F-15 was the greatest, and that it would never settle for anything less. Of course, in the long term the USAF was to buy the F-16 in numbers much greater than the F-15, but that does not alter the fact that the F-15 never had a bad reputation and I never heard anyone 'knock' it.

Today the USAF is regarded by most Europeans with awe, because of its strength in depth in such assets as PhDs and computer terminals, in its vast funds, in its ability to do things 'across the board', and in its colossal political power. But half a century ago the Army Air Corps was relatively tiny, with money and political power to match. We in Europe tended to regard the 'Air Corps' with disdain, especially after we started fighting and they didn't. Such an opinion stemmed from ignorance. In fact the USAAC, from top to bottom, was a highly professional group of men (no women, then). They tried to get everything right, and after analysing what was happening in Europe sometimes took action quicker than did the RAF!

To some degree our totally unjustified poor opinion of US airpower stemmed from an enduring belief that Americans talked big and achieved rather less, a view strenuously promoted by C.G.G.—Charles Grey Grey, the cantankerous and eminently controversial Editor of *The Aeroplane*. For years we had been used to the French filling their annual Salon de l'Aéronautique—then a small static exhibition in the Grand Palais just off the Champs Elysées—with fantastic 'prototypes' which obviously could knock any rivals into a cocked hat, if it were not for the fact that they were really only mock-ups and would never be seen again. We tended to regard each new American prototype in the same light. The more fabulously advanced it seemed to be, the less we took it seriously. To some degree this was an instinctive wish to defend our own outdated British industry, churning out Gladiators, Harrows, and Stranraers, and trying to get the bugs out of the awful Ensign. It arose mainly because in those days nobody actually went to the USA—it was a week's journey—so we completely failed to understand that the Americans were not in the

habit of displaying mock-ups, and if they rolled out a 'noo airplane' it was real, and
what's more liable to do a good job.

Having recently been subjected to such things as the P-38 and P-39—neither of
which I took seriously, partly because of the flamboyant maker's advertising—I was
all set to be critical of the Martin Model 179, the first XB-26, when it appeared in
late 1940. One has to remember that we were at that time suffering from the nightly
visits of fleets of extremely operational black-painted bombers in what we called
the Blitz. In contrast, this shiny example of almost perfect streamlining, with the
blue and red stripes on its tail, seemed light-years away from the harsh realities of
war.

Of course, my schoolfriends and I were almost totally ignorant of what the XB-26
was really like, but we could hardly fail to notice that, by contemporary standards,
it had a wing that was much too small. It was by designing the wing for the cruising
regime that designers Peyton Magruder and William K. Ebel met the very
challenging Air Corps requirement for a speed of 350 mph. Normally the wing is
designed to meet the more severe cases of takeoff and landing, where you crank in
a (low) speed and come out with a (quite large) wing area. For example, a typical
1939 He 111H had a loaded weight of 25,000 lb and a wing area of 943 sq ft. This
wing was a lot bigger than necessary in cruising flight, and made the Heinkel rather
slow. In contrast, the XB-26 was expected to weigh 26,625 lb (later it added 12,000
lb to this!) and had a wing area of 601 sq ft.

You seldom get anything for nothing, and the penalty was naturally that the
Martin was from the start 'a hot ship'. Other medium bombers of the day had a
landing speed of 75-90 mph, but the Martin was typically brought in at 140 and
touched at 130. Takeoff run was also obviously very long, always over 3,000 ft and
soon to be much greater, or roughly double the run needed with the B-18 and other
types which the B-26 was designed to replace. Long runs and very high rolling
speeds demanded paved runways, and these had to be smooth because the big four-
blade Curtiss Electric propellers almost touched the ground. These propellers also
had to clear the fuselage, and because the fuselage was so fat and of circular section
the very powerful engines had to be mounted unusually far out from the centreline.

In those days Pratt & Whitney had a slogan: 'Dependable engines'. The XB-26
was the very first application of the big R-2800 Double Wasp engine, which began
at 1,500 hp and by 1945 was giving twice this power (for brief periods, with water
injection). In the XB-26 it was rated at 1,850 hp, and it needed the big prop to turn
this into thrust, to meet the challenging performance demands. Despite the
immaturity of the engine, it proved, as P&W promised, to be dependable. The same
could not be said of the propeller. It was a maintenance nightmare. The carbon
brushes rubbing on a slip-ring caused endless failures of the electrical supply,
partly because of dirt and partly because of changing clearances due to wear. The
supply invariably failed if the batteries were not fully charged (it was partly for this
reason that, after building 201 B-26s, Martin continued with the B-26A with a
24-volt electrical system). At least in the early years, the propeller caused more
serious trouble than everything else in the B-26 put together. Any failure of supply
caused the blades immediately and rapidly to rotate into a superfine pitch, called
flat pitch. I never understood why this was permitted; it would have been simple
to have inserted fine-pitch stops at an angle giving less drag and positive thrust
(once speed had bled off). As it was, the failed prop acted like a gigantic airbrake,

giving no thrust whatever and causing violent engine overspeed. The shriek of the maltreated engine could be heard for miles. As the drag was so far outboard, the yaw was powerful and violent, far outside the experience of any pupil. Moreover, unless this all happened at high speed, the wing behind the failed propeller not only fell back but also stalled, throwing the heavily loaded bomber into a snap roll with vicious loss of height. Not nice on takeoff.

Well, I won't go on about the B-26; you've already got the message. It was almost named the Martin Martian, which I think might have been appropriate, but the name finally chosen was Marauder. I suppose it was inevitable that, after the first spate of crashes by inexperienced pilots—first at Patterson Field, before it was joined with Wright Field, in Ohio, and then at the big school at McDill Field in Florida—that this bomber should have become the Martin Murderer. Everyone laughed at 'The Flying Prostitute' (because it had no visible means of support). Every pupil reporting to McDill soon heard the jingle 'One a day in Tampa Bay', and I flew with one B-26 pilot who on two separate occasions had to fly the McDill circuit with not one but two funeral pyres of black smoke marking where crews had died minutes previously. Not for nothing was the B-26 called 'The Widow-maker'.

Everyone knew from the start that the B-26 would be a handful, and that loss of an engine on takeoff would require immediate powerful action, especially on the rudder. Yet from the first flight, piloted by the man who designed her (Ken Ebel), on 25 November 1940, the XB-26 seemed to need little change, apart from reversing the direction of the rudder tab because the surface proved slightly overbalanced. There was no prototype and deliveries to the Air Corps began as early as 25 February 1941. It was only later that, at the conversion schools, pupil casualties (mostly complete crews) mounted at such a rate that, at the start of 1942, production was suspended and a special board of enquiry was set up under 'Tooey' Spaatz to investigate the B-26 and recommend on whether production should be continued.

In the end Martin was told to carry on, and indeed a vast new plant was built at Omaha to double production (later Omaha switched to the B-29). Meanwhile, instructors gingerly learned how to cope with engine failures on takeoff and even runaway propellers, and found that, with quick thinking, skill and powerful muscles, these conditions were survivable. Demonstrations of these emergencies did a bit to remove the B-26's reputation, and ease the fear gnawing at the vitals of every pupil assigned to fly it, but what the pupils lacked was skill; and it doesn't help if you start out lacking confidence and scared stiff.

Martin kept on modifying the B-26, partly to make it better and partly to make it do a bigger job. Self-sealing tanks, armour, and about a ton of extra equipment were added, and instead of four small guns of 0.30-in calibre the armament grew to eleven big ones of 0.50-in! Partly because of the extra armament the crew grew from five to seven, and instead of weighing about 26,000 lb the later Marauders turned the scales at 38,000! Fighting back, Martin extended the wingtips, increased the wing incidence, tilted up the engines (which incidentally gave a few more inches of ground clearance), and improved the flight controls. But by far the most important changes were that, as pilots and maintenance crews became proficient, inflight failures became rarer and rarer, crashes tailed off until they almost never happened, and instead of being a terror the B-26 became loved as a willing and capable friend. Altogether 5,266 were built, and in every theatre they eventually established the lowest loss rate of any medium bomber; in the ETO (European theatre of ops) it averaged 0.5 per cent in 1943–4 and 0.4 in 1944–5.

So why all the bother? Unquestionably, the major cause was release to the Air Corps before the propellers had been properly developed and before line crews had learned how to look after them. Once pilots and ground personnel had learned how to 'hack it', most of the dangers melted away. But the Marauder was to the end an aeroplane that could make big demands on its pilots. Let me quote from *Flying Combat Aircraft*, copyright Airforce Historical Foundation, B-26 chapter by Lt-Col Douglas C. Conley:

We were letting down in a six-ship formation to enter the pattern to land; we were the left wingman, lead element, in a left turn at a comfortable 200 mph when the right engine froze with a sudden, final shudder. As quickly as we perceived what had happened, both the pilot and I stomped the left rudder to the floor; the plane did a half snap roll right through the middle of the formation, past the nose of the No. 4 aircraft, and ended up in a vertical right turn. I never saw our formation, during or after our recovery, because I was completely occupied with trying to regain control. (I can only imagine what would happen shortly after take-off at low airspeed if an engine froze.) Now for one of those rare single-engine landings to get her down safely. J.C.'s face had an ashen pallor, and again I was glad there was no mirror to reflect my own color. Something about the look on his face and the way his knees were shaking struck me as funny, and I managed something less than a hearty laugh. I'm sure this helped to relieve the tension as we set about trimming her up and preparing to land.

28

20 April 1941

Death of the Aces II

World War Two was long and tough, and very, very few combat pilots who were in at the start survived it. Ironically, some did so only to meet their death unexpectedly. One who 'got the chop' very early on was M.T. St John Pattle, a South African who served in the Middle East and Greece. He was killed near Athens on 20 April 1941, but nothing was reported in the papers. Hardly anyone in Britain had heard of him, and he did not appear in any of the post-war histories, official or otherwise. Only gradually, helped by the Ops Record Books of RAF No 80 Squadron and, especially, No 33 Squadron, was it realized that his score must have been at least 34, and was almost certainly considerably more than 51. Belatedly, despite his early death, he was recognized as Britain's greatest ace of the war.

The top ace of the United States was Dick Bong (Major Richard I. Bong, USAAF), who certainly knew how to fly a P-38. After scoring 40 in the Pacific, he was sent home. On 6 August 1945, as the first atomic bomb fell on Hiroshima, he climbed aboard a sleek P-80 Shooting Star jet on a beautiful day, crashed on takeoff, and was killed.

Another top USAAF ace was luckier. Col Dave Schilling (22.5 victories with the 8th AF in England) survived the war. He stayed on and flew intensively, in all the foulest weather of northern Europe. On 22 September 1950 he flew his F-84 Thunderjet non-stop to the USA, with three inflight refuellings (Lt-Col Ritchie, who accompanied him, ran out of fuel and baled out over Labrador). On 4-17 July 1952 he led 51 F-84s of his 31st Fighter Escort Wing from Georgia to Japan. Then on a beautiful day in England—14 August 1956—he got into his Allard sports car and slammed into a concrete bridge pier at high speed (why, we don't know). He was killed instantly.

At least he had this accident by himself, which is more than can be said for the Luftwaffe's greatest night-fighter ace, Heinz-Wolfgang Schnaufer. To destroy 121 enemy aircraft is no mean record, but to destroy 121 aircraft, all of them large bombers and all at night, is surely amazing. Just for good measure he was several times fired at by his own flak. Unlike so many of his comrades he survived the war, fighting to the end (on almost his last mission he destroyed seven Lancasters). He got a job as a commercial traveller. In July 1950 he was driving in France when a huge *camion* came from a side turning and drove straight into him. He is believed to have survived the impact, but his car was then crushed flat under the weight of many tons of gas cylinders which broke free from the truck.

The Luftwaffe day fighter pilots made all previous definitions of an ace rather laughable. Many of them scored ten in a day—one bagged 13 confirmed in a single mission—and they had to devise different ways of recording the score on their aircraft. An élite few put '200' in a laurel wreath and then started again from scratch. One of the very greatest of this select band was Austrian Walter Nowotny. First to reach 250, he then lost out by being appointed to command a school and then help develop the Me 262 twin-jet. On 8 November 1944 he destroyed a B-17, and then returned to Achmer. When he was within seconds of reaching the runway his Me 262 simply exploded. The cause was never discovered; no Allied aircraft was near, and one theory put forward is that he was a victim of Achmer's own flak.

Perhaps the strangest end of all lay in wait for another of the 200-plus scorers. Heinz Bär was the very personification of a fighter pilot. Off duty he was called 'Pritzl', seemingly a man who lived for fun and high spirits. In the cockpit he became a deadly killing machine. He ended the war as one of the handpicked exponents of the Me 262 with Galland's special Jagdverband 44. His rank was Oberstleutnant, and his confirmed score 220. On 28 April 1957 he went for a flip in the third Zaunkönig. The Zaunkönig (little king) was an ultralight designed during the war at the Brunswick Technical Institute. It had incredible STOL performance, and was designed to be totally uncrashable and the safest thing in the sky. John Fricker often flew one in the immediate postwar years, and had I known him better then I'd have asked him to let me have a go. It must have seemed like a time-warp to cruise at 46 knots. Well, the amazing thing is that Bär managed to fly this paragon of safe features beyond its design limits. It came apart and he was killed.

29

22 June 1941

The Red Air Fleet

Operation Barbarossa, Hitler's invasion of the Soviet Union in June 1941, suddenly gave Britain a mighty new ally. But we knew next to nothing about its air force. And here is a very curious thing. Because we were so ignorant, we jumped to the strange conclusion that the Russians could do nothing for themselves. Virtually every single aeroplane that they possessed was said to be a copy of some familiar Western type. And this is odd, because in fact, from 1913 onwards, the Russians have had a track record of remarkable originality in aircraft design.

To use *The Aeroplane Spotter* once more as our guide to contemporary thought, issue No 31, dated 31 July 1941, devoted a page to the chief types of the Red Air Fleet. Pictures and brief specifications were given of 14 types. Two were labelled 'designer unknown', presumably because the writer could not make up his mind which non-Soviet type had been copied. One, in a joking fashion, was called 'most original', because he could not even think of a type it could have been copied from. Every one of the other 11 aircraft was said to be a copy of some non-Soviet type, or in some cases two non-Soviet types, apart from 'the 2PA' which was the Seversky 2PA built under licence and the R-10 which was the Vultee V-11 built under licence.

We can tick them off one by one. The I-15B was called the Chato, despite the fact that this was not its name but a rude epithet (meaning flat-nosed) applied by its Nationalist opponents in Spain. It did, in fact, have a name: Chaika (Seagull). It was not the 15B but the 15*bis*, though the heavily retouched picture looked more like a 153. The engine was not the 1,000 hp M-63. It was said to be 'derived from the Curtiss Sparrowhawk', presumably because both were radial-engined biplanes. Polikarpov actually had designed a series of such fighters from 1925 onwards. Next came the familiar I-16B Rata. Whenever this appeared during the war, it would be identified as a Rata, because we failed to realize that, far from being its proper name, this was again a derogatory nickname (meaning rat) applied by its enemies in Spain. Obviously their propaganda was better than that of the Republicans, whose name for the same aircraft (Mosca = fly) was unknown. Also unknown were the 27 true designations for the various sub-types (I-16B was just invention). Again the engine was said to be the M-63, but this was fitted in the very last batches only. This aircraft, the world's first cantilever stressed-skin fighter with retractable landing gear, was said to be copied from 'P-26 and Gee Bee'. One has only to think for a moment about this to see it as pure rubbish.

Next came the I-17, 'copied from Me 109 and Spitfire'. We need not worry about this as it never went into production, but it would have been difficult for Nikolai Polikarpov to have copied the 109 and Spit because his prototype flew on 1 September 1934! Next came the '2PA', a single example of which was imported in 1937; there was never the slightest intention of getting a licence for it. The R-5 followed, with the comment 'designer unknown'. The fact that this was not known to be another Polikarpov is surprising, because it first flew in 1928 and over 6,000 were built. The picture was retouched to look unlike any R-5 I ever knew! Then came the DI-6. Yet again this had a '1,000 hp M-63' (actually it didn't), and was designed by Polikarpov (no, it was S.A. Kochyerigin). It was 'derived from Curtiss Helldiver', a patently ludicrous suggestion. Next came the R-10, and this was in fact an original design by the KhAI (Kharkov Aviation Institute), owing nothing whatever to the Vultee V-11, two examples of which were imported a year after the R-10 entered production.

The SB-1 was said to be the ANT-39, 'derived from Glenn Martin 139W'. In fact Tupolev did study the Martin Bomber (so did a lot of other people), but hardly in order to copy it slavishly. There was no SB-1; the SB (ANT-40) was followed by the mass-produced SB-2 and variants. Far from being a mere copy of a 1930 design, the SB was the best fast medium bomber in the world at the start of the Spanish civil war in 1936, and in every respect it surpassed the Blenheim (but that did not save hundreds being shot down by 109s in 1941). Then came S.V. Ilyushin's CKB-26, which was actually the DB-3. This was yet another type with '1,000 hp M-63 radial motors' (no, various M-85 to M-87B of 765 to 950 hp). Bombload 1,100 lb for 500 miles (no, 3,307 lb for about 2,100 miles). As for 'derived from Boeing Y1B-9A', one might as well have said the Gladiator was 'derived from Sopwith Camel'.

The DB-3A followed (actually DB-3f, later Il-4). Then came the TB-1 (ANT-4). Amazingly, this was the correct designation, and they got Tupolev right as well. Then they spoilt it by saying 'Derived from Junkers Ju 52', which was not very likely as the Ju flew (in its original single-engined version) in 1930 while the ANT-4 flew in 1925! Before the first Ju 52/3m took to the air, the 218th and last TB-1 had been delivered. Next came the TB-3B (ANT-6). This was almost right, though none of the ten TB-3/ANT-6 versions was called TB-3B. This was again said to be 'derived from Junkers designs'. I'd like to know which. These superb heavy bombers were the first in the world to be four-engined cantilever monoplanes, and they were much bigger than a B-17. The first was rolled out in 1929, and in seven years a total of 818 were delivered. Far from being a mere 'copy', these tremendous machines were in service when the US Army heavy bombers were Keystones and Condors, and the RAF used Virginias (we hadn't yet got the Heyford), all fabric-covered biplanes.

Last but one was the TB-6B (ANT-41). This was the 'most original', the designer being Tupolev, with 1,000 hp M-100 engines. In fact the aircraft was the DB-A, designed by V.F. Bolkhovitinov, powered by 970 hp AM-34RN engines bearing no relationship to the M-100. (There was, in fact, an ANT-41; it was a twin-engined torpedo bomber derived from the SB family.) The DB-A was famed as the scarlet 'N-209' which on 12 August 1937 left Shchelkovo for a flight over the North Pole and was never seen again. Last of the 'Red Air Fleet' types was the L-760, derived from the *Maksim Gorkii*. This was really the ANT-20*bis*; L760 was merely its civil registration. It served with Aeroflot, not with the air force, and the comment that its bombload was 'big but unknown' is wide of the mark, as it was never intended to carry bombs. There was only one 20*bis*, and many Soviet groups are sad that it was scrapped during the war; there are not many aircraft around today with a span of nearly 207 ft.

To round off this carefully compiled page summarizing what we knew in July 1941 about Soviet airpower, we were told 'Most of the Russian types have been developed from American, German, Italian or French prototypes. The Heinkel He 113, Consolidated 28, Savoia S.55, Vultee V-11, Republic 2PA and Macchi C-94 are all built under licence.' The Consolidated 28 most certainly was; the GST was the Soviet Union's main long-range patrol flying boat. Not one of the rest was even considered (as we have seen, the He 113 did not exist). I am especially intrigued by the C.94, because only 12 (possibly 13) examples of this very undistinguished Italian flying boat were ever built, and there is no record of any Soviet interest in it. But the *Spotter* completely overlooked the chief transport of the Soviet Union in World War Two: the DC-3, built under licence as the PS-84, later redesignated Li-2 in honour of Lisunov, who managed the protracted negotiations with Douglas and the State Department, as well as the 1,293 engineering changes.

In the very next issue there appeared a description of the CKB-26. Again it was said to be based on the Boeing Y1B-9A of 1931, and the silhouette published was certainly just that! In fact this drawing bore only a very general resemblance to the CKB-26, predecessor of Ilyushin's DB-3 bomber, which was a totally different and much more modern design. On the facing page was a picture of the famed ANT-25 long-distance record-breaker, with the comment 'now modified for bombing'. One began to wonder where such totally untrue reports stemmed from; were they all deliberate invention? Again, as late as 28 August 1941 we were told that 'the Russians use the Republic 2PA as their standard amphibious fighter.' Now where could that bit of misinformation have come from?

Too much in this vein becomes boring. In World War Two everyone pulled together, and did the very best he or she could. The Russians, even as our Allies, were not easy to get on with. Trying to prise information out of them on even their most standard types of aircraft was not easy. Yet is it not amazing that, a year after Luftwaffe intelligence officers had clambered all over Il-2s, Yak-1s, La-5s, Yak-4s, MiG-3s and Pe-2s, virtually nothing was known about these—the *real* Red Air Fleet—in Britain? Just down the road from me lives 'Wag' Haw, one of the four members of RAF 151 Wing to receive the Order of Lenin (the only ones given to any Allied personnel during World War Two). One of his first missions was to 'escort Russian bombers'. He pictured fabric-covered monsters doing about 100 knots. He had a shock: they were Pe-2s, which were unknown in Britain, and at absolute full throttle, fearing blowing up his Hurricane's Merlin, he could just about keep up!

30

7 December 1941

The Rising Sun

Though tension had been building for some weeks, the attack on the US Pacific Fleet at Pearl Harbor by carrier-based aircraft of the Imperial Japanese Navy will probably go down in history as the most famous of all unexpected sneak attacks. It was carefully timed to hit at around breakfast time on a quiet Sunday (date above). By amazing good fortune a brand new surveillance radar had just become operational on the hills to the north. The operators were excitedly learning how to get the best results. Suddenly, they began to see lots of 'blips' (echoes'), moving swiftly towards them. No problem; it was just an expected formation of B-17s, the first on the islands, due in that morning from California, so there was no need to report what was happening! Of course, the really crucial bit of good luck is that not one carrier was in harbour; they were all at sea, and these, plus others newly commissioned, were what destroyed the Japanese fleets in the decisive battles of 1942-3.

If we had known little about the Soviet air forces in June, we now discovered we knew next to nothing about the Japanese in December. Maybe intelligence was harder to get in Japan. In that country a European stands out like a sore thumb. So what knowledge we had was completely out of date; out of 18 known types, information on which was urgently disseminated in British recognition manual AP.1480J, 16 were to be dismissed as 'obsolete in 1941' in the classic book by Dr René Francillon, *Japanese Aircraft of the Pacific War*!

As we had little idea of the true designations of Japanese aircraft we began by inventing some. While we were about it—yes, you guessed it—we also invented some Japanese aeroplanes. Temple Press, wartime publishers of *The Aeroplane*, also produced an outstanding series of recognition books. Pearl Harbor made them stop and think for a bit. Indeed, the thinking went on until February 1943. Then at last they produced their recognition book on Japanese aircraft. The Foreword commented on how much painstaking and diligent research had gone into it 'from many and widespread sources'. It was described as 'the most complete and accurate compendium possible at the present state of knowledge . . .', and as we had by this time been in all-out war with the Japanese for 15 months one might have expected the inventions to be replaced by realities (even if we didn't know what all of them were called).

The first entry was the Aichi KT-97, a single-engined biplane seaplane. Full details were given, but no photographs (only drawings). This was probably pure imagination, but it may have been intended to be the E3A; if so we certainly never encountered any. The next aircraft was much more formidable: the Aichi KT-98. This was a fine-looking three-engined monoplane seaplane. Well might the accompanying description say 'apparently derived from the Cant Z.506B of the Regia Aeronautica'. Again we had full details—things like 'Weight loaded 26,400 lb, Fuel capacity 880 Imp gals'—but again drawings replaced photographs. Not surprisingly we learned 'Very little has been seen of this machine in action . . .'; in fact I doubt if any Allied fighter pilot ever got one in his sights, because the whole thing was again pure invention. But how could it happen?

Passing the 'Kawanishi KT-94', which was in reality the widely used E7K (but all the wartime examples were E7K2s with a radial engine), we came to the 'Kawanishi H-97-2'. This big four-engined flying boat was simply the Japanese version of the French Lioré et Olivier H-24-6. We learned that 'Little is known about the Japanese version except that it appears to resemble the French boat in almost every respect, and is probably made from the same drawings . . .'. It could not have been quite the same, however. The Kawanishi H-97-2 bristled with machine guns and bombs, while the French boat was a 26-passenger transport for Air France. Only six were built, for services in the Mediterranean. In the 1950s I asked the great Georges Hereil, President Directeur-Général of SNCASE (who had been top man of Lioré et Olivier before the war) if the Japanese had taken a licence for the H-24-6. He seemed to regard the question as a joke, and replied 'What on Earth gave you that idea!?'

Next we came to an old favourite, the 'Mitsubishi Navy B-96-1 Otori'. The description commented that 'the original civil version . . . flew non-stop from Tokyo to Bangkok, 2,000 miles, in 1936'. Few figures were given—'No other details available'—and this is odd, because the Otori actually existed. But it existed only as a single example built for the *Asahi* newspaper.

One of the valid entries was the Mitsubishi G3M (though called the OB-96-4, in conformity with the belief that the Japanese used such prefixes as S, KT, OB, and G, for particular missions, which they did not). This aircraft was somewhat in the class of the Wellington, and was likewise noted for its range. The principal service versions were the G3M2 (maximum range 2,722 miles) and G3M3 (3,871 miles). In this 1943 book, however, we were told the range was 1,615 miles, and there is evidence that this gross underassessment resulted in Japanese bombers appearing in places thought by the Allies to be 'impossible', a notable example being the destruction of the Force Z capital ships *Prince of Wales* and *Repulse* by bombers flying from Saigon (also see 'OB-01' later). Another small oddity is that this 1943 book, compiled when several shot-down G3Ms had been examined, reported that the prominent side gun blisters were staggered, 'the starboard blister being much further forward . . .', and this is how the silhouette was drawn. This might make sense if you have two waist gunners, but in fact the blisters were directly opposite each other!

Next came the 'Mitsubishi Navy S-97'. Again there were no good photographs, though one of the drawings could have been a retouched photo. It showed an 'S-97' on the ground, with a ground crewman obscuring the landing gear (and this could have been significant). We learned that the Navy S-97 was 'the first Japanese fighter to have a retractable undercarriage. It is a direct development of the Nakajima Army S-97 . . .' The silhouette and drawings showed an aircraft looking very much like the Nakajima fighter (which actually was the Ki-27), but obviously bigger (span 40 ft), tougher and with retractable gear in place of the spatted landing gear of the Ki-27. Two auxiliary tanks were shown scabbed on the underside of the wing, behind the retracted wheels. This was a distinctive and unusual option for the Ki-27. So what do we make of this entry? First, Army aircraft were not developed into Navy aircraft. Second, Nakajima aircraft were not developed into Mitsubishi aircraft (though it once happened the other way round). Third, the S-97, 'known to have been in service in China' and presented with the fullest numerical details, was another example of pure invention.

In contrast, a most notable absentee from the book was the Nakajima Ki-43 Hayabusa (Allied name, Oscar). This was by far the most numerous and important Army fighter in World War Two, and by February 1943 it had been encountered on literally hundreds of occasions. I simply cannot understand how it could have been omitted from a 'most complete and accurate compendium' published at that time. The retouched photo of the 'Navy S-97' could well have been a Ki-43, with a few changes and with the ventral tanks drawn in. If this was indeed the case, why take a photo of a real aeroplane and alter it to look like an invented one? And who dreamed up all the details of the 'Navy S-97'?

A bit later we found the 'Navy S-00' which, we were told, 'should be called the "Double Oh" and not the Zero, which is wrong' (wonder who thought that up?). Next came the 'Mitsubishi Navy OB-01', actually the G4M, and again we had a gross underestimate of range ('about 2,000 miles', the true figure being 3,749-3,765 miles). In view of the large number of G4Ms that by 1943 had been inspected it is also rather surprising that the engines were thought to be '1,050 hp Mitsubishi Kinsei . . .' instead of the Kasei of 1,825 hp.

There followed the 'Nakajima Navy G-96'. This ancient biplane, in the class of the Vildebeeste (ie pre-Swordfish), was the only Japanese torpedo bomber known to exist in December 1941. Accordingly, it was credited with amazing powers. The excellent British annual *Aircraft of the Fighting Powers* said in Vol iii that these aircraft had torpedoed the US fleet at Pearl Harbor and sunk the capital ships of British Force Z three days later, 'a feat which would have been deemed impossible a few weeks earlier'. In fact these biplanes were not Nakajima G-96s but the Yokosuka (Navy Arsenal) B4Y1. What's more, they were not in action at all. Francillon comments that by December 1941, 'the few B4Y1s still airworthy were operated in a training capacity'.

Next we came to a spread of photos of lesser-known types. Two were not only real but important: the 'Sasebo KT-00' was the Mitsubishi F1M and the 'Mitsubishi SSH-00' was the Nakajima A6M2-N. The Kawasaki S-95 was the Ki-10, a real biplane fighter but an extremely obsolete one, and the Nakajima AT was another real aeroplane which led to the Army Ki-34 transport. The 'Tatikawa Army Ambulance' was another real type, but hardly important. A tiny biplane, powered by a 120 hp Cirrus Hermes, it could carry two stretchers. Actually the Tachikawa KKY, it flew in 1934 and 23 were built, all donated by private subscription.

This left three types on the spread unaccounted for. The Nakajima Navy S-01 might have been meant to be the same company's Army Ki-43, though the engine was said to be a Kinsei and the speed was given as 387 mph, about 70 mph too fast.

The 'Mitsubishi B-97 Darai' was quite a nice looking medium bomber, which was pure invention. And the 'Osaka Army RK-97' army co-op aircraft, looking like a Cessna Airmaster or a Beaver, was another type (and maker) which seems to have had no basis in fact whatsoever.

There followed the Nakajima Navy S-97, which never received any naval designation because it remained a prototype, which lost out to the A5M. This was followed by the Nakajima SKT-97, a mid-wing monoplane seaplane with two open cockpits. Another of the extraordinary absentees from this book was the Aichi E13A, the most numerous and important of all Japanese reconnaissance seaplanes; but this was a very different machine, much bigger and more powerful, with an utterly different shape and a crew of three under a long greenhouse canopy. I have often wondered why the 'SKT-97' was invented. Needless to say, the accompanying specification was highly detailed.

A bit later we found the Kawasaki Army OB-97. Though said to have a gross weight of only 20,900 lb, this was described as a heavy bomber. We learned that it 'has not been reported in this war, although it may have been used and not recognized'. It had a few odd features; for example there were no bomb doors, and there was an enclosed tandem cockpit exactly where the bomb bay ought to have been. It was full of interesting features, and somehow provided room for a crew of 'five to seven', but after a fair amount of research I can only conclude that this was another bit of pure invention.

We moved on through various Mitsubishi Kariganes (the KB-98 Karigane III was actually nothing to do with this family but was the Tachikawa Ki-36) to 'one of the world's ugliest aeroplanes', the Mitsubishi Army OB-98. Again, one wonders what this was. It had a lot in common with the Ki-2 bomber of 1933, though this was a smaller aircraft of just half the weight. Certainly the Japanese never built any aircraft remotely answering to the 'OB-98' description. A minor point is that '98' meant our year 1938, whereas the aircraft depicted would obviously have been 1930 technology, had it existed.

Passing the Nakajima T-94 (actually the Ki-4, long since obsolete in 1941) we came to the Showa SB-99. This, 'claimed by the Japanese to be the Showa Type 98, is really the United States Vultee V-11GB attack bomber'. Old Gerard Vultee did pretty well with his V-11, one of the first aerodynamically clean stressed-skin attack bombers. It was widely exported (which it wasn't), built in quantity in the Soviet Union (which it wasn't) and built in quantity in Japan (which it wasn't). There was no such thing as the 'Showa SB-99'.

The final page of this compilation depicted 'foreign types in Japanese service'. Of course, almost all of them weren't. One of the most curious of these types was the Heinkel OB-98, the 'He 111K' with radial engines. As an illustration an He 111H was used, the engines airbrushed to look like radials. Again, I never understood where this idea came from. Heinkel did fit BMW 132 radials to two He 111 prototypes. At first called He 111G-3s, they later, in 1938, entered airline service with Deutsche Luft Hansa as He 111Ls. No other He 111 was ever fitted with radial engines, and the Japanese never got as far as talking about a licence. So this, too, was pure invention. Another of the foreign types was the Potez B-01, the French Potez 63B2 twin-engined fighter bomber. There were many variations on the Potez 63 family, but I have never been able to discover the slightest connection between any of them and Japan. Yet another type was the four-engined Heinkel He 116, called the 'Army Y-98'. Two pre-production examples of the He 116 were sent to Japan, but they were civil transports used by Manchurian Air Lines. The 'Army Y-98' was a figment of someone's imagination, as were Japanese Messerschmitt Bf 109s and 110s.

One of the strange puzzles, not only of our beliefs regarding Japanese aircraft in World War Two but at many other times, such as Soviet aircraft in the 1950s, is that, while we have been eager to invent all sorts of fictitious aircraft, these have almost never had the happy knack of resembling any of the real ones. In the same way, while we have produced long lists of aircraft of foreign design, erroneously supposed to have been adopted and made under licence, we have failed to notice the real ones. Thus, we appeared to be ignorant of the manufacturing licences which, after careful evaluation of imported aircraft, were obtained for the Bücker Jungmann primary trainer and the North American NA-16R advanced trainer, the latter being one of the fixed undercarriage relatives of the T-6 Harvard. Also conspicuously absent from this most earnestly compiled book were the Douglas DC-2 and DC-3. The former was made only in small numbers, but the DC-3 was one of the most important Japanese transports of World War Two. After evaluating 20 imported before the war, a licence was obtained in 1938 and announced by Douglas at the time. As the L2D, differing from US versions mainly in that the flight-deck windows were extended much further to the rear, 416 were made by Showa and 71 by Nakajima. Francillon notes that 'These were met throughout the Pacific theatre . . . and often led to tragic recognition errors', but presumably the news failed to reach London?

As noted in the story on the A6M Zero (page 121), a tiny US team in Melbourne hit on the idea of inventing code names for Japanese aircraft, to try to reduce the confusion. The only problem was that another group in the CBI (China, Burma, India) theatre was assigning different names to the same aircraft, but the CBI names were soon dropped. Francillon listed all the names in his classic book. I won't bore the reader by repeating all the nonsenses, but the comment 'Fictional type' is common, and so is 'Erroneously believed to be . . .'. Among the types reported in the Pacific War were the Fw 190, Fw 200, Ju 87, Ju 52/3m, Bf 109E, and Ju 88! All pure invention; or maybe the chaps just weren't very good at 'aircraft rec'?

As so often happens, this little story has a twist in the tail. One of the favourite dodges of the fictitious-aircraft inventors was clearly to pick on some commercial transport known to have been supplied to the particular foreign power, and then invent a bomber version, said to be used by that air force. In the case of Japan that procedure twice actually happened. In 1930 a licence was obtained for the gigantic Junkers G38, two of which had been supplied to Deutsche Luft Hansa and were common sights around Europe. The Imperial Army thought they would make fine bombers, and in great secrecy Mitsubishi turned the G38 into the Ki-20, called by the Army the Type 92 Super Heavy Bomber. Six were built, each with a bombload of 11,023 lb and a crew of ten. They were completely obsolete by December 1941.

Now in the mid-1930s Douglas Aircraft had begun planning a large four-engined transport to become the DC-4, to meet the future needs of American, United, Eastern and, originally, PanAm and TWA. The result, flown on 7 June 1938, was an aircraft that looked both extremely modern and, by the standards of the day, enormous. The wing resembled that of a DC-3 scaled up to a span exceeding 138 ft, and the huge main wheels of the tricycle landing gear retracted inwards into the wing roots. Unfortunately, it was not an inspired design, and Douglas and the airlines decided to start again with a fresh DC-4 that was somewhat smaller, much simpler, more efficient, and very much cheaper to build and to operate. To Douglas's delight they found a buyer for the original DC-4, which by this time had become the DC-4E (E for experimental). The Japanese government had been looking for a suitable large and modern four-engined aircraft, because the Japanese industry lacked experience of such aircraft, especially one of stressed-skin construction. Douglas sold the DC-4E in January 1939, and it was at once flown to Japan. The transaction was fully reported at the time, the recipient being named as Japan Air Lines.

So we come to 1942-3, when numerous enthusiasts, experts, non-experts, and inventors of fictitious aircraft were busy trying to put together comprehensive lists of Japanese Army and Navy aircraft. Some must have pondered on this huge prototype. What was it doing today? Was it in production? More ominously, had the Japanese developed it into a bomber? Of all the inventors of fictitious aircraft, not one had the nerve to suggest such an unlikely thing as a giant bomber based on the DC-4E. And that is ironic, because that is just what did happen. Indeed, before the big Douglas reached Japan the Imperial Navy had told Nakajima to get ready to produce a bomber version. The American prototype was instantly dissected and studied. Nakajima didn't hang about; they got the first G5N1, powered by four 1,870 hp Mamoru engines, flying by December 1939. Others followed, but their bomber was if anything even less of a success than the DC-4E, though it looked tremendous. Strange that the inventors of fictitious aircraft always miss the real ones!

31

23 June 1942

Air or Water

On the date above, the Adjutant of Luftwaffe Gruppe III/JG 2 became lost and disorientated after a succession of combats with Spitfires and landed in error at RAF Pembrey, in South Wales. It gave the RAF a valuable prize: a flyable Fw 190A-3. Not only did this aircraft confirm the reports of every RAF fighter pilot who had met the 'Focke-Wulf', that it was an extremely formidable aircraft which could outfly the Spitfire in every respect except sustained turn radius, but it also showed British industry how to install an aircooled radial engine.

Previously the combat reports had been doubted. At first there lurked a supposition that these radial-engined fighters might be captured Curtiss Hawk 75As, but their performance and heavy cannon armament, as well as their totally different appearance, soon disproved this notion. But there remained nagging disbelief; how could a radial-engined fighter be so good? This was an odd viewpoint. For one thing, almost all the RAF's fighters between the wars had had radial engines: Woodcock, Grebe, Gamecock, Siskin, Bulldog, Gauntlet, and Gladiator, punctuated only by the Hawker Fury, which had a water-cooled V-12 engine and, despite its shape, was slower than the Gauntlet and Gladiator.

But the Schneider Trophy seaplane races exerted an enormous influence on everyone from chief designers to chiefs of the air staff, and the answer seemed to be that, if you want speed, you have to use some form of 'inline' engine. Strictly, I would use this term only for an engine with all its cylinders in one row, such as a Gipsy Six, but very loosely 'inline' can mean an engine of V, inverted-V, H, or various other configurations. Of course, such engines do not have to be cooled by liquids. Getting rid of surplus heat is best done by maximizing the difference in temperature between the cylinder and the cooling medium, and even on the hottest tropical day the difference between the fins on an air-cooled cylinder head and the outside air may be 250 to 350°C, whereas the difference between cooling water and the air is unlikely to exceed 80°C.

Unfortunately, aviation is full of emotion, fashion, and unproven beliefs. The fact that the Short Crusader, the only post-1924 Schneider contender with an air-cooled radial engine, did not exceed 246 mph and then crashed (because the ailerons were connected in reverse) proved only that you don't go as fast if you have less power. But as soon as Lord Trenchard and the other air marshals saw Richard Fairey's Fox bomber in 1925 they were hooked on pointed spinners and what looked like streamlined engine installations. The only drawback was the big radiator sticking out into the slipstream, and in 1931-5 enormous efforts were made, mainly by Rolls-Royce, to perfect an engine cooled by the condensing of steam in radiators flush with the leading edges of the wings. This seemed a marvellous idea, because it added no drag and in fact might slightly have increased speed by adding energy to the airflow. What killed it was partly supposed greater vulnerability to gunfire, but mainly the fact that during aerobatics, as in combat, the water and steam changed places and spoilt the cooling flow.

Rolls-Royce, the unchallenged leader in Britain of the liquid-cooled engine, gradually perfected pressurized cooling systems filled with ethylene glycol and then with mixtures of water and glycol. Among many other things this brought down the size of radiator needed, which in turn reduced drag and also the very considerable weight of the cooling circuit and the liquid it contained. Towards the end of World War Two Rolls-Royce succeeded in developing radiators which gave net thrust, operating like a low-temperature ramjet. But there is no reason why a properly cowled air-cooled engine should not give net thrust as well, in this case operating like a slightly hotter ramjet. The idea, of course, is to ram in air at the front, pass this through a duct of expanding cross-section to convert velocity into even higher pressure, pass it through the radiator matrix or past finned cylinders where heat is added, and then let it escape by accelerating to high velocity through a constricted 'propelling nozzle'.

In the United States almost every engine was air cooled. In 1931 Pratt & Whitney had tested a rather advanced water-cooled engine, the 20-cylinder R-2060, but got such poor results they dropped liquid cooling until 1935. Then, partly because of supposed limitations of air cooling and partly because of British development of high-power engines with multiple liquid-cooled sleeve-valve cylinders, Pratt & Whitney began developing a series of impressive liquid-cooled engines. The programme got ever bigger and harder. Meanwhile, the company's ordinary air-cooled radials made rapid progress. From the 575 hp Hornet their power went to 1,000 hp with the Twin Wasp in 1935 and to 1,850 hp with the Double Wasp in 1940. On 1 October 1940 one of these early R-2800 Double Wasps powered the XF4U-1, prototype of the famed Vought Corsair fighter, to a level speed of 405 mph. This was almost certainly the first time any aircraft, other than a pure racer, had exceeded 400 mph.

Unlike Britain there was no prejudice in the USA against the air-cooled radial. Luke Hobbs, newly appointed P&W Chief Engineer, told Army Air Corps chief 'Hap' Arnold that, while the complex liquid-cooled X-1800 and H-3730 would be likely to miss World War Two, Pratt & Whitney could build equally powerful radial engines that would make it. Arnold immediately authorized termination of the liquid-cooled programme and substitution of the 28-cylinder R-4360 Wasp Major. This passed its first tests in June 1942, and a year later had been qualified for production at 3,000 hp. By the end of the war it was in volume production at 3,500 hp.

All this would have seemed heresy in Britain, especially before we captured the Fw 190. Consider the Hawker fighters built to Specification F.18/37. One was the N-type (N for Napier Sabre), which became the Typhoon, and the other was the R-type (R for Rolls-Royce Vulture) which became the Tornado. Both these complex liquid-cooled engines were in deep trouble. Eventually the Tornado, which had actually been placed in full production at A.V. Roe at Manchester, was cancelled completely. This was purely because of the failure of the Vulture engine. Yet with an alternative engine the Tornado could have been a very superior aircraft. Back in November 1940 Roy Fedden at Bristol had sent Hawker Aircraft a prototype of the 18-cylinder sleeve-valve Centaurus aircooled radial. Sydney Camm scraped together stock spare parts, and a fuselage built at Langley, and managed to put together a third Tornado prototype, HG641. This was fitted with the Bristol radial, and it flew on 23 October 1941, a month after the Tornado programme had been cancelled. Test pilot Philip Lucas found, probably to everyone's surprise, that the radial-engined aircraft handled better, was quieter, and had a much higher all-round performance. Level speed was 421 mph, considerably faster than anything previously reached by any British fighter.

As a result the few open-minded people realized that the best engine for the new family of Hawker fighters was the Centaurus, but prejudice against radials remained. In my biography of Sir Roy Fedden I wrote (and I stand by it): 'Development of a good British fighter with a radial engine was—in Fedden's view—deliberately prevented by official bias, centred around Air Marshal (later Air Chief Marshal Sir) Wilfred Freeman, Air Member for Development and Production. Freeman disliked Fedden as intensely as he liked Hives and his team at Rolls-Royce. The antipathy was quite open . . . Camm managed to get a Centaurus fitted to one of his new thin-wing Tempests, which then (August 1942) was called the Typhoon II. Freeman was furious, and had the engine taken out again. In return Fedden said he wondered whether he could get Freeman impeached for seriously undermining the war effort. The Centaurus fighter was not allowed to fly until 28 June 1943, by which time the excellence of the Fw 190 and American P-47 Thunderbolt had made it difficult for Freeman to insist that a radial-engined fighter must be inferior.'

Now of course this gives Fedden's point of view. Truth did not lie down the middle, because there is no doubt that pulling the Centaurus out of the Typhoon II prototype LA602 really did delay the development of an extremely important fighter programme—despite the fact that Freeman is widely remembered as a great and patriotic man, not too given to petty and erroneous decisions. But there is no doubt that during almost the whole of World War Two it was tacitly assumed in Britain, much more than in any other country, that aircooled radials might be all right for lumbering transports and such machines as the Swordfish and Walrus, but were very much a second-best choice for fighters.

Even as late as 14 May 1942, when the Fw 190 had firmly established its ascendancy over any fighter the RAF could pit against it, the magazine *Flight* was so overcome by our own propaganda and wishful thinking as to call it 'a serviceable commonplace type . . . It can be assumed that if the Luftwaffe had at their disposal any inline powerplants of an output commensurate with up-to-date fighter requirements they would have taken a different course. Instead they had to make a virtue out of necessity, and indulge in the application of the available engine type for their new fighter.' This was sheer rubbish. First, we knew perfectly well that the meticulously planning Germans were hardly likely to forget to provide the engines they would need. At Daimler-Benz Technical Director Fritz Nallinger's main problem was that he had far too many new types of fighter engine, most of them with complex multi-stage supercharger systems. Second, the Fw 190 was deliberately designed with a radial engine partly to avoid overloading the demands on liquid-cooled engine production but mainly because the radial was appreciably more powerful. The result was a tremendous aircraft whose only shortcoming was a fall-off in performance at high altitudes. It was purely to meet the high-altitude demand that the Fw 190D-9 and Ta 152 later used liquid-cooled engines, the BMW-powered fighters remaining in full production.

In Italy there were no suitable high-power engines for fighters, and so aircraft designed by Fiat, Macchi, and Caproni-Reggiane were all re-engined with German liquid-cooled engines. For example, many accounts of the development by Ing. Mario Castoldi of the Macchi C.200 and C.205 fighters all emphasize how different his creations were from those of Mitchell in Britain. Both had built streamlined Schneider seaplanes with pointy-nose liquid-cooled engines. But, whereas Mitchell had carried on the good work with the Spitfire, Castoldi had been forced to use what a British author called 'a bulky drag-producing aircooled radial'. But in August 1940 'the infinitely superior MC.202' had made its first flight with an imported German DB 601A liquid-cooled engine, giving it a front end very like a Bf 109. Later Alfa Romeo made the DB 601 under licence and Fiat made the more powerful DB 605, resulting in 'far superior fighters no longer encumbered by the drag of a radial engine'. But this is a superficial and erroneous view. Switching to the German liquid-cooled engines added more than 1,000 lb to the empty weight (1,350 lb with coolant and other items), reduced manoeuvrability because of the greater engine length and also—though in a fighter this is a minor consideration—approximately doubled the capital and operating costs. The extra speed came simply from having 1,475 hp instead of only 870. So what we are really saying is, fighters go faster with more powerful engines.

There are plenty of examples where the engine change was the other way round. I have mentioned the Hawker fighters, which began with nothing but liquid-cooled engines and after the war finished up with nothing but the aircooled Centaurus radial, in the Tempest II and the whole Fury family. The Halifax heavy bomber started with Merlins but overcame its performance problems by switching to Hercules radials. In the Soviet Union the clumsy and indeed dangerous LaGG-3 fighter was transformed by a radial engine into the superb La-5 and its successors, while in Japan the Mitsubishi Ki-61 was given a radial engine as a panic emergency measure and became so much better that the quick lash-up was put into production as the Ki-100. And after the war it was certainly a mistake on the part of Canadair, prodded by Trans-Canada Airlines, to build the DC-4M with Merlins instead of the original Twin Wasp R-2000 radials.

Today RAF No 8 Sqn still thunders aloft on the last remaining hours available on Rolls-Royce Griffons. These are an anachronism. Virtually every other high-power piston engine in the world, outside the world of unlimited racers and power boats, is an air-cooled radial. And virtually every piston engine in General Aviation, from agricultural aircraft through luxurious twins to the humblest Cessna, is also air-cooled. OK, you say, so air-cooled engines finally won. Well, like most things in aviation, it's not as simple as that. Since 1975 one or two water-cooled engines have made their appearance. Since 1980 they have started to become important. When in December 1986 Dick Rutan and Jeana Yeager made their fantastic non-stop flight around the world, the engine they used for 99.9 per cent of the flight was liquid-cooled, using a 50/50 glycol/water mix just like many wartime engines. They selected this engine because its fuel economy was better than that of the air-cooled front engine of the Voyager aircraft, the two engines otherwise being of the same make and almost identical.

So the answer is clearly that air-cooled engines are definitely better than liquid-cooled engines, unless it's the other way round.

32

13 June 1944

Flying Bombs

I was amazed recently to find that many young people do not know what a Doodlebug was; they had no idea that from the date above until 30 March 1945, five weeks from the end of World War Two in Europe, London, Manchester, Brussels, Antwerp, and a few other places, were attacked by pilotless jet-propelled flying bombs. Today we would call such weapons cruise missiles. The 'Doodlebug'—actually the Fieseler Fi 103, but also known as FZG 76 and by the code name Kirschkern, meaning cherry stone—was an extremely simple miniature aeroplane made mostly from sheet steel, with a launch weight of about 4,800 lb. There were several versions, the most common being 27 ft 4 in long and having an untapered wing of 17 ft 4 in span.

The bomb was propelled by an intermittent-firing pulsejet duct with a frequency of about 47 Hz (cycles per second). Each bomb was launched along an inclined ramp incorporating a high-pressure steam catapult similar in principle to those used on today's aircraft carriers. The speed naturally varied with the thrust, which varied with fuel flow, which was determined by various types of fuel metering device. Dozens of test bombs averaged about 370 mph, but the earliest ones fired in anger in the summer of 1944 often cruised at a mere 280 mph or thereabouts. Changes were made to aneroid capsules and diaphragms, and speed thereafter settled at 385–400 mph, making these tiny targets *very* hard to destroy. This short story merely asks a few questions and adds personal reminiscence on a fascinating episode near the end of the greatest war ever.

By the summer of 1944 the citizens of London were quite used to bombs and to air attack generally. I was then 17, and lived at 93 The Chase, Eastcote, Middlesex, about 15 miles north-west of Piccadilly Circus. Even here we had more 'incidents' than I could count, the most serious being the arrival of a parachute mine in October 1940 which simply removed eight houses from the map, damaged about 100 others, and among many other things removed the roof, garage doors, and front gates of No 93. With my best friend, Roy Webster, I got the Headmaster's permission to stay at home next day and help clean up. I remember our laughing at finding a kitchen sink in the garden, and our inability to hold on to a heavy glass-filled carpet which we tried to shake from an upstairs window. A day or two later a Ju 88 came over at roof-top height dropping SC50 (110-lb) bombs at about one-second intervals.

Excitement and interest overcame self-preservation and I rushed out to watch, in time to see two bombs eliminate a house across the road (No 66 I think) and a bungalow dead in line with us in the next street, Deane Croft Road. In 1946 a friend in the US Army (Pte Chuck Loudermilk, from Bowling Green, Kentucky) rang the door bell, and I showed him some of the sights. I pointed to the neatly cleared places where the stick of SC50s had fallen, and Chuck said, 'Sure was good luck they fell there, and not on any houses.'

From May 1941 things had been pretty quiet; the Luftwaffe was elsewhere. When we were at Air Training Corps camp at Upper Heyford in 1943 several of our mob (ATC 628 Sqn) saw an Me 410 come screaming across the airfield, very low. They said there was no doubt about it, and the only puzzle was that it just went on into the distance. A few weeks later I happened to be at Hastings when, surprise, surprise, what should happen along but an Fw 190 at full throttle and very low. It passed within about 200 yards of me, and I couldn't take my eyes of the large bomb that detached itself from the 190 and plunged into a sea-front hotel. To my amazement the bomb reappeared out at the back, this time climbing and tumbling wildly. It seemed to take an age to arch over and disappear again. Still no explosion. Almost an anti-climax.

Like millions of families we had a Morrison 'table shelter', a simple steel box strong enough to bear the weight of a collapsed house. I was sleeping in this when everything happened at once on 13 June 1944. I don't need to be told this was a Tuesday; I won't forget it. The sirens announced a raid, I began to hear the sound of an aircraft, and flak bursts came rapidly nearer, all within the space of about a minute. Nothing like this had ever happened before. I got up quickly, but it was all over so fast I saw nothing. The thunderous, throbbing aircraft seemed to pass right over No 93, very low, and the flak bursts were so low they were shattering windows. The hubbub swiftly died away into the distance. Then a few seconds later there came a heavy explosion, not so much a bang as a shaking like an earthquake. My famous quote was, said to my mother, 'Well I take my hat off to that chap!' Though it didn't sound like a 190 I couldn't think what else it could have been.

I was still puzzled the next morning. As soon as we could, Roy and I got our bikes and went to look for where the bomb had fallen. The track had been roughly north-west, and 20 seconds at 360 mph would be two miles, so that gave us a reasonable circle of probability. In fact we went straight to the spot. There had obviously been 'an incident' just off Bury Street, Ruislip, in open fields just south of Mad Bess Wood. There was a huge crater and a lot of what at first glance looked like bits of aircraft. Most of the police, wardens, fire and other official people had departed, and there were few sightseers. There was no sentry on guard.

Roy and I were perplexed. A crashing 190, even with a big bomb on board, would have left quite different bits of wreckage. Here there were just a few bits of what, from their weight, were obviously steel—and a strange device which looked like the inlet to a circular duct containing a barrier filled with springy flap valves. Roy and I, there and then, pieced together in our minds the design of the Argus 109-014 pulsejet duct, and how it worked. Having done that, there was only one possible conclusion. This had been some kind of pilotless missile.

A day later the newspapers broke the story: Britain was being attacked by what were officially called P/Ac (pilotless aircraft) but code-named 'Diver', some purists insisted on calling 'reaction-propelled crewless aeroplanes' and 486 (NZ) Tempest

Squadron called Doodlebugs. Obviously, the slick name stuck, and quite right, because 486 was part of Bee Beamont's Newchurch-based wing which eventually shot down 638 of the bombs, far more than any other unit. Yet another name for the things was 'V1', from the German Vergeltungswaffen (reprisal weapon) No 1. Soon the Air Ministry was insisting that there was only one type of bomb, while other groups identified a host of others. With hindsight it is clear that some, such as the 'butterfly' model with strange sweptback elliptical wings, were pure invention. Some others have never been proved to exist, but on the other hand there were many thousands made of at least three variants. At least 29,500 of these missiles were delivered, the main assembly centre being the gigantic Mittelwerke underground slave mine near Nordhausen where 9,000 of the workers died in 1944 alone.

To me flying bombs typified all that was evil in the Nazi regime. I never felt any animosity toward Luftwaffe aircraft, and wasn't in the least bothered by the A4 (or V2) rockets, where the first thing you heard was the explosion, followed by 10 seconds or more of diminishing rumble—man-made thunder, in fact—which was the sound of the huge rocket's supersonic approach. But I hated the flying bombs. You could hear them coming from miles away, always flying (like a mindless machine) dead straight and level, never to be put off by fear of the defences. Cruising height varied from about 500 to 2,500 ft, though I would guess nearly all the ones I saw were not much above 1,000 ft. Their noise was hideous and absolutely distinctive. And when it stopped you could be certain of a colossal explosion not long afterwards. At school I was taking my Higher Schools Certificate, a bit like today's A-levels. We sat each paper in the Hall, where there was no cover and lots of glass, but an observer on the school tower could press a button in emergency. One couldn't help being distracted, because in July 1944 the unearthly throbbing went on day and night, but only once was the button pushed. The bomb passed overhead and the whole school shook soon after. It hit Addison Road, Northwood. A few days later I got on my bike to see another site, and found a huge area of devastation at Woodway Crescent, Kenton. The crescent goes downhill from Gerard Road, and I saw something that made me get down on hands and knees and feel the road. The bomb had actually scraped along the road surface, travelling at a shallow angle and leaving a deep groove with pale blue paint marks, before hitting a house at the bottom about 100 yards further on and exploding. I was puzzled by the groove until I discovered that under the bomb was a strong angle girder driven by the catapult piston on takeoff. Remarkable that it could groove the road without detonating the warhead.

Most bombs went down much more steeply. Contrary to the popular belief, the fuel was not cut off nor were the elevators depressed. The range was determined not by a clock but by an air-log propeller on the nose. When the log had rotated the preset number of times a dive control unit was triggered which: locked the elevators neutral; severed the air pipes to the rudder relay, holding the rudder neutral; and released small spoilers under the tailplane. The spoilers put the bomb into a dive, and it was negative g causing fuel starvation which cut off propulsion.

The technological excitement of being under flying bomb attack wore off rather quickly. Thereafter one soon grew tired of hearing the things, and seeing enormous palls of smoke around the distant horizon—and they were the ones that didn't come near you. At night an oncoming bomb could be seen as a dot of yellow light; the eye could not detect that it was really 47 separate dots per second.

I have many memories of those six months. I had a lot to do with the London Philharmonic—I was paid but unofficial assistant to that superb orchestra's librarian, Tom Russell—and was impressed that, at a rehearsal at Wembley Town Hall, not a single member stopped playing even when a bomb cut out overhead. It fell about a mile away. Afterwards the handsome leader, Jean Pougnet, asked the conductor, Basil (later Sir Basil) Cameron, if he had heard it. The reply, appropriate for a conductor, was: 'I'm not deaf!' On a grey Sunday another friend, Derek Pool, let me watch from the roof of his office on King's Cross station (he was an LNER permanent-way engineer). About a mile away, in the City, a bomb arched down at high speed and hit a large office building. The warhead appeared to light up all the windows from inside, with a golden glow. When the usual pall of smoke and debris drifted away the building was no longer there.

When Beamont's wing moved to the Continent Sir Harry Broadhurst told them, 'Over here the targets fight back!' So shooting down flying bombs might have been thought a 'turkey shoot'. In fact it called for skill (because of the tiny target), courage (because of the likely massive explosion), and every ounce of aircraft performance. Do not forget (Story 33) that the published maximum speeds of piston-engined fighters refer to the full-throttle height, such as 22,000 ft. At flying-bomb height it was a different story. At 1,000 ft the 448 mph Spitfire XIV could just reach 365 mph, while the 435 mph Tempest V could manage about 383 mph. Thus the margin of speed over the small and elusive bombs was close to zero. Many organizations worked wonders providing 150-grade fuel and fuel containing 2.5 per cent monomethyl aniline or injection of nitrous oxide, and modifying the engines so that they didn't blow up. What amazed me is that none of this was done beforehand, during the almost two years warning we had of this weapon.

We knew about these flying bombs in increasing detail and accuracy from November 1939. By autumn 1943 we had quite a detailed knowledge of the bombs. Why then did we do nothing to organize our defences until the attack started? And why did we do nothing to fill the Channel with flak from the French coast to our own? We had command of the sea, we had tens of thousands of AA guns from 20 mm upwards, and we had no end of ships, hulks, landing craft, and other floating platforms which could have been anchored along the known lines of approach from the launch sites. As a diversion on a long 747 flight I even designed an idealized floating flak platform. We did nothing like this, and instead, even after an urgent large-scale redeployment, still left vast numbers of AA units eating their heads off on land and sea in places where the Luftwaffe never came and flying bombs couldn't.

33

8 May 1945

The Jet Lead

The date given above is that of VE (Victory in Europe) day. Actually, nothing much happened on that day: the instrument of German surrender was signed on the 7th and formally ratified on the 9th. Anyway, in this piece I intend to outline how complete at that time was the superiority of the Allies in jet engines, except that maybe it was the Germans who had the superiority. I will also attempt to answer the question: 'What was the first jet fighter?' So this cannot avoid being violently controversial.

Let me say at the start that, for various reasons (some outlined in Story 14), we in Britain completely threw away our seven-year lead in the invention of the turbojet. Thus, on VE day, Britain had a mere handful of jet engines bolted into what were essentially piston-engine type airframes with piston-engine performance, while the Germans had many thousands of the new engines installed in several types of aircraft which were often of significantly higher performance, with a *daily* engine production rate in autumn 1944 which exceeded Britain's production for the entire year. Does this not seem almost beyond belief?

Let's start with the question of who invented the turbojet. As explained earlier, Whittle invented it in October 1929, and wrote it all down with diagrams and thermodynamic calculations. These formed the basis for his patent specification submitted a very short time later. Hans-Joachim Pabst von Ohain independently invented the turbojet in October or November 1935. He had a small model of his idea built by gifted automotive engineer Max Hahn. In April 1936 Ohain and Hahn joined Ernst Heinkel Flugzeugwerke, and were able to gather a complete team dedicated to getting a jet aircraft into the sky as fast as possible (an objective denied to Whittle until nearly four years later). Other workers, such as Mélot, Lorin, Morize, Harris, Leduc, Lysholm, Campini, and Griffith, can be eliminated, either because they were later or because they either did not use a compressor or else used a reciprocating engine to drive it.

Next, when was the first turbojet run? Whittle knew exactly what he wanted to do and, after overcoming more than six years of disbelief and disinterest, got his WU (Whittle Unit) running on 12 April 1937. Ohain's first test apparatus, the HeS 1, was first run in late March 1937. This would appear to antedate Whittle, but we are comparing apples with oranges. Whereas the WU was in all respects a complete turbojet—a bit clumsy for aircraft installation, but perfectly capable of it—by no stretch of the imagination could the HeS 1 be called a 'turbojet' at all. It was instead a laboratory demonstration rig, intended to solve some of the mechanical problems. The thorny problem of combustion was sidestepped by using hydrogen gas, and if the machine was disconnected from the laboratory gas supply it could not run. Next came the HeS 2, first run in October 1938. This was started on hydrogen and run on petrol (gasoline). It was unsatisfactory, and was followed by the HeS 3A and 3B. There are no other contenders for 'first turbojet'.

What about the first jet flight? This was made by the Heinkel He 178, flown by Flugkapitan Erich Warsitz (borrowed from Wernher von Braun's group at Peenemünde), at Rostock-Marienehe airfield. Taxiing tests began on 24 August 1939, and a short hop of a few seconds was made on that day. The first proper flight followed early on the morning of Sunday 27 August—a small bird being ingested at the start of takeoff. This was yet another test flight programme begun more than a week before the war in a public place which remained (so all the records suggest) completely unknown in Britain!

On 27 August 1940 the Italian Caproni-Campini N.1 made its first flight. This was a distressingly clumsy experimental aircraft with a jet produced by the power of an ordinary piston engine. Its performance would have been improved if the engine had been connected to an ordinary propeller. The first jet fighter, the Heinkel He 280, flew as a glider on 11 September 1940 and, after 41 test flights as a glider, made its first twin-jet powered flight on 2 April 1941. The British Gloster E.28/39, powered by a Power Jets W.1, made its first flight on 15 May 1941. There are no other contenders.

So what about 'the first jet fighter'? This question, so beloved of the quizmasters, is invariably answered by 'the Messerschmitt Me 262', but it is not as simple as this. I just called the He 280 'the first jet fighter', and this it surely was; but it depends what you think the expression means. The following is a brief chronology. We have already seen that the He 280 flew as a glider at the height of the Battle of Britain and powered by two HeS 8A turbojets on 2 April 1941. In my opinion this aircraft unquestionably qualifies as 'the first jet fighter', and the sixth prototype flew with production engines and full armament. The He 280 is in no way disqualified by the fact that it was dropped in 1943 and did not go into production.

The Me 262 was first flown on 18 April 1941, but in a form totally unlike that with which we are familiar; it had no jets, but a piston engine driving a propeller in the nose, and it also had a tailwheel. On 25 March 1942 it flew with the piston engine plus twin jets (which failed). The first proper twin-jet flight, with the production engines, was made on 18 July 1942. The first flight with a (fixed) nosewheel came on 26 June 1943. The American Bell XP-59A Airacomet first flew on 1 October 1942. Because of the outrageous situation between Power Jets and Rover the British Gloster Meteor did not fly until 5 March 1943, and then on the power of two de Havilland (Halford) H.1 Goblin engines.

Let's now turn to 'the first jet fighter in service'. This is by no means simple to pin down. A good case can be made out for the Bell YP-59A Airacomet, examples of which between 30 September and 5 November 1943 were delivered to the USAAF, US Navy, and RAF, and flown by all three recipients in their own countries. On 5 May 1944 the first three Meteor Is were accepted by the RAF at the CRD (Controller of R&D) unit formed at the RAE Farnborough under G/Capt

H.J. 'Willie' Wilson. They lacked guns, but did intensive development, being joined by three more later in the month. But before this, on 30 April, the Luftwaffe had formed Erprobungskommando 262, the Me 262 test unit, and these had about 20 Me 262A-la fighters which were in almost all respects combat ready—even if no pilots were. On 23 May Hitler learned to his fury that his order to build 262s solely as *Blitzbombers*—lightning bombers—issued in November 1943 had been ignored. He now furiously repeated it: he wanted 262 bombers to repel the imminent Allied invasion. It has often been said that the Führer's order seriously delayed the programme. I have no doubt whatever it did not delay it by one hour; the pacing item (obviously) was always the Jumo 004B engine.

Another criterion is the first jet fighter with a combat unit. There is no doubt that the answer here is the Meteor I, with No 616 (S Yorks) Squadron from 12 July 1944. The aircraft and pilots mainly came from CRD and were fully operational. The first Luftwaffe operational unit to fly the Me 262 was I/KG 51, which was formed on 22 August 1944 by renaming Ekdo Schenk, which had done the service testing of the Me 262A-2a fighter/bomber version.

What about the first jet fighter to engage in combat? An Me 262 of Ekdo 262, flown by the CO, Capt Thierfelder, was (according to Luftwaffe records) shot down over Bavaria on 18 July 1944; the Allied victor has never been discovered, and it is generally believed that Thierfelder was a victim of his own flak and that there was no Allied aircraft involved. On 25 July an Ekdo 262 aircraft spent 15 minutes trying to destroy a PR Mosquito, which eventually escaped into cloud. The 262 began scoring with a B-17 on 8 August, but four days earlier, on 4 August, RAF No 616 Squadron had destroyed the first of their 'V1' flying bombs. The jet fighter's guns failed to fire, and F/O Dean downed the missile by tipping it over with his wingtip, so some purists might claim this was not a 'combat'. But on the following day several bombs fell to Meteor guns. So the reader can decide this one.

While on the subject of who was ahead in timing, I don't think anyone would quarrel with the contention that the Germans did the best they could and, despite a fair amount of bickering, abrasiveness, and personality intrusion, could not have knocked more than perhaps a week or two off their timescales. In the most startling contrast, we in Britain wasted not weeks, or even months, but years. For a start, nobody showed the slightest interest in Whittle's radical new engine until well into 1938, nine years after the invention. Even then nothing tangible happened until in January 1940 the Power Jets work, previously disinterestedly tagged as 'long-term research', was suddenly recognized as 'a potential war-winner'. It was accorded Al, the highest national priority for scarce materials, labour, and other requirements. Then, after the collapse of France in June 1940, Lord Beaverbrook's sweeping crisis measures concentrated solely on production of established types (such as the Whitley and Blenheim!) and removed all priority from the jet engine. Whittle recalls: 'For a week or two this looked like the end of the project; then we were told we could proceed, so long as we did not in any way interfere with other essential production work.' The company which had made the sole Whittle engine, BTH, regarded the whole thing as 'a dead duck', stopped all jet activity and moved personnel to other jobs.

It was a long uphill struggle to get anything going again, and even in August 1941 only two Whittle engines existed. Moreover, tiny Power Jets were required by the Ministry to hand complete sets of drawings, specifications and 'all experience' to all the big firms being drawn into the growing jet industry, and this stopped the country's only established jet team from getting on with their real work. Worse, these big intruders immediately began competing with Power Jets for all the scarce parts, such as fuel pumps, turbine blades, and bearings. Perhaps worst of all was the disastrous link between Power Jets and Rover Cars, which instead of producing engines produced such acrimony that by late 1942 the two firms were hardly on speaking terms, and almost nothing was happening. Then Whittle managed to get Rolls-Royce to replace Rover, and British jet engines at last got going almost overnight. For example, running time on the W.2B engine for the Meteor totalled 24 hours in December 1942 and 414 hours in January 1943!

As explained in Story 14, according to Whittle, 'The succession of avoidable delays may have totalled about seven and a half years. The RAF could have been equipped with Meteors and Vampires or the like by about 1937, and bombers having turbofan engines, based on our LR.1, by about 1939 . . .' Makes you think.

I will round this appraisal off by comparing the German and British engines and aircraft. Wisely, Whittle stuck to centrifugal compressors. This was despite the scorn of such ivory-tower people as Griffith, who did not have the remotest idea of what it meant to develop a real engine. Unlike the awesome complexity of the multi-stage axial, the centrifugal was more or less a known quantity. Indeed, thanks to Whittle's incredible knowledge and skill, his centrifugals had a considerably *higher* performance, in terms of airflow, pressure ratio, and efficiency, than contemporary German axials, besides being lighter and far less prone to damage. Their only adverse feature was that they resulted in engines of greater diameter, but this caused no significant difference in aircraft performance. Don't forget, jet installations are not 'solid' but have air flowing through them. The fact that a tall man can stand upright inside a 747 engine inlet does not stop the aircraft flying at 600 mph! And to show the kind of margin I am talking about, the Jumo 004B, the most important German turbojet of 1944, weighed 1,585 lb, had a 'brochure' thrust of 1,980 lb (though the average of three tested at random by the MAP in June 1945 was 1,605 lb static at sea level), and had an eight-stage compressor with a pressure ratio of 3.1; specific fuel consumption was about 1.59. In contrast the Rolls-Royce Welland, the productionized Whittle engine used in the Meteor I, weighed only 850 lb, had a guaranteed thrust of 1,700 lb, and had a one-piece compressor with a pressure ratio of 4; specific fuel consumption was 1.12. So the 'crude' British engine was superior all round.

Now I'm one of those odd people who believe in numbers rather than in emotions. I have often read that British wartime jets were in some way backward because they used centrifugal compressors. Certainly the great A.A. Griffith held this view, and it's the kind of opinion that is catching. I shall elaborate on this later (Story 42). Let's just say such a belief is unsupportable by the facts.

Whilst writing this I received an Australian magazine in which was an article on the 50th anniversary of the Jet Age. Apart from claiming that today's F404 engine 'puts out about 16,000 lb thrust *unreheated*' (my italics) it includes the statement: 'To the victors went the spoils. Britain, the US and France grabbed the axial flow research undertaken by the Germans.' I have never seen such a claim before, and I challenge author David Carter to name a single British engine that owed anything whatsoever to German axial-flow research. In France the SNECMA Atar was originally an all-German design, and SOCEMA used Jumo technology in the

TGAR 1008. Much later, in the USA, the top Junkers designer, Dr Anselm Franz, masterminded the T53 helicopter engine, which later led to the T55 and then to the ALF502 (engine of the BAe 146). But Britain grabbing German axial know-how? We didn't even grab their aerodynamics (next story).

Of course, you can look at most things in two ways. In July 1945 two British engines, a de Havilland Goblin and a Rolls-Royce Derwent I, were tested in the mighty Herbitus high-altitude test plant adjoining the BMW works at Munich-Allach. The skilled German technicians who had been rounded up by their new masters were amazed and impressed to find that the British engines could be run for 150 hours without attention, or six times as long as any of the German engines. So we were ahead; or were we?

If the Ministry had settled for 25 hours TBO (time between overhauls) then a little of the wasted seven and a half years could have been recovered, and the RAF could have had a Meteor squadron at least in May 1943. Around 1931 Lord Trenchard, 'Father of the RAF', gave a major staff lecture in which he insisted that, where fighters are concerned, performance and armament are far more important than long life or time between overhauls. In a famous phrase, he said that squadrons equipped with short-life but otherwise superior fighters would 'cut through the enemy formations like a knife through butter'. This is precisely the situation that the Allies faced in 1945. By this time the Germans had lost the war, and it is nonsense to talk about the German jets having the power to stave off defeat or even result in German victory; but if they had been available in greater numbers sooner then the final advance through Germany would have been much tougher.

Why was the Me 262 so much faster than the Meteor? Mainly because the British aircraft was a rather pedestrian design, conceived along totally traditional principles. So, indeed, was the Me 262, but it had wings of reduced thickness/chord ratio and appreciably lower overall drag, especially at Mach numbers over about 0.78. What it did not have were sweptback wings. The mean chord of the centre section was actually slightly swept forward, and that of the outer panels was slightly swept back to give the correct centre of pressure position, aft of the centre of gravity. Critical Mach number was unaffected. Messerschmitt knew all about the advantages of sweepback, but abandoned it for the 262 in 1942 because of undesirable stability effects which, at that time, they did not know how to correct. (By 1945, however, his designers *were* using swept wings, but the prototypes never got into the air.) I was never within miles of 'having a go' in an Me 262, but those fortunate enough to fly one said it was a beautiful aircraft in all respects. Despite this, even with such pilot view, handling, performance, and devastating firepower, the Me 262 almost certainly killed more German pilots than Allied pilots.

Incidentally, do not be misled by mere single figures for 'maximum speed'. Engineers think in pictures, and when the question of maximum speed arises a performance engineer pictures speed plotted against altitude. Aircraft such as the P-51D, Spitfire XIV, and Tempest were fastest at one particular height, above or below which the maximum fell away very sharply because that's how the engine supercharger gears and boost system was arranged). A jet, such as the Meteor I, showed little difference in maximum speed at different heights; the plot would show a gentle curve increasing slightly from sea level to 30,000 ft, thereafter falling away to the ceiling. (Today's supersonic jets, with full afterburner, show a plot resembling that of piston days, because structural strength does not permit more than about half the Mach 2 maximum at low levels, but that is beside the point.)

To sum up, the German jet aircraft that fought in the war were very good aircraft but not outstandingly advanced. They did not have sweepback in order to postpone compressibility effects, and having axial engines did not make any significant difference. Far more important was the fact that, while the Germans built as if they were fighting a war, around 1,300 Me 262s (for example) being completed, we built as if we had already won the war (Meteors on strength on 31 May 1945 = 58). In any case, how could anyone contrive to waste seven and a half years?

34

July 1945

'Haven't We Won the War?'

The history books tell us that, having in 1815 won the Battle of Waterloo, the British Army was not disposed to change anything until its terrible deficiencies and errors were exposed by the Crimean War 40 years later. The British seem, at least in the past, to have been predisposed towards feelings of blind superiority. This was certainly true in the summer of 1945.

Back in 1944 both the Soviet Union and the United States had held big meetings to plan missions to Germany as soon as possible after that country was occupied, in order to see what was worth finding out or grabbing. These missions were to embrace every kind of activity, but especially military, air, and naval subjects. Everything was planned thoroughly, to reap the maximum benefit. We in Britain did nothing. So by VE day (8 May 1945) over 600 specialists from our Allies were already combing Germany, while we were beginning to think maybe we ought to do something as well. Eventually, as far as aviation was concerned, three tiny teams were sent out, totalling 27 people in all. Overcoming endless difficulties, always feeling second-class citizens in comparison with their Allies, and bereft of the slightest back-up or interest from London, they nevertheless brought back a rich harvest. How could they fail? In between the rain-filled bomb craters, the face of Germany was littered with technology we had never thought of.

To give a flavour of that summer among the ruins, the following comes from my biography of Sir Roy Fedden:

The mission spent the first three days at the LFA laboratory, also called the Hermann Goering Institute, at Volkenrode, near Brunswick. This had been discovered by American troops a few weeks before. It was easily the biggest aeronautical research laboratory in Europe. Fedden had heard before the war such an establishment was being planned, but there followed only conflicting rumours, some prisoners saying it was in East Prussia and others claiming it had been planned but never built. Now it had at last been discovered. Never in the thousands of reconnaissance flights over Germany had its presence been suspected, though photographic interpreters had looked at it in numerous prints. It had no main road, no rail link, and no overhead power line. The whole series of services were brought underground from Brunswick. Yet the place was gigantic. It covered about 1,100 acres in a thickly wooded area. It contained dozens of huge buildings, a great array of wind tunnels far surpassing in size, Mach number and power anything even planned in Britain, and large complexes of laboratories for engines, structures, explosives and weapons (including rocket propulsion and various classes of guided missiles). Yet, so good was the camouflage, even former members of the staff were continually getting lost and having to make huge detours. The biggest wind tunnel, for example, operating up to Mach 1.8, was under thousands of tons of earth in which were growing grass, bushes and small trees.

This mighty establishment was just the first of a succession of surprises. Members of the mission walked miles through ruined machine shops and laboratories to study and discuss huge piston engines, jet engines, rocket engines and new research tools. They discovered a range of optical interferometric methods of picturing aerodynamic flow, and even got a tunnel working with a swept-wing model in it. The use of sweepback to delay com-pressibility drag-rise had been known before the war, but subsequently forgotten and ignored in Britain, but in Germany it was being accepted as standard in all the latest jet aircraft. While the airflow round the model was being explored a team breezed in from Boeing; next morning Fedden was piqued that the swept-wing model was nowhere to be found (guess who had it). A day or two later Fedden had made up two huge truckloads of books for Cranfield from Göttingen. They were about to leave when the loads were commandeered by US troops, on the instructions of a rival US team. Fedden could see there would be trouble, and sought the advice of the Allied Control Commission. They did not want to know, and the rule seemed to be the law of the jungle. Fedden had no inclination to steal things off the Americans, and it was galling when he was robbed of the things he had managed to find for Britain. As he had no troops and could get no backing he had to let the trucks be driven away.

Thus, the British came off third- or fourth-best in combing Germany for new technology, largely because the newly elected government was utterly uninterested. Despite this, between August and October 1945 various exhibitions were staged in London, at Farnborough, and at Hendon of German aircraft and equipment. The whole idea appeared to be: 'This is what we defeated; now we can put it in a big pile and put a match to it.' There was never the slightest idea that anyone might learn anything. For example, the doughty *Aeroplane Spotter*, having noted that a particular exhibition of German aircraft equipment, materials, accessories, and parts 'would have taken some days to examine, appreciate and thoroughly digest', continued: 'From these static exhibits the observer could judge that, far from being superior to British equipment, many of the German counterparts were far behind in efficiency and practical application.' After all, when you have fought a propaganda battle non-stop for six years, it's hard to change and become objective!

Chief designers are much less inclined to adopt a stance based on propaganda, but they often become hooked on the rightness of their own ideas and can see only the flaws and shortcomings—real and imagined—in the ideas of their rivals. For example, Sydney Camm, splendid character though he undoubtedly was, showed extreme reluctance in 1934 to switch to stressed-skin construction and instead covered the Hurricane with fabric. With the F.18/37, which became the Typhoon, he had no option but to use metal skin from the outset, but based his aerodynamic sums on faulty tunnel results and chose a thickness/chord ratio more appropriate to a heavy bomber (and also devised an odd cockpit with car-type doors and no rear view!). By the end of the war Camm had a really excellent fighter in production, the Tempest V, with the Fury well advanced in testing. It is therefore perhaps understandable that, when in July 1945 he was shown drawings and models of advanced German designs, about three generations later in conception, he totally failed to take them seriously. Shown a drawing of the Messerschmitt P.1110, which Fedden had found in a project design department near Oberammergau, Camm looked at it for about a minute and then said: 'Did you ever see anything more ridiculous?'

I am not trying to 'pick on' Camm. I am merely citing his reaction as typical of British industry. He had heard of Whittle and his jet engine, of course, but nobody in the entire British industry had done anything about jet aeroplanes apart from George Carter at Gloster and the de Havilland company. All Camm had done was draw a few sketches seeing how Whittle-type engines might fit into the fuselage of a traditional fighter. Soon he hit on the idea of the bifurcated jetpipe—to make it sound complicated Lord Hives of Rolls-Royce always said 'birfucated'—so that a fuel tank could be put in the rear fuselage. Camm's first jet fighter (which actually had this feature), the Sea Hawk, reached the customer, the Royal Navy, in 1953. This was eight years after the end of the war, and the Sea Hawk had 'straight' wings and a lower critical Mach number (0.83) than the Me 262! Of course, the Sea Hawk met the official specification, N.7/46, which said nothing about swept wings, but I am surprised that nothing happened to alter things during those eight years.

I think I've got the general message across, that in 1945 all these axial engines and swept or delta wings were considered to be outlandish rubbish, far removed from reality. If anything, the German deltas were thought even more ridiculous than the swept wings. Who'd have thought that at the Farnborough Airshow in 1952 Hawker Siddeley would dish out thousands of carrier bags bearing the slogan '1952—DELTA YEAR'! (We delivered our first delta fighter and bomber four years later.)

Though it's not exactly aeronautical I'll finish with another extract from the Fedden biography:

On 17 July 1945 Fedden went back to Germany to witness the jet testing on the Herbitus plant. He took Peter Ware with him, and as they were driving along the repaired Autobahn Fedden pointed to a signpost to Fallersleben, mentioning that in 1938 General Milch had taken him there to show him the production line of the new People's Car, the Volkswagen. Ware was quite excited, and asked if they could pay the works a visit. They found it badly bombed, and with a B-17 Fortress still in the main erecting hall, whence it had entered via the roof. Fedden commandeered a Volkswagen, brought it back to England in a Dakota, and called a conference of British motor-industry leaders to study it. One and all were scathing. Ford in particular saw not one good feature, and ridiculed the use of an air-cooled engine mounted in the rear. The only man who did not actually laugh was Billy Rootes, and his attitude was one of pity. 'It's actually got some ingenious features. Indeed I'm grateful to you Roy, for bringing it over. But of course it's all a waste of time. Even if the Germans try to go on making it, it'll never sell.'

35

31 January 1946

Through the Barrier

To any Briton the story of the Miles M.52 ought to be of the most supreme importance. Who can say how many million or billion pounds, or how many tens of thousands of jobs, might have ridden on the back of it over the subsequent 30 years? Sadly, like so many great British enterprises, it was cancelled at the stroke of a pen after almost all the design problems had been solved, and just as it was coming to fruition. And, as the government of the day desperately hoped, Fleet Street hardly noticed, and today many—perhaps most—aviation enthusiasts have never heard of it.

When young Frank Whittle was a cadet at Cranwell his amazing strategic vision made him think about aircraft that could fly at great heights, where their thermodynamic efficiency would be much greater. In turn, this led him to invent the turbojet. He saw at once that such an engine would free aeroplanes from their existing universal limitation on speed imposed by the propeller. Indeed, he saw with absolute clarity that, provided aircraft had the correct shape, flight control system, and structural strength, jet aircraft could even fly faster than sound. But this was clearly far in the future. Meanwhile, in the mid-1930s, he also invented the aft-fan (he called it an augmentor) and jetpipe reheat or afterburning. Both these additions were to be used in the design for the world's first supersonic aircraft, the M.52.

According to the Ministry of Supply, 'In the summer of 1943 information from German sources suggested that active consideration was being given to aircraft capable of 1,000 mph . . .' Overlooking the fact that Germans think in kilometres, not miles, this was considered plausible enough to require some kind of response. After some heart-searching—because it all seemed slightly in the realm of fantasy—specification E.24/43 was raised. It did not ask for an aircraft to meet a string of requirements: merely that it should take off from and land on a normal aerodrome and fly at 1,000 mph at 36,000 ft! This is the kind of specification that results in real advances.

In World War Two the British aircraft industry more or less consisted of staid, established, and accepted firms, among whom the lush contracts were parcelled out, and Miles. This little firm at Reading were simply terrible. They designed aircraft in half the time they ought to, built all sorts of amazingly unconventional machines (sometimes—one must say this in a whisper, it was so wicked—without even telling the Ministry), and generally seemed to think they could flout the rules laid down by the officials. In 1943 they dared to offer a design, called the X.11, to meet the Brabazon I specification for a non-stop transatlantic airliner. The officials had decided on political grounds to award this giant contract to Bristol, and took it for granted they would easily find reasons for rejecting the upstart X.11. Unfortunately for them, the X.11 was in most respects ahead of the Bristol 167 technically, even after the officials had (either mistakenly or deliberately) downgraded all the figures by assuming use of Rolls-Royce Griffon engines instead of the much more powerful and highly efficient RR Pennine.

Suddenly a way out was seen: as a sop, give Miles the E.24/43. This seemed so 'far out' that not a few officials secretly hoped the Reading bad boys might make a complete hash of it. But I am over-simplifying things. George Miles, brother of chairman F.G. Miles, told me: 'No one, not even the decision-makers, ever really understands the true reasons for placing major contracts. In the convoluted logic of power, Ministers and Civil Servants are fundamentally influenced by expediency, personalities, patronage and prejudice, rather than by such secondary factors as

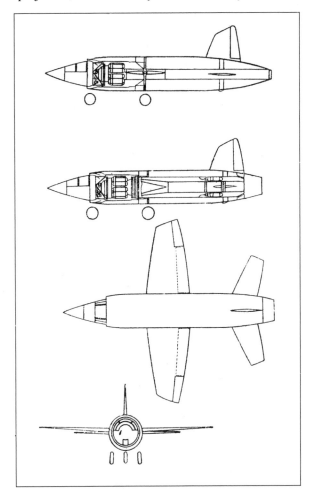

Ministry of Supply drawing of the M.52 showing the installation of the W.2/700 engine (top), the other three views showing the added ducted fan and afterburning with the nozzle enlarged to 37 in diameter.

technical competence, experience and energy. I happen to believe that we were the most competent organization to undertake the formidable problems and hazards of the E.24/43; I also think the support of Sir Stafford Cripps was a factor.'

Miles got the go-ahead on 8 October 1943. They were to work in the greatest secrecy, but in close collaboration with the Royal Aircraft Establishment at Farnborough and with Power Jets Ltd. Both partners showed enthusiasm at the great challenge; after all, unlike Ministry officials, actual workers in the industry love nothing better than to push ahead into the unknown. P.A. Hufton at the RAE played a major role, and of course G/Capt (later Sir) Frank Whittle's brilliant team pulled out all the stops to provide the propulsion system. But at Reading only six people were allowed at first to be 'in the know': Fred and George Miles, project engineer L.C. 'Toby' Heal, chief aerodynamicist D.S. Bancroft, chief designer and assistant test pilot Don Brown, and chief stressman H.S. Wilkinson. I was privileged to discuss the E.24/43 challenge and the resulting Miles M.52 with all of them.

Don Brown said: 'You say that it is surprising that so small a team could take so many seemingly radical yet correct decisions in such a short time, with so little to guide them. In my view the *only* way to do any job speedily and successfully is to have a small team. A giant consortium is the best way of getting nothing done over considerable periods.' I did say Miles were a terrible lot!

I asked George Miles whether the very small size of the firm, and lack of facilities, did not prove a handicap. He replied, 'No other firm had a high-speed tunnel either. Such crude supersonic equipment as was then available in Britain was at Farnborough, and we were their nearest neighbours. With Don Brown and 'Bush' Bandidt I went to Volkenrode towards the end of the war in an attempt to gain temporary use of the big German supersonic tunnel before either the Russians or our own people started to dismantle it. That trip was worthy of a Peter Sellers epic, but failed in its main objective, even though we had a four-foot stainless steel model ready and waiting to go into what was then the world's most advanced high-speed tunnel.'

In all essentials the M.52 was a thoroughly sound design. For obvious reasons it was rather like a mid-winged projectile, and perhaps the main thing we would not do today would be to use a peripheral annular air inlet with the cockpit inside the centrebody. This cockpit was carried on four steel-tube vee struts attached to the first main circular bulkhead behind the inlet. Cordite charges could sever these struts in emergency, ram pressure in the engine plenum chamber then blowing the drogue-equipped nose section clear. The wing had a biconvex section with a sharp leading edge which resulted in the name Gillette. Thickness/chord ratio was 7.5 per cent at the root, quickly tapering to just over 4 per cent at the tip. Normal by modern standards, this seemed dauntingly thin in 1943, and flaps were at first considered impossible. A full-size wooden replica of the wing, with flaps, was fitted to a Miles Falcon (naturally called the Gillette Falcon), and this aircraft also successfully test-flew the M.52's one-piece 'slab' tailplane. I cannot think of any aircraft programme that accomplished so much true pioneering so quickly, and for such modest expenditure.

Power Jets, despite having to battle for survival throughout the war, welcomed the challenge of creating the M.52's propulsion system. The basic engine was to be a Whittle W.2/700 turbojet, rated at a maximum of 2,500 lb. This was considered marginally enough for preliminary test flying. All fuel and the main landing gears were to be housed in the cylindrical fuselage, of 60 in diameter. The engine diameter was 42.5 in and that of the long straight jetpipe 18.5 in. But for 1,000 mph much more thrust was needed, and Whittle's team designed, built, and quickly tested the definitive propulsion system. This comprised the W.2/700 plus the No 4 augmentor plus full reheat. The augmentor comprised a free-running two-stage turbine carrying double-deck blades with fan blades as extensions. Britain made no use of this Whittle patent, but when it expired in 1959 General Electric of the USA certainly did, in such engines as the CF700 and CJ805-23B. The fan blades handled an enormously augmented airflow. For supersonic flight additional fuel was burned both upstream and downstream of the added fan turbine, and, especially, in the fan airflow. The jetpipe would have terminated in a nozzle variable in diameter up to 37 in. Static thrust at sea level would have been about 17,000 lb. At 36,000 ft thrust was calculated to be 1,620 lb at 500 mph, 4,100 lb at 1,000 mph, and about 6,000 lb at 1,500 mph. Power Jets began static testing the whole bypass combustion system on 27 June 1945.

With a thrust of 4,100 lb, even assuming a lift/drag ratio as pathetic as 4, there would have been enough power for an aircraft weighing 16,400 lb, whereas making pessimistic assumptions the calculated gross weight of the M.52 was 7,710 lb. There is not the slightest doubt in my mind that the M.52 would have gone well beyond Mach 1. Heal and Bancroft were hoping to reach 1,500 mph. Everything was going like the proverbial train when, at about Christmas 1945, the Director of Scientific Research, Ben Lockspeiser, visited Miles. George Miles told me: 'He informed me that his department wished to take a new look at the project, because of the mass of captured German material on the advantages of high sweepback for transonic flight. I was left with an uneasy feeling . . . It was a pity my brother happened to be away at the time, since I think he would have had more politically intuitive reactions to the discussion.'

The brothers were utterly unprepared for what happened on or about 31 January 1946. The Ministry of Supply curtly informed the company that the M.52 contract was cancelled! Work was to cease immediately; all jigs, tooling and parts were to be destroyed, and all research reports and other information were to be sent to Bell Aircraft in the USA. Bell, of course, was building the XS-1 (later X-1) research aircraft to do exactly the same thing as the M.52, namely, to reach well beyond Mach 1. And, of course, it had a completely unswept wing, because swept wings are used for aircraft that do *not* exceed Mach 1.

Miles Aircraft were specifically told they were not to inform the Press, or even refer to the M.52 publicly in any way. Thus, nobody outside a tiny security-cleared circle even heard about the M.52 until six months later, in June 1946, when a display of British aircraft was staged at the RAE at Farnborough. What *Flight* called 'a belated and inconspicuous exhibit' was a model of the M.52. It was explained that this had been abandoned 'for reasons of economy', and that instead smaller rocket-propelled models fitted with autopilots would be dropped from aircraft. This was announced at a big Ministry of Supply press conference on 18 July 1946. Lockspeiser, who by this time had been knighted for his good work, never referred to the M.52, but said: 'The impression that supersonic aircraft are just around the corner is quite erroneous, but the difficulties will be tackled by the use of rocket-driven models. We have not the heart to ask pilots to fly the high-speed models, so we shall make them radio controlled.'

From that time on a hornet's nest was let loose, though it had little impact on the general public. First of all, Sir Ben was talking rubbish. Nobody had ever dreamed of putting pilots in the models, only in the M.52. Second, they were not radio controlled. Third, Ken Waller, Chief Test Pilot of Miles who would have flown the M.52 from Boscombe Down, stormed around (he was normally the most placid man) saying nobody had asked him, and he had been longing to fly the M.52. To embarrass the MoS further, a German test pilot who was a prisoner of war said that, if British pilots were barred, perhaps he might be allowed? Surely nobody would mind if he broke *his* neck? In fact, danger to the pilots was merely a ridiculous excuse invented by the Ministry to try to explain the cancellation.

The Ministry desperately tried to hush up the whole affair, repeatedly calling the M.52 'a piece of dead research'. They eagerly awaited the start of the model programme, the models being produced mainly under B.N. (later Sir Barnes) Wallis at Vickers-Armstrongs, Weybridge. They were dropped from Mosquitoes flying from St Eval to beyond the Scilly Isles. It was intended that, said Lockspeiser, models would be made in batches of six, there possibly being as many as 18 batches each having a different shape. Surprisingly (if the M.52 was 'dead research') the first batch were scale models of the M.52! Between 30 May 1947 and 10 October 1948 numerous missions were flown, on which models fell off, blew up, dived into the sea and did almost everything except work properly. At last, on the latter date, a model did a good run, reaching Mach 1.38. The amount spent on the model programme at that time exceeded £800,000, or just over eight times the amount spent on the M.52. Odd sort of 'economy'!

What had the model programme accomplished? Nothing, except to show that the aerodynamic design of the M.52 had been completely correct. And by this time it was all a bit late, because on 16 October 1947 Charles E. 'Chuck' Yeager had gone supersonic in the Bell XS-1. Today 'Yeager' is more famous than 'Waller'!

In March 1950 the staff of Farnborough's Supersonics Division completed R&M (Reports & Memoranda) No 2835, dealing with the RAE/Vickers model programme. The M.52 was still a hot potato, so, unprecedentedly, R&M 2835 was held back for four years and published only in 1954. It stated: 'With the gradual accumulation of knowledge it became clear that the E.24/43 was unlikely to reach sonic speed, and when wind-tunnel model tests indicated . . . serious loss of longitudinal stability at high subsonic speeds . . . the wisdom of continuing with this design was questioned . . . Early in 1946 the contract for the E.24/43 was cancelled since, in addition to the adverse feature already mentioned, there was now added . . . the impossibility of safe escape for the pilot.' It is the simplest thing in the world to disprove each of these three statements. But Britain has a long heritage of disastrous Government interference in aeronautics, often followed by a sterile search for excuses and explanations.

In February 1955 the Government's own *White Paper* on 'The Supply of Military Aircraft' stated, on the cancellation of the M.52, 'It is easy to be wise after the event, but it is clear now that this decision seriously delayed the progress of aeronautical research in the UK.' And in 1970 Rolls-Royce Bristol came to the conclusion: 'Re-examination of the M.52 in the light of present-day knowledge has shown that it incorporated sound principles and was capable of meeting the specification requirements.' In 1977 I asked Lockspeiser about the real reasons for the cancellation. He replied: 'Old men forget . . .'

36

6 March 1946

More Poke, Less Speed

Some of my best friends work for Rolls-Royce. In fact, you don't 'work for' R-R; it's rather like Japanese industry, where you are part of the company, and for life. I just hope none of those friends think I'm getting at them, or at the company.

My first car was a Ford Consul convertible, 1953 vintage. If I remember correctly it had 1,508 cc, while the other kind of British Ford, the Zephyr, could boast 2,553. I claimed to be able to outrun any unmodified Zephyr ever made (one could do this kind of thing in those days) and I never lost a bet. Maybe I just had a particulary good engine, but you surely wouldn't think that possible, *n'est-ce pas*? In the same way, when a year or two later my chums on *Autocar* tested the Vauxhall saloons, the 4-cylinder Wyvern, and otherwise similar 6-cylinder Velox, they were bemused to find that, overall, the car with the big engine burned less fuel. This story is about the funny results you get—rather like these—when you put lots more power into jet fighters.

The last aeroplane I ever flew in the RAF, on 1 July 1948, was a de Havilland Vampire F.3. Then a very new aeroplane, it was a delight. The cockpit was just like any other RAF fighter of the day, it was a basically simple machine, and I'd never before been able to fly at 500 mph. My abiding impression is that, rather like when I was given a ride in a pre-war MG, you felt extremely close to the ground. In the MG you could, I think, touch the road if you gave enthusiastic arm signals (as people did in those days) and I felt in the Vampire that, if there hadn't been a canopy, I might have touched the runway as I sank on to it.

The only possible criticism was 'lack of poke'. Halford's Goblin engine was a fine achievement in late 1942, and it scored a little over the Power Jets/Rolls-Royce engines in that the inlet(s) rammed air straight into the eye of the single-sided compressor instead of having to flow all round the engine to get in to both sides of a double-sided impeller, which also required that the engine be installed in an oversized box called a plenum chamber instead of being tightly cowled. About three years later my boss on *Flight*, Wing Commander Maurice Smith (one of the nicest men I ever met, who sadly died suddenly at 71) did a pilot appraisal of the Vampire (I think it was an F.3) for the magazine, and in extremely restrained terms commented that, compared with some later fighters, it was a trifle short on brute thrust. In those days the British aircraft industry thought it could tell even a magazine published weekly since 2 January 1909 what to write, and what not to write. We lost de Havilland advertising for a whole year.

Common sense suggests that 3,000 lb in 1948, or 1951, would soon not be enough, though anybody who saw what Teddy Tennant could do with 1,640 lb in the Folland Midge might disagree. Anyway, Halford, Moult and Co very quickly got on with the Ghost, rated for fighters at 5,000 lb. But before this was ready another 5,000-lb engine was produced: the Rolls-Royce Nene. Designed and built in six months, it first ran on 27 October 1944, and was at that time unquestionably the most powerful aircraft engine in the world. In Britain, unlike almost every other industrialized country, practically nothing was done with it. It was, however, fitted into one of the third production Vampire F.1s, TG276, which made its first flight with the powerful engine at the Rolls-Royce flight test establishment at Hucknall on 6 March 1946. With thrust increased from 3,000 lb to 5,000 lb it was fractionally slower than before!

Hucknall accordingly designed an improved installation with prominent dorsal ram-type inlets above the engine to feed more air to the rear of the compressor. Called 'elephant-ear' inlets, these were not particularly beautiful, but from the first flight of the next Nene-Vampire, TG280, on 4 July 1946, it was clear they were doing some good, because at low altitude this aircraft was able to reach 565 mph, instead of 548 with the little Goblin. A third conversion was TX807. All were obviously unsatisfactory, but in the post-war era nothing tended to happen for months at a time. Eventually, in November 1949, Boulton Paul Aircraft at Wolverhampton received a contract to develop neat wing-root inlets and bifurcated ducts able to handle the Nene's airflow of 40 lb/s on each side (80 lb/s total) instead of only 31. BPA based their inlet and duct design on that of the Hawker N.7/46 (prototype Sea Hawk), and test flying was done by 'Ben' Gunn, who later survived the tricky Nene-powered BPA deltas to become manager of Shoreham Airport. But Australia had already adopted the Nene-Vampire with crude elephant ears, and these were on their Mks FB.30 to 32. The French started off building Vampires with the Goblin, so by the time (1950) they switched to the Nene they could use the BPA inlets, renaming the aircraft the Mistral. At last it behaved like a Vampire with 67 per cent more thrust, maximum speed at low level going up from 548 to 576 mph, and initial climb from 4,800 to 7,090 ft/min.

At this time Australians still looked towards 'the Old Country', but when in 1950 they wanted to select a modern fighter to replace the Meteor in the RAAF we had absolutely nothing to offer. Hawker tried to interest the RAAF in the idea of a fighter derived from the P.1081, but the more sensible thing to do was buy a fighter that actually existed, especially as the RAAF was involved in the war in Korea. I recall poor old 77 Sqn singing 'All we want for Christmas is our wings swept back'! The obvious choice was the North American F-86 Sabre, but the Australians quite reasonably thought the Rolls-Royce Avon might with advantage replace the General Electric J47. The latter was based on almost prehistoric technology, with its roots in the TG-180, the pioneer American axial turbojet designed in 1942–3 and first run in April 1944. The Avon promised much more power in a shorter and lighter engine, with considerably reduced fuel consumption. In any case, Australia was eager to continue the long and fruitful association with Rolls-Royce. Accordingly, when in October 1951 the Australian government signed a manufacturing licence for the Sabre it was for a modified version fitted with the British engine, and with the standard armament of 'six fifties' replaced by two 30 mm Adens.

CAC, Commonwealth Aircraft Corporation, had had a team at NAA since May 1951. By the time the licence was signed it seemed clear that there would be no significant technical problems in effecting the modifications. The schedule was for all drawings to be issued within six months and for the prototype Avon-Sabre, called the CA-26, to fly on 1 April 1952. In fact it made its first flight on 3 August 1953, a week after the Korean war ended! I don't think the ungainly word 'horrendous' had been coined then, but if it had the Aussies would have used it. I won't bore readers with a list of the 665 engineering changes required, but the supposed simple modification turned out to result in a new aircraft. More than 60 per cent of the fuselage was completely redesigned, and one of the major problems was the way one change invariably led to another. There were spin-offs into the fuel system, flight control and many other areas. For example, to give a reason for some of the bigger changes, the Avon not only needed a larger inlet duct and jetpipe all the way from nose to tail but, being lighter, it had to be mounted further back. Consequently it could not be cantilevered off the fuselage to allow the entire tail to be pulled off for maintenance. This meant the forward (main) fuselage had to be considerably lengthened and the tail end shortened, and so the changes multiplied.

Even the CA-26 was far from being the definitive fighter, and after many further changes the CA-27 at last flew on 13 July 1954, becoming the first 'Sabre Mk 30'. In turn this was replaced in production by the Mks 31 and 32, which contrived to get out of step with NAA and switched from a slatted wing to the so-called '6-3' hard leading edge just as NAA had decided to go back to slats! The changes needed not only swallowed up the Avon's weight-saving of 400 lb but added a lot more, so that instead of having an equipped empty weight about 400 lb less than the 10,890 lb of the F-86F the Avon-Sabres typically turned the scales at 12,020 lb. I remember 'Old Scherg'—Air Marshal Sir Frederick Scherger, RAAF Chief of the Air Staff— saying: 'What we got at the end of it all was a fighter just about as good as the F-86F but three years later and costing twice as much. I'll tell you: we'll never go through all that again!' One of the few people who flew almost every type of Sabre, R.N. 'Bob' Broad, has no hesitation in saying the best of the lot was the Canadian Sabre 6. This also had a different engine, the Orenda 14, but somehow they shoved this Avon-power engine in without changing much else, and there was no need for more than very local modification. Bob reckoned the Sabre 6 'the best dogfighter of its day, better even than the FJ-4 Fury'.

So the project to put a Rolls-Royce engine in the Sabre rather backfired, leaving everyone involved saying 'never again'. And this was extremely tough, because of course by the time the troubled Avon-Sabres were in service they were no longer the last word in fighters. CAC was still delivering the Sabre 32 in 1959, a year after the RAAF had drawn up a list of possible replacements. It was quite a short list. Thanks to Duncan Sandys (Story 41) 'the Old Country' again had nothing to offer, so—after casting a wistful eye at the amazing new McDonnell XF4H-1 Phantom II—the list boiled down to the F-104 Starfighter, F8U Crusader and, as an outsider, the French Dassault Mirage III. Back in 1958 Rolls-Royce's Ronnie Harker had gone to Canberra to see what fighter the RAAF might select, and to make sure it would have an R-R engine. He discovered that one of the desirable requirements was the ability to ferry non-stop from Darwin to Singapore, bypassing Indonesia which was in the throes of President Soekano's belligerent 'confrontation', which with Soviet support was making claims on Malaysia and Singapore.

Back at Derby, Harker and R-R engineers looked at the Mirage and found that, with two drop tanks and powered by the Rolls-Royce RB.146 (Avon 300 series), it would have a ferry range of over 2,400 miles, enough for Darwin-Singapore with a safe margin. The existing Mirage, with the SNECMA Atar engine, could not fly so far because of the French engine's higher fuel consumption. It looked as if the Avon-Mirage would be the obvious choice. Harker then went to Dassault, and argued the case for the British engine. Technical Directeur-Général Henri Deplante showed no enthusiasm, pointing out that the Avon was bigger and heavier, would need larger inlets and ducts, and did not have a big enough afterburner (R-R had consistently lagged behind the USA, USSR, and even Sweden in afterburners). In any case, said Deplante, the Atar was good enough and was French, so that was that. Undaunted, Harker got Chief Installation Designer Tom Kerry to come up with an installation drawing of the RB.146 in the Mirage IIIE. One of the things I have never understood is why some people apparently think you cannot work on two things at once. According to Harker, Kerry's ultimate boss, Engineering Director Adrian Lombard, saw him working on the Mirage and said, 'Don't waste time with that, concentrate on the Conway in the 707 and DC-8'. This is odd because, quite apart from the fact that 'Lom' was a sensible man for whom I had profound respect, the Conway had then already been sold on both aircraft. What's more, no matter how hard Kerry worked, it was only going to be sold on a total of 69 aircraft (out of a combined total of 1,519 civil 707s and DC-8s), so it was of very little importance. The Mirage, on the other hand, was likely to run into four figures if the Avon could become the standard engine, as seemed very likely.

To cut a long story short, Deplante finally agreed that Kerry's drawings could be translated into metal, and R-R's Managing Director, Sir Denning Pearson, agreed to provide an engine, Dassault agreed to provide an airframe, and the result was the Mirage IIIO; Dassault salesman Bernard Wacquet said, as the IIIA already existed, they'd called it 'O for Orstralia'. In June 1960, while the Avon-Mirage was being designed, an Australian mission had visited Lockheed and Dassault, and among other things flown the F-104C and Mirage IIIA-01. They were impressed by both but, despite the French offering a manufacturing licence, various small changes to meet RAAF needs and a barter deal involving Australian wool and wine, the RAAF finally picked the F-104, in the upgraded F-104G version then about to fly. After all, it's not easy to import wine into France. Derby got wind of this, sent frantic signals and got the Australians to hold off for a few weeks in case the Avon-Mirage could really demonstrate its unique ability to stage from Darwin to Singapore.

The Mirage IIIO, with Rolls-Royce engine, flew on 13 February 1961. The Avon 67 gave 12,825 lb dry, compared with 9,436 lb from the Atar, and 16,450 lb with full afterburner compared with 13,625. It raised gun-firing height by 10,000 ft, and increased ferry range by over 600 miles. Yet, amazingly, the Australians picked the Brand X aircraft. This time they could not claim they were afraid of having another agonizing saga like the Avon-Sabre because the Avon-Mirage already existed, and a super aircraft it was. Harker thinks the French underpriced the Atar aircraft by quoting prices in Australian pounds (which were 20 per cent cheaper than Sterling). The clincher, he says, is that some nit in Derby refused to supply a more powerful afterburner at the original price, reasoning that 'it wouldn't be economic for a batch of only 30 aircraft'. So the one good R-R re-engining effort came to nothing. Of course, the 30 Atar-engined Mirage IIIO fighters for the RAAF was just for starters; successive batches brought their total up to 100, and there is not the slightest doubt that the all-round superior performance of the Avon-Mirage would have seen it sold in place of the Atar in a high proportion of today's 1,410 similar aircraft. This would have helped in a small way to fill the gap in British industry caused by having no warplanes of our own.

I won't mention putting the Spey in the Buccaneer. This was an eminently sensible move which caused few problems and performed as advertised. The same can be said of replacing the unsatisfactory TF30 in the Vought A-7 Corsair II by the Allison TF41, which was a slightly enlarged Rolls-Royce Spey produced by the British and US companies in partnership. This story concentrates on fighters, and the biggest fighter programme for many years was expected to be the USAF/USN TFX, which was intended to replace almost everything in sight in both US services. To give an idea of how big this programme was expected to be, it was calculated (mostly by Defense Secretary McNamara, whose brainchild it was) that developing versions of the same aircraft for the Air Force and Navy would *save* over a billion dollars. Three companies bid for the engine, one being Allison. Had the Allison/Rolls-Royce AR.168, an advanced afterburning version of the TF41, been chosen I don't think there is the slightest doubt that the TFX would have had a much happier subsequent history. As it was, the contractors were eventually *instructed* to use the TF30. Anyone who knows anything about the F-111, which is the designation of the aircraft that resulted from the TFX competition, knows that the problems with the engine, and especially with the engine installed in the aircraft, were for six years simply terrible. But of course, nobody had the slightest inkling of this when the AR.168 was rejected, simply because it was tainted by being 'foreign'.

While all this was going on, McDonnell Aircraft at St Louis was churning out F-4 Phantoms, which the F-111 was supposed to replace. In fact they did rather better than the F-111 programme because while the latter ended at No 562 the F-4 came to an end at No 5,211 (not 5,057, 5,081, 5,195 or any other popular total). If these figures had been known to the Top Brass of the USAF or the DoD planners in the Pentagon in 1960 they'd have had a fit. And 'Mr Mac' nearly produced a swing-wing Phantom! So, instead of being instantly replaced by the swing-wing wonder, while F-111 production ended in January 1976, the old F-4 went on pouring off the lines at St Louis until 26 October 1979.

A small proportion of these 5,211 aircraft (168 I think) had Rolls-Royce engines. It was one of those things that seemed a good idea at the time. When I heard that 'British Phantoms' were going to have afterburning Spey engines instead of the General Electric J79 I felt that, though obviously the aircraft would cost more, they would be very superior in almost every way. But the love-affair between the Royal Navy and the Phantom went back to 1960, and well it might! When you compared the McDonnell aircraft with the Royal Navy's Sea Vixen and Scimitar, which were similar only in approximate size and the amount of metal they consumed, you couldn't help thinking something had gone wrong with the British procurement machine.

But in the early 1960s both the RAF and RN were working with Hawker Aircraft on the P.1154, an extraordinarily advanced supersonic jet-lift aircraft—rather like a Harrier that thought it was a Phantom. At the time, jet lift was internationally important. Air forces as well as navies recognized that there was little point in spending billions on modern combat aircraft if you then park them on the very places picked as juicy missile targets by the enemy. Today we seem to have forgotten this obvious fact, so everyone needs runways (apart from Harriers), and if this book ever has a sequel I'll include a think-piece about why 'no airfield' aircraft are the only ones that might see Day 2 of a war. Here there is room only to note that, after all sorts of vicissitudes, including a campaign by Rolls-Royce (that man Harker again) to get the P.1154 fitted with twin vectored Spey engines, the RN gradually ceased to regard the P.1154RN as what it wanted, and spent the second half of 1963 in increasingly detailed discussion with Mr Mac, not just about Phantoms but about Spey-Phantoms. On 27 February 1964 Defence Minister Peter Thorneycroft announced cancellation of the P.1154RN. He described adoption of a Spey-Phantom as 'the most attractive solution'. In February 1965 the new Labour Government cancelled the P.1154RAF as well. Prime Minister Wilson gave as the reason 'the P.1154 will not be in service [planned date 1968] in time to serve as a Hunter replacement. In these circumstances . . . it will be necessary to expand the late Government's purchasing programme for Phantoms and use this aircraft as a partial replacement for the Hunter. This is the only way of closing the time gap. They will have British engines . . .' The die was cast, and it was full steam ahead on the F-4K which became the Phantom FG.1 for the Royal Navy and F-4M which became the Phantom FGR.2 for the RAF.

Wilson's government was delighted. As always they told the public wonderful figures of cost reduction, including a saving of £20 million by buying RN Phantoms on 'credit terms' (which is what you always do, of course) and £40 million by not buying the 'interim aircraft which would have been necessary had we persisted with developing the P.1154'. At the time I asked what the 'interim aircraft' was to be. The Ministry of Aviation said 'We have no idea', so could someone tell me where the £40 million saving was coming from, so proudly announced by Defence Minister Healey on 4 August 1965? Just to help things along, the Ministry costing staff added a £20,000 contingency to the price of each Spey, making the price of the pair for each Phantom £314,000 instead of £274,000. Arguments raged, the Civil Servants refused to back down, and so, to hold the original price, Rolls-Royce degraded the engine. In Harker's words, 'Some very expensive materials in the turbine section were deleted, with the result that the top speed was limited' (can you believe it?).

From the start McDonnell had no doubts about the improvements that would result from using the British engine. Though fractionally larger in diameter than the J79, and at 4,093 lb about 200 lb heavier, it promised 'greater thrust/weight ratio, lower specific fuel consumption, greater acceleration potential, more bleed air for boundary-layer control flap blowing, higher thermal efficiency and the ability to give maximum power for sustained high-speed performance . . . giving significant improvements in performance and combat radius'. Later some figures were forthcoming, including '30 per cent shorter takeoff, higher top speed, up to 24 per cent greater combat radius or equivalent greater ordnance loads, 30 per cent lower sfc and 20 per cent quicker climb to high altitudes'. The RN customer was especially concerned about spool-up time for carrier waveoffs, and was assured of 'faster response to throttle movements' by Mr Mac as well as by R-R.

The totally different installation needed by the Spey was designed jointly at St

Louis and Derby, while the many other changes needed for the British Phantoms, such as inverse-slatted tailplane, extra-extensible nose legs, quick-fold radomes, a strengthened arrester hook, many avionics changes and, for the F-4M, numerous further modifications, were almost all done at St Louis. The British Government did, however, insist that as many things as possible were to be made in Britain. Thus, items produced in the USA in huge quantities at rates high enough to justify many kinds of special tooling were, for the British aircraft, made in small numbers at very low rates without special tooling by people completely unfamiliar with the job. This obviously was going to put up the price from the announced £1 million per aircraft. On the other hand, the development of the Spey 25R went well. For the Phantom FG.1 the Spey Mk 203 was produced, with ultrafast afterburner light-up for carrier waveoffs; for the RAF the Spey 202 was adequate. Dry and afterburning thrust was set at 12,250 and 20,515 lb, respectively, and everyone was looking forward to the upgraded Phantom with these engines.

The first YF-4K flew at St Louis on schedule on 27 June 1966. But by this time the British Government had announced that it would eliminate Britain's aircraft carriers (which made the Falklands campaign a bit harder). This meant that, whereas the RN squadrons could have kept P.1154s, eventually the FG.1s would be handed to the RAF. It also meant that the FGR.2 did not need carrier equipment, which had originally been planned. Eventually the first YF-4M flew at St Louis on 17 February 1967. Mr Healey had no intention of reminding anyone that this was one month later than the originally planned date of the first *delivery*. Moreover, it was soon apparent that there were various problems, the most serious being poor engine response to varying power-lever position and unacceptable afterburner behaviour. It was also gradually made evident that drag was much higher than estimate.

In his Defence speech in February 1967 Healey announced that the first RN squadron would now commission in March 1968 and the first RAF squadron in '1968-69'. He seemed pleased, saying the delay would 'save several million pounds in the current budget'. In fact he was a bit adrift even at this late date, because the first operational RN squadron, No 892, began to convert on 31 March 1969. The first RAF squadron, No 6, became effective on 6 May 1969. Thus, having cancelled the P.1154RN because of the fact that 'it will not be in service until 1968' the Royal Navy actually got an aeroplane in 1969. In the case of the P.1154RAF late delivery was the *sole* reason given for cancellation, and again the US aircraft was a year later than the planned date for the British one. But in the case of the 1154RN price was another factor. Frank Hopkins, who I had thought the best-ever DNAW (Director of Naval Air Warfare) and who had become Fifth Sea Lord, told me in November 1963: 'There is absolutely no way we are going to buy the P.1154 at a unit price of £1.5 million.' So instead they bought the nice cheap Phantom at about £1 million, except that by 1966 it had become £1.15 million, by 1967 £1.25 million, in 1968 £1.4 million, in January 1969 £2.05 million and in the 1970s, when everything had to leak out, it was found that the actual unit price was almost exactly £3 million, or just double the estimate for the cancelled British aircraft.

That might not have been so bad if the F-4K and F-4M had indeed turned out to be super aircraft. At low levels they are pretty much what you might expect: big, tough battlewagons with 'bags of poke' which can accelerate impressively and also start off upstairs rather better than an F-4E or J. But except at low level the British

Phantoms turned out to be anything but super. Even in the matter of combat radius the Spey installation increased aircraft drag so much as to wipe out all the planned gains. It is very difficult to compare like with like but, making all the same assumptions, the combat radius of an RAF Phantom FGR.2 in the CAP (combat air patrol) mission is 150 nm and the radius for a USAF F-4E is 250 miles or 217 nm. At 36,000 ft the time to accelerate on the level from Mach 0.9 to 1.6 came out to 157 sec compared with 120 for the F-4J or E. Maximum speed in level flight at the peak height, about 36,000 ft, is 2.2 for the J79-powered Phantom and 1.9 for the ones with the more powerful engines. So for 20 years any RAF Phantom pilot will tell you 'We have the biggest, most powerful, most expensive and slowest Phantoms in the world.'

It wasn't planned that way. Incidentally, I know politicians are prone to rewriting history, especially their own history. Remember how Mr Wilson announced, at the very start of the RAF Phantom buy, that 'They will have British engines and incorporate as many British components as possible'? He even went on: 'We are urgently examining the possibility of manufacturing or assembling these aircraft . . .' In view of the delays and cost-escalation it's a good thing we didn't do that. Mr Healey said at the time: 'The Goverment can take credit for this excellent match of a British engine in an American aircraft, which provides an excellent solution to the problems we faced when we entered office.' Now try what he said about the Phantom a few years later. '. . . I was forced to Anglicize it to give work to the aircraft industry. The result of all that mucking about was that it cost twice as much in total and just as much in dollars, and we could have had twice as many Phantoms if we had bought them off the shelf.'

In the past 20 years Rolls-Royce has not had much opportunity to replace other engines in military aircraft, though for a while there was a chance that B-52s might fly with four 535E4s in place of eight J57s or TF33s, which would have had a fantastic effect on combat radius, reliability, noise, and almost everything else. Even today it is still possible that the same splendid engine might replace the F117 in a later batch of McDonnell Douglas C-17s, though I regard this as a very long shot indeed. Isn't it a good thing for the US industry that the rest of the world doesn't mind buying 'foreign' products?

There are also about ten million MiGs around the world, seen by such companies as Raytheon, Hughes, Smiths, Dowty, Kaiser, Honeywell, and, yes, Rolls-Royce as possible vehicles on which they could bolt their goodies. So far Mr Tumansky's engines have resisted all attempts to replace them. Augmented Speys or Tays would multiply TBO (time between overhauls) and dramatically reduce the fuel bills, but Third World air forces tend not to have the money to pay for them. But there is a twist in the tail of the story of the Spey.

In his autobiography *Not Much of an Engineer*, which I greatly enjoyed writing, Sir Stanley Hooker describes the prolonged visits to the People's Republic of China—most definitely not to be confused with the Republic of China, as an unfortunate R-R person once did—and supplications to HM government which were necessary before, four years from the start of negotiations, a manufacturing licence for the Spey 202 was signed on 13 December 1975. The Chinese built a special factory at Xian to produce this complete engine, and by 1979 they delivered two Chinese-built engines to Derby which sailed through their Type Tests at the full dry and afterburning ratings. Everyone was delighted, and I naturally put it all in the Engines section of *JAWA* (*Jane's All the World's Aircraft*). Then absolutely nothing more happened. Chinese delegates at Paris and Farnborough never knew anything about the Spey, and it seemed clear they had dropped the whole idea. I even read articles in Western magazines explaining how they had found the Spey 'too complicated' or, in two US newspapers, 'obsolescent'. Eventually I got the permission of my Editor, John W.R. Taylor, to delete the whole entry, and if you look in the 1988-9 annual you won't find a mention of it.

This went to press just as we were going to the 1988 Farnborough. There what should we find but a model of the Xian-built H-7 multirole attack aircraft in the class of the Tornado or Su-24. The engines? Why, for the next few years at least, twin Spey 202s! The first H-7 was then about to fly. We ought to have know that, to the timeless Chinese, a mere gap of ten years is of no consequence; and with the time we are taking in the West to develop new weapons, especially multi-national ones, I think they are right.

37

July/August 1951

Swift and Hunter

The point is made elsewhere in this book that after World War Two Britain, unlike the other victorious Allies, adopted the remarkable policy that, as the British Government had decided there wasn't going to be a war for at least ten years, there was no need to bother about such expensive things as supersonic research or modern military aircraft. Such a policy strikes at the very heart of the aircraft industry. Politicians love to believe you can always make up for lost time in a sudden 'crash programme', but if you haven't moved with the times the crash programme won't work. This story tells how tough it was trying to provide the RAF with a modern fighter.

The accompanying diagram shows graphically how far we had fallen behind our Allies. Indeed, in order to let the RAF have something a bit more modern than Meteors and Lincolns we were forced to equip squadrons with American-designed F-86 Sabres (made in Canada) and American B-29 bombers, and also P2V-5s and AD-4Ws. It is particularly worth noting that the United States flew a jet bomber in 1946 and five in 1947, including the six-jet 100-ton XB-47 with fully swept wings and tail and the eight-jet all-wing YB-49, which had much in common with today's B-2! As for fighters, the immortal F-86 Sabre first flew in 1947, an order for the first 221 was placed before the end of the year, and on 15 September 1948 a standard F-86A complete with armament and combat equipment was flown by Maj Richard L. Johnson (who appears as a Lt-Col in the next story) to a new world speed record.

In the Soviet Union the MiG-15 was similarly coming off the production line in 1948—and with the powerful British-designed Nene engine which, for some reason thinking this would 'curry favour' with our former ally, we had sent to Moscow. But in Britain we ourselves sat on our hands. The famed creators of the Hurricane flew the P.1052, with a swept wing, on 19 December 1948, and the P.1081, with a swept wing and tail, on 19 June 1950. The famed creators of the Spitfire flew the Type 510, with a swept wing and tail (and tailwheel landing gear) on 29 December 1948. But not one of these aircraft was in any way the prototype of a fighter. They were simply things to play with, to try to gain some knowledge of what high-subsonic

Right After World War Two the British Government took little interest in new fighters and bombers, with the result seen here. The supersonic Lightning flew as a prototype in 1957 and entered service in 1960.

Jet Fighters

Prototypes

GB: Hunter · Swift ★

USSR: La-160 · MiG-15 · La-174 · La-176 ★ · Yak-30 · La-15 · Su-15 · Yak-50 · MiG-17 · La-200 · La-190 · Yak-25 · MiG-19 · Sukhoi S-1 · MiG-21 versions · F3H-2

US: XP-84 · XP-86 ★ · XF-87 · XF-89 · XF7U · XF-88 · XF-91 · XF-90 · XF4D · XFJ-2 · XF3H · XF9F-6 · YF-100A · YF-102 · XF-104 · F11F-1 · YF-102A · F-101A

Production

US: P-84B · F-86A · F-89A · F7U-1 · FJ-2 · F9F-6 · F-100A · F4D-1 · F-102A · F11F-1

USSR: MiG-15 · La-15 · MiG-17 · MiG-19F · Yak-25

GB: Hunter → Hunter in RAF · Swift FR.5

Years: 1946 1947 1948 1949 1950 1951 1952 1953 1954 1955

Jet Bombers

Prototypes

GB: Canberra · Valiant · Vulcan · Victor

USSR: H-22 · Tu-12 · Tu-78 · H-28 · Tu-82 · Tu-14 · H-30 · H-28 · Tu-88 (Tu-16) · H-46 · Tu-95 (Tu-20) · H-54 · Tu-98

US: XB-45 · XB-46 · YB-49 · XB-48 · XB-47 · XB-51 · YB-52 · XA3D · A3D-1 · RB-66A · XB-58

Production

US: XB-43 · B-45A · B-47A · RB-66A · B-52A

USSR: H-28 · Tu-14 · Tu-16 · Tu-20

GB: Canberra · Valiant · Vulcan

Years: 1946 1947 1948 1949 1950 1951 1952 1953 1954 1955

★ Dive beyond Mach 1
☐ Supersonic in level flight

aviation was all about. Meanwhile, many hundreds of F-86 pilots were able to make sonic bangs and shoot down MiG-15s in Korea.

The story of the design and development of the Hunter and Swift is well known, and my intention here is merely to comment on the technical and political aspects that are ignored in many of the published accounts. As the Hunter ran slightly ahead in timing I will deal with this first, but some Ministers appeared to get odd advice from their minions in Whitehall. In March 1956 Reggie Maudling, who had succeeded Sandys as Minister of Supply, said: 'Of course, the Hunter was designed before 1950, when our knowledge of guided missiles was very rudimentary. The Swift, which was designed later, was always intended to be the first aircraft to carry guided missiles.' I can only say, this was news to me.

In fact nobody thought much about AAMs (air-to-air missiles) when either aircraft was designed. One of the early armament schemes, suggested to both Hawker and Supermarine, was a formidable blunderbuss with a calibre of 4.5 in. Other ideas were batteries of spin-stabilized rockets, twin 30-mm Aden cannon and (rather pie in the sky at that stage) the primitive Blue Sky beam-riding AAM developed in a truly pioneering effort by Fairey Aviation and destined to go into limited production in 1955 as Fireflash. Unlike many other things, armament for the new fighters was given careful consideration, just as it had been in 1934 when Sqn Ldr Ralph Sorley's calculations had led to the unprecedented armament of eight forward-firing machine guns. This time the choice fell on the Aden, a British 30-mm copy of the pioneer German Mauser MG 213 revolver-fed cannon which just missed the war. Four were to be fitted; if this proved difficult, two guns were to be fitted but with an increased supply of ammunition.

Camm's designers came up with a remarkable package containing four Aden guns, each with a theoretical 150 rounds (in practice about 135 were loaded, to ensure feed reliability). This hefty load could be hoisted into its housing under the cockpit by three standard bomb winches. To reload, the four barrels were unscrewed and left in their fuselage blast tubes while the rest of the pack was winched down and either replaced with a loaded one or else given a fresh ammunition tank. Such packs had been used before, especially by the wartime Luftwaffe, but never to fit inside the aircraft in this way.

Chief test pilot Neville Duke, very soon to be a household word and national hero in a way that his distinguished wartime record could never have accomplished, flew the first of three prototype Hunters on 20 July 1951. The biggest and best book on the Hunter fails to note that on this first flight, while the elevator forces were unacceptably heavy (because it was considered preferable to disconnect the hydraulic power boost), the ailerons were unacceptably light (because the power boost was working and had a ratio of 14:1). I doubt if there has ever been any other first flight in which the longitudinal control demanded all the muscle power of both arms while the lateral control was so twitchy the pilot wanted to let go of the stick entirely!

The first two prototypes had Rolls-Royce Avon engines while the third was powered by an Armstrong Siddeley Sapphire. At first everything seemed 'set fair'. The Hunter was a true thoroughbred, and looked it. It had the backing of a big, experienced, and dedicated team of designers and engineers under the legendary Sydney (Sir Sydney after the 1953 Coronation Honours) Camm. It had a choice of two engines which ought to have been world-beaters. It had excellent backing from a host of other contractors, notably Fairey Aviation for the flight-control power units. It had devastating armament. Soon after the first flight I walked around WB188, the first prototype, and said to myself, 'I expect it will not look quite as beautiful and clean in production, but this looks a real winner. We should have squadrons very soon.'

During the 1950s I was Technical Editor of *Flight*, and from time to time Camm would send his chauffeur-driven Armstrong Siddeley Sapphire (in this context, a car) to bring me to Kingston for a long solid chat. He did the same for Freddy Meacock, my opposite number on the rival *Aeroplane*, and for Derek Wood of *Interavia*. Unlike so many others of equivalent stature in Britain, Camm valued the technical Press, and I think our chats were beneficial to both sides. On my first such visit I told him of my thoughts as I walked round WB188 at Dunsfold, and he said: 'It's my most beautiful aeroplane. But I'll have to fight to keep it that way. They'll want me to hang things on it, and the rotten engines burn so much fuel they'll want a flight-refuelling probe next . . .' The trouble with Camm was that you never knew how far he was joking. He had a lifelong act of professing to despise the makers of engines (Story 18 gives an example). In 1927 he angrily complained that the Bulldog beat his Hawfinch only because the prototype Bulldog had a better Jupiter engine, and in 1936 he complained that the shortfall in the Hurricane's performance was due to the Merlin engine not giving the advertised power. In this last assertion he was right, and Dr Stanley Hooker soon discovered that the fault lay in the traditional way powers had been calculated (so that explained previously puzzling shortfalls in the performance of the Spitfire, Bf 109 and everything else!).

The Hunter was fortunate in having a choice of two engines. The Rolls-Royce AJ.65, later named Avon, was designed for 6,500 lb thrust, and for the first three years (1945-8) was probably the most problem-ridden gas turbine in the world. In Hooker's words: 'It was difficult to start, wouldn't accelerate, broke its blades and was a Hell of a mess!' It nearly broke his giant heart—and indeed was one of the underlying causes of his deeply emotional bust-up with Hives and departure to Bristol. In contrast, the Metropolitan-Vickers F.9 Sapphire was designed for 7,000 lb, with specific fuel consumption lower than that of the Avon, and worked pretty well from the outset. This was mainly because, unlike Rolls-Royce, Dr D.M. Smith and K. Baumann had plenty of experience with axial compressors. Perhaps brashly, the Ministry in its wisdom arbitrarily said in 1947 'There are too many engine firms, Metrovick must go' and, despite the angry protestations of de Havilland's Frank Halford, the Sapphire was given to Armstrong Siddeley Motors at Coventry.

Here it was obviously destined to be No 1 engine. It eventually powered the Javelin, Mk 1 Victor, and various other aircraft, and was made under licence in far greater numbers as the Wright J65 in the United States. Of course, when Armstrong Siddeley took it over they redesigned it, because that is what firms always do, and when Wright Aeronautical in New Jersey got their hands on it they redesigned it again. It all helps to use up time and spend money (to be fair, some of the J65 redesign was an improvement). Thus the Hunter had a choice of either engine. At first, up to 1950, the Sapphire looked and behaved better in every way, but from the start the Avon was favoured, solely because of the reputation of Rolls-Royce. In November 1948 two prototypes were ordered with the R-R engine and only one (No 3) with the Sapphire. So the Sapphire Hunter did not fly until 30 November 1952, more than 16 months after the Avon version.

The Korean panic in 1950 focused entirely on the Avon, so in October 1950 Hawker were told to tool up for massive production of the Avon-Hunter. This, of course, happened, and almost every production Hunter had the Avon in one form or another. Armstrong Whitworth built just 45 Hunter F.2 and 105 F.5 aircraft with the Sapphire. They were faster than the Avon-powered F.1 and F.4 (brochure figure 698 mph versus 693) and had engines that, to anybody not using them, appeared to cause no trouble at all, apart from the fact that occasionally synthetic turbine oil would bleed back from a vent and dissolve the squadron insignia. In his definitive book on the Hunter, Roy Braybrook comments that the Sapphire in the early Hunters 'provided not only better performance but vastly superior handling'.

Reality was somewhat different. Hearken to Colin Buttars, who flew with 257 Squadron:

We most definitely were never allowed to fire our guns for practice, although we flew fully armed in case we had to fire in anger. We were not allowed to participate in fly-pasts over London . . . it was considered that our engines were not reliable enough . . . In all my time in 2TAF I cannot recall any cases of engine failure on an F-86, yet they were a weekly occurrence in 257. This despite the fact that we usually had 20 serviceable F-86s on the line every day and flew them hard, compared with one or two a day serviceable on 257.

There are certain bands of revs on the Sapphire that we were forbidden to use, because of vibrations, but had to accelerate or decelerate through these bands as quickly as possible. This in itself was a hazard, since the Sapphire did not take kindly to quick throttle movements. I recall one case of N.D. McEwan slamming the throttle closed as he broke into the circuit and the engine seized completely. He received a Green Endorsement for landing the aircraft with impeller blades spewing out of the intakes and the whole fuselage aft of the wing oxidised white from the heat of the rear end of the engine and jetpipe.

I could go on forever about similar incidents. Flame-outs for no reason, which after a dead-stick landing would start first time and show no faults, until they decided to do it again a day or so later. Engines which, no matter what the pilot did to the throttle, would select their own revs and stay there—sometimes for a few minutes and sometimes for the rest of the trip. Again, after shut-down they would usually start again and behave normally . . .

But the chaps with the Avon were no better off. By 1952 the engine itself seemed at last, after seven years of 'blood, toil, tears and sweat', to be 'out of the wood'. The early Mk 101 was giving good service in the Canberra, and the Hunter's Mks 113 and 115 were not very different. Believe it or not, it was not until well into 1953, with the Hunter F.1 about to enter service with 43 Squadron, that it was found that firing the guns caused violent surging in the Avon engine. The main problem was ingestion of gun gas. This had been swallowed without difficulty by the Sapphire, and we were so lacking in imagination that all the manufacturer's gun-firing trials had been done with WB202, the Sapphire prototype. The Avon's compressor surged at the slightest excuse, and the problem was manifest at almost all speeds, heights, and angles of attack. So 43 Squadron, followed by 54 Squadron in February 1955, received Hunter F.1 aircraft that were useless as fighters because their guns could not be fired above 25,000 ft or above 350 kt IAS! Rolls went back to trying to improve the Avon, while Hawker added a fuel-dipping switch in the gun-firing circuit, so that if you fired the guns the fuel flow to the engine was drastically reduced, just when you needed more poke to counteract the massive recoil.

This was just a part of the problem. Another was the unacceptable nose-down pitch when the guns were fired, which of course meant you missed the target. Yet another was that when you fired the guns the spent links and shell cases poured from their ejection slots and slammed back into the underside of the fuselage. I was bemused that nobody seemed to know what was happening. Some people said that the links, being light, were more inclined to hit the fuselage, while others said the damage was caused by the heavy closed ends of the cases. The adopted cure was to collect the links in large bulged boxes which were promptly called Sabrinas after an equally bulbous starlet of the day. Much later the Swiss fitted even bigger Sabrinas to collect the cases as well, to end complaints from farmers near the firing ranges.

Even this was not the end of the Hunter gun-firing problems. The nose-down pitch was worth bothering about only at high altitude, and it was cured at some cost in drag by fitting muzzle deflectors to direct the blast downwards. Muzzle blast and vibration also caused structural cracking of the forward fuselage, necessitating local reinforcement with stainless steel and restricting firing to pairs of guns instead of all four. Yet another problem was accumulation of gun gas in the nose, which on one occasion caused an explosion serious enough to blow the front cap off the aircraft. About the only armament problem not attributable to Hawker or Rolls-Royce was the incredibly protracted effort to achieve reliable operation of the electrically fired ammunition. In 1953 this was much less reliable than the almost identical ammunition of the MG213 had been in 1944!

There simply is no room to relate all the Hunter's other problems, one of the most basic of which was such inadequate internal fuel capacity that, after a short training sortie, a 12-mile diversion resulted in the loss of six out of eight aircraft, with one pilot killed. If you design a fighter with inadequate fuel capacity it is hard to do much about it, but in the case of airbrakes it is possible to try various alternatives. The Hunter airbrake has become one of the classic sagas of getting it wrong and then trying to get it right. Obviously, it is marvellous if you can use your main wing flaps as airbrakes, and this 'two for the price of one' concept seemed to work well on the P.1052 and 1081. The split flaps could be selected at any speed up to 620 kt, above which speed a relief valve in the hydraulics restricted flap angle and prevented overstressing the structure. On the Hunter, however, the nose-down trim change on selecting airbrake was totally unacceptable, except at low speeds (I liked the RAF's official language: 'The pilot headed for the canopy').

Hawker already knew about the problem (I suppose this might have been expected, as they had been flying Hunters for more than two years). They tried twin lateral brakes, but these were no improvement (they are still on the original first prototype WB188, now at RAF St Athan). Next came every arrangement imaginable, one which nearly made it being to divide each flap into inboard and outboard sections and use just the inner 40 per cent sections as the airbrakes. This worked well except at just one combination of IMN (0.95) and IAS (550 kt). In the end, between July 1953 and July 1954, the answer proved to be a single door-type airbrake hinged under the rear fuselage. Months of cut and try, involving various lengths and angles of brake, addition of external strakes and changes to the upstream fairing, were needed before a satisfactory arrangement was reached. Even then it was just what it looked; instead of being recessed flush, as it would be on any self-respecting aircraft, it was stuck on externally, forever proclaiming itself an afterthought and prone to damage from spent links or cases.

I have not even mentioned the months of effort put into curing pitch-up and trying to obtain good flight-control qualities. Four modifications, quite late in the day, transformed the aircraft into an acceptable fighter. Mod 188 changed the aileron system from 14:1 Fairey boosters to full power, with spring feel. Much later Mod 457 changed the aileron gearing upon reversion to manual control, to ease stick loads. Mod 365, long overdue, made the elevators fully powered, again with spring feel and with an electrically driven follow-up tailplane. Mod 533 added nine square feet ahead of the outer wing leading edges, cambered downwards and ending at a sharp dogtooth kink at the inner end.

All this took until May 1956, by which time Hunters had reached 30 RAF Squadrons! More were coming off the line every day from the five factories in Britain and the Benelux countries. It all sounds like a terrible indictment of Hawker Aircraft, so it may come as a shock to readers unfamiliar with the Hunter to learn that from the start it was really a fighter possessed of many outstanding qualities. Many would rate it, if not the best fighter and ground-attack aircraft of its day, at least in the top three, especially after it was utterly transformed by the 200-series Avon, which owed a lot to the Sapphire. These more powerful aircraft were called 'large-bore' Hunters. In 1957 Switzerland carried out an extremely thorough evaluation of six types of aircraft and finally selected the Hunter, which 33 years later remains a major combat type in the Swiss air force. It has equipped the national aerobatic team for 31 years despite evaluations of the Mirage III and Northrop F-5E.

As for the RAF, British politicians love to pretend that major items of defence hardware are about to be withdrawn from service. The reason is sometimes so that money can be saved by not allowing updates or improvements. For example, in 1956 the Suez campaign drove home the lesson that the Hunter needed to be cleared at much higher weights in order to fly with four 230-gallon drop tanks, but no funding was made available for three years, by which time the modification cost more. In 1960 several air forces had fitted Sidewinders to their Hunters, but despite a clamour for this handy missile from the RAF squadrons nothing was done, 'because the Hunters are about to be withdrawn, with less than two years to serve'. In 1965 the incoming Labour government, having decided to chuck all Britain's new military aircraft on the scrap-heap and replace them with American aircraft, then had to look for a reason that could be 'sold' to the public. In the case of the supersonic jet-lift P.1154 the reason was 'These aircraft . . . cannot be in service before 1969, long after the Hunters must be withdrawn.' What actually happened is that No 8 Squadron remained operational with Hunter FGA.9s until December 1971, and the Tactical Weapons Units, 237 OCU and Royal Navy No 899 Squadron, will fly Hunters into the 1990s.

This story has turned out much longer than I intended, even without mentioning one particular Hunter built in Belgium. One day its Belgian pilot decided, in preference to a dead-stick landing, to eject; the Hunter carried on and eventually, at about 200 mph, hit some trees and went through a stone wall. Hawker bought it, grafted on a new two-seat nose and flew it as an Indian T.66 at the 1959 Paris airshow. It then served more than four years as G-APUX, the company demonstrator, being used by Bill Bedford for impressive airshow performances including 13-turn spins at Paris and Farnborough. Next it became a T.66A of the Iraqi air force, going on three years later to see seven years of active warfare in the Lebanon, almost continuously in action. In 1973 it became a T.72 in Chile. Like

I said, the Hunter possesses outstanding qualities, one being toughness.

Today the fame of the Spitfire exceeds that of the Hurricane, Typhoon, and Tempest combined, and I think after 1945 most people expected Joe Smith's team at the Supermarine design office at Hursley Park, a stately home near Winchester, to come up with something special in the way of jet fighters. They began in the most basic way possible, by putting a Nene-powered fuselage on the wing of the Spiteful. Aircraft design is harder than it looks; the Spiteful wing, designed for better performance at high Mach numbers than the wing of the Spitfire, actually turned out to be inferior, especially in comparison with the wing of the final Spits from Mk 21 onwards.

After the war, with all the pressure off, not much happened. At the end of 1948 the Supermarine 510 began to show the disbelieving British that an aircraft with swept wings and tail could actually fly (this at a time when the MiG-15 and F-86A were in volume production). Unusual features of the 510 were traditional landing gear, with twin tailwheels, and (in December 1951) a pivoted rear fuselage to investigate the idea of a 'slab' tailplane.

In 1948 an order was placed for the Type 517, with an afterburning Nene, but taildraggers (Story 2) had at last gone out of fashion! Criticism of the landing gear was so universal that the 517 was replaced by the 535, with a forward retracting nosewheel as well as the twin tailwheels. The Nene had a primitive on/off afterburner, with a two-position eyelid nozzle. If it opened and the afterburner failed to ignite, the best you could hope for was about 4,050 lb thrust instead of the planned 6,800. The 535 flew on 23 August 1950.

Two months earlier the Korean war had broken out, and almost overnight the pottering about with research aircraft was expected to yield throbbing production lines of swept-wing fighters. But Supermarine had fallen into the same trap as Hawker. During what you might call the Locust Years, when nobody gave a thought to defence, the essential groundwork for modern fighters had not been laid. As with the Hunter, it seemed impossible to get there all in one jump (and nobody realized just what giant leaps would be needed). Joe Smith was immediately given an ITP (instruction to proceed) with two fighter prototypes, to be powered by the axial Avon engine. The Sapphire, not being politically favoured, was not even considered. In four weeks a plan was drawn up for four marks of production fighter, named Swift. The Mk 1 would have two Aden 30-mm guns. The Mk 2 would have four Adens. The Mk 3 would have four guns and an afterburning Avon. The Mk 4 would be a Mk 3 with an all-flying tail, similar to that pioneered by the F-86E Sabre in which the tailplane was power-driven as the primary control surface, the elevators following up to increase camber. It could all have been done at once, but breaking the work into four stages was expected to avoid any difficulties.

While Supermarine desperately tried to recruit staff and skilled production workers, work went on almost 24 hours a day trying to design the Swift. In November 1950 a production order for 100 was placed, starting with the F.1 and moving on to the 2, 3, and 4 'at the earliest possible date'. It was planned to have the F.4 released for service in January 1953. In August 1952 the Conservative government—elected the previous October and even more eager to make up for lost time—placed a further order for 100 with Shorts at Belfast, followed by further orders for 300 from each factory by January 1953. Offshore procurement was confidently expected to take the total to more than 1,200. Outwardly this looked like the beginning of a terrific programme. The stage was actually set for a major disaster which even got into the British daily papers.

The first of the two prototypes, and not generally regarded as a Swift, was the Type 541 WJ960. Outwardly almost identical to the 535 except for its curved Küchemann-type wingtips, WJ960 had an early Avon RA.7 engine, revised fuel system and provision for two Adens under the inlet ducts. It first flew on 5 August 1951. Almost from the start severe tail buzz (high-frequency buffet) was encountered, and this soon broke the linkage to the fuel cock, stopping the engine. There were other problems, some affecting the elevator spring tabs, which is hardly to be wondered at since the company had no high-speed tunnel in which to try things out before flying them. Three days before the 1951 Farnborough show test pilot Dave Morgan had total engine failure and had to make an immediate crash landing.

The first Swift, WJ965, had a redesigned fuselage which, together with 90 gallons in each wing, increased internal fuel capacity from 360 to 778 gallons. This compared with the ridiculous total of 330 for the Hunter F.1, and together with the planned development to the Mk 4 standard with afterburner and all-flying tail (things not planned at that time for production Hunters) led to enormous effort being put behind the Swift. Much later, in February 1955, the Minister of Defence, Harold Macmillan, said: 'All the earlier reports, up to fairly recently, were that the Hunter would not be so successful as the Swift.'

The first of the initial batch of 100, WK194, flew on 25 August 1952, so the 535, WJ960 and WK194 were each just a year apart. At WK213 production switched to the four-gun F.2, first flown on 12 December 1952. There was no gun pack as in the Hunter, but a conventional installation of the four guns in the bottom of the fuselage under the cockpit. Unfortunately, there was nowhere to put the ammunition for the two extra guns until the inboard wing was extended slightly forward, resulting in a slight kink in the leading edge.

By this time, in late 1952, the test pilots were getting up to high speeds and beginning to think of diving beyond Mach 1. Unfortunately, when WJ965 got to about 550 kt it (in Dave Morgan's words) 'practically dissolved'. Few people had ever encountered such severe wing/aileron flutter. The ailerons were unpowered, but in desperation the spring tabs were removed. This left lateral control extremely poor, unless you had Herculean strength, but it did allow higher speeds to be reached, and on 18 February 1953 Morgan got a lot of 'Mach 1 plus' indications. On 24 February there was no doubt about it, and on the 26th he planted a sonic bang on the company test airfield at Chilbolton. This was encouraging. By late February 35 Swifts had flown, and output from South Marston (backed up by Southampton and Trowbridge) and Belfast was rising almost daily.

It was then that two things happened. One was an almost unbelievable unreliability of the Avon engine, which with totally unacceptable frequency took to shedding its compressor blades. The other was the distressing discovery that the seemingly unimportant alteration to the leading edge in the F.2, 3 and 4 had resulted in pitch-up. When pulling even modest g at Mach 0.85 or above at high altitude the nose kept rising. Incremental g was modest, but the aircraft would enter a high-speed stall and the pilot then had to recover with minimal loss of height. All useless for an operational fighter!

As for the engine failures, it seemed obvious that the fault lay in the Swift's intakes and inlet ducts, and frantic efforts were made to find a cure, while more than 45 trial modifications to the wings sought to alleviate pitch-up. For the Coronation flypast on 15 July 1953 it seemed essential to include some modern aircraft, even if they were a long way from reaching the RAF, and so four Swift F.1s were taken, plus the sole F.4 prototype, WK198, and fitted with absolutely new Avon engines. Everyone crossed their fingers as they brought up the rear of the flypast and thundered off into the haze. Moments later Mike Lithgow in the F.4 did have engine failure, but just managed to reach Chilbolton. Over 50 hours of flying had been done with modified inlets to try to stop the engine failures when, the day after the flypast, a red-faced Rolls-Royce admitted the cause lay in the engine. It so happened that the Swifts all had Mk 105 engines made by one of the crash-programme licensees. This firm had introduced a seemingly trivial change into the root fixings for the compressor rotor blades, and this had caused all the failures.

I won't go into further detail on the F.2, 3, and 4, except to say that nobody even discovered half the problems, far less solved them, until hundreds of Swifts were coming off the production lines. To quote P.B. 'Laddie' Lucas, a former wing commander and in 1955 an MP, 'It wasn't until Wing Commander Bird-Wilson was able to test the swept-wing fighters at the Central Fighter Establishment that we began to know the truth about these aircraft operationally.' The whole programme reflected the politicians' belief that you can make up for lost time by a mad rush. Thus in November 1953, with production in full swing, a Swift got to Boscombe Down for the first time. It suffered a fatal crash, so in December it was replaced by 'the next aircraft off the production line'. Boscombe's role is to evaluate aircraft *before* production starts! In January 1954 a 'limited release' of the F.1 and F.2 resulted in these equipping a famous RAF Squadron, No 56, from late February. Poor 56 were forbidden to climb above 25,000 ft, pull any significant g, spin, exceed 550 kt indicated or Mach 0.91, or do almost any of the things fighter pilots need to do. Two Swifts were lost, and the type was temporarily grounded.

Matters came to a head in February 1955, and in the House of Commons on the 23rd of that month Harold Macmillan had the unenviable task of explaining why an unacceptable fighter was pouring off production lines at two factories. He said: 'It has been decided that the Marks 1, 2 and 3 cannot be brought up to an acceptable operational standard . . . After further tests on the Mark 4 it has been decided that production of this mark should be restricted to a limited number . . .' Inevitably the situation attracted the attention of Fleet Street, especially after the Select Committee on Estimates commented: 'As the difficulties with the aircraft increased, so, it appeared, did the number on order.' Selwyn Lloyd, Minister of Supply, defensively said: 'At the time these decisions were taken, only two prototypes had been ordered.'

Short's contract was cancelled. Supermarine did retain a small ongoing programme for developments of the F.4: the FR.5 with two guns, a lengthened nose with three cameras, frameless canopy, belly tank and afterburning Avon 114; the long-span PR.6 (cancelled); and the long-span F.7 with Avon 116, slab tail and Blue Sky (Fireflash) beam-riding missiles. These later Swifts were far better than the early ones, but still lacking in certain qualities. Wing Commander R.N. 'Bob' Broad tried out an FR.5 against a Hunter at the Air Fighting Development Squadron in 1955. He recalls: 'I was flying an elderly Hunter 4 without the powered tail, and my squadron leader was in front in the Swift. We went to 20,000 ft and to start things off I got into the 6 o'clock position at 400 yards; the idea was that the Swift would start a maximum-rate turn and I would try and follow. I thought the Swift, which did have a good tail, would get into its turn much more quickly, but that I would then be able to out-turn it. The effect of reheat could then be investigated. However, what actually happened was quite astonishing. On the word GO, the Swift rolled smartly into its turn. Its attitude changed dramatically as its plan view came into sight, but it did not get out of my line of flight. Instead it came rushing back towards me, and I had to work quickly to avoid it . . . Although the term "agility" had not then been coined, we were only too well aware that the Swift was lacking in it.'

In 1977 I had to write the story of the Swift, and sent the draft to six people for their comments. None of the RAF people had much to say, but the Supermarine men virtually exploded. Dave Morgan called the RA.7 'a lousy engine', insisted that '56 Squadron were delighted with the aeroplane; I know, I was there', and claimed 'The shortcomings of the aircraft . . . were greatly exaggerated in order to support the cancellation of the Mk 4 fighter version, which was in any case a logical step in view of the reduction in world tension at the time.' One thing is certainly beyond dispute: in the pre-computer world nearly 40 years ago to put an unknown quantity into mass production was courting disaster.

38

March 1952

Superpriority and Offshore Procurement

As we have been celebrating what happened 50 years ago, most aviation enthusiasts probably know about the appointment of the newspaper tycoon Lord Beaverbrook as Minister of Aircraft Production in May 1940. The German Blitzkrieg had struck in the West, eliminating all opposition in its path, and it was a time of dire emergency. Previously, aircraft production had been handled by a department of the Air Ministry which on the outbreak of World War Two had been evacuated to Harrogate. Now, newly appointed Prime Minister Churchill, realizing it was a time for desperate measures, created the new MAP.

He told 'The Beaver' to double, treble, quadruple aircraft production. So Beaverbrook picked such types as the Hurricane, Spitfire, Blenheim, Wellington, and even the Battle, and tried to cancel all the oddballs and new prototypes such as the Mosquito. To be frank, he worked wonders, though his roughshod manner, with endless business conducted at around 3 am, made him a tough boss, which is just what he meant to be. His results were amazing, Air Chief Marshal Dowding writing in 1946 that in the Battle of Britain 'aircraft wastage ceased to be the main problem'. Fortunately, the system was sufficiently flexible for Beaverbrook's competent henchmen, such as Trevor Westbrook and Patrick Hennessy, to restore the more important of the brashly cancelled programmes, so we did later get some modern aircraft.

In passing, the Luftwaffe's leaders had the same Beaverbrook outlook, and with some justification, because what impressed Hitler were sheer numbers. So the Bf 109 and 110, He 111, Ju 87 and 88, and many other old stalwarts never did get replaced by modern types, but just had to carry on being built in improved versions.

In 1945 the scene changed completely. The great conflict ended, and Britain elected a Labour government which had not the slightest interest in anything to do with defence, or future air technology, or anything of a related kind that might take money from the National Health Service or such sacred cows as the Ground Nuts Scheme. The effect on the aircraft industry was progressively catastrophic. We fell flat on our faces in the new realm of supersonics (Story 35). Total lack of urgency resulted in stretchout of the few remaining programmes, except when—as in the case of the Comet and Viscount—the manufacturer's own professionalism and *esprit de corps* kept things going. Worst of all, the lead time (time between placing an order and getting delivery) on almost any major bit to be built into an aircraft grew from an average of 4.5 months in 1945 to 42 months in 1951.

To pick an example at random, when in 1949 Boulton Paul wished to order forgings for main legs for the Balliol they were quoted 1953 delivery. In the end they managed to get them from Belgium.

The Government remained completely unconcerned. In matters of defence it was applying the Ten-Year Rule, a rule which arbitrarily assumes that there will be no war for the next ten years. Thus, in 1949 there was to be no war until 1959 at the earliest, and in 1950 no war could happen until 1960. Unfortunately, the North Koreans didn't know about this rule, and on 25 June 1950 they invaded South Korea and all hell broke loose. There was panic in Whitehall, because now very suddenly the cherished belief of politicians that you can always make up for inaction by some kind of crash programme was about to be put to the test.

Orders for defence hardware were showered on a weak and debilitated industry. As the capacity of each company had almost vanished, material had to be ordered from several firms. For example, where aircraft were concerned, the Canberra B.2 was suddenly ordered not only from English Electric but also from A.V. Roe, Handley Page, and Short Brothers, and the Rolls-Royce Avon engine was ordered not only from the parent firm but also from Bristol, Napier, and Standard Motors. The costs in tooling alone were astronomic, and there were various unexpected side-effects. Rolls-Royce were only too well aware that the big Avon contract would at last jerk Bristol into the jet age and force them to acquire the capabilities they needed to become a serious competitor. What nobody expected was that another of the licensees would introduce a seemingly trivial change into the finish-machining of compressor blades which led to a serious fatigue problem and caused numerous Swifts to make dead-stick landings (Story 37).

When the Government had had time to think—which took almost a further two years—someone thought of the brilliant idea of resurrecting Beaverbrook's methods. It was called 'Superpriority'. This was simply a scheme for giving selected defence items absolute priority over everything else in 'the supply of scarce materials, components, labour and technical services'. It was a typical invention of politicians, because on paper it sounded marvellous, and so could be 'sold' to the public. Where aircraft were concerned the chosen types were the Canberra, Hunter, Swift, Valiant, Gannet and 'either the D.H.110 or the G.A.5'. The 110 became the Sea Vixen and the G.A.5 the Javelin. Nothing quite like this scheme had ever been adopted in Britain, even in wartime, and it was thought necessary as a method of making good seven years of neglect or at least appearing to do so.

Unfortunately, in practice the grand Superpriority scheme accomplished practically nothing. Nobody could be found who knew how it was supposed to work in the real world. Its net result was that, while non-Superpriority customers often never got served at all, the most critical items, such as machine tools, tooling, and Nimonic 90 bar stock for turbine blades, had to be allocated between the Superpriority contractors, each of whom had a prior claim on all the others. As an example of how the scheme worked we can look at the mighty Hawker Siddeley Group. Chairman Sir Thomas Sopwith said in August 1952: 'Labour is also presenting a problem, which would be very serious if machine tools were in better supply. Superpriority cannot find us one extra worker.' And Managing Director Sir Frank Spriggs said, at the same time, 'We placed machine-tool orders worth £24 million as far back as May 1951, but nothing has been delivered yet . . . We are at last beginning to get the jigs we need to build Hunters at Gloster, Coventry and Blackpool, because we are getting them from abroad, from such Italian firms as Macchi, Breda and Fiat. Superpriority? It's all nonsense. It doesn't help one whit trying to get blood out of stones.'

Of course Duncan Sandys, the newly appointed Conservative Minister of Supply, had to say how wonderful the idea was. According to him, 'The scheme is providing special alloys six to twelve months earlier than would otherwise have been the case.' When I visited Henry Wiggin & Co in Hereford (the crucial Nimonic people) they said 'Rubbish, how could it?' In December 1952 Superpriority was extended to take in the Vulcan, Victor, Comet, Viscount, and Britannia, the last three being commercial transports quite unrelated to the war in Korea. In 1953 this war was terminated by an uneasy armistice, Britain's industry recovered a little of its wartime capability, and Superpriority was allowed to fizzle out, unlamented, in 1954.

At exactly the time Superpriority was introduced, the US Congress overrode objections from its industry lobby—which in the early 1950s was not very powerful—and passed the OSP (offshore procurement) bill. This was nothing less than a bill to enable the US Government to spend the money of its taxpayers on the purchase of defence hardware manufactured by America's allies. The idea was that, with hot war in Korea and a general intensification of the Cold War, lots of weapons were needed, and fast, and that making them in friendly nations was cheaper than US production. The OSP bill also was intended to strengthen Allied industry. It was separate and in addition to the Marshall Plan, which specifically set out to finance the rebuilding of the shattered primary industries of continental Europe. The Marshall Plan did not include Britain, except peripherally, but OSP was of greater benefit to Britain than to any other country, because only Britain had a full range of suitable military products.

Originally, OSP applied only to the dollar purchase of spares and services for aircraft and other military equipment. In June 1952 Fred Anderson, Special Representative for the MSA (Mutual Security Agency, which administered OSP), announced in Paris that the plan was being extended to cover complete aircraft. He said: 'The United States will be free to choose for co-ordinated production in Europe of any locally designed aircraft that is judged, after careful evaluation of the characteristics of European aircraft for operational requirements, to be as good as, or better than, US types.' There were one or two provisos, one of the tricky clauses being that 'Communist firms' were to be excluded; indeed it was intended that no Communist sympathizer should be in a position to make a contribution (positive or negative). This was a touchy question in Italy, where the relevant trades unions were Communist dominated. In 1954 some Italian contracts for the F-86K and Javelin were cancelled on this ground.

Another possible source of embarrassment would have been rejection of a candidate aircraft as unsuitable, but so far as I am aware this never happened. This is remarkable, because one of the candidates was the Swift, and the evaluation team, appointed by the US Air Force, included such men as Maj-Gen Albert Boyd, Col Frederick J. Ascani, Lt-Col Richard L. Johnson, and Maj Charles E. Yeager. They had no brief to overlook any shortcomings. On the whole they enjoyed the assignment, and a junior member of the team, Capt Davies, sent Marcel Dassault into ecstasies by diving a Mystère IIC faster than sound, unaware that this had never been done before. This led to a big OSP Mystère order, as described later, which really put Dassault 'on the map'.

The first group of OSP orders was published in October 1952. It totalled $225 million, and one of the stipulations was that all deliveries had to be completed by the end of US Fiscal Year 55, ie 30 June 1955. This time-limit curtailed some purchases, and certainly would have ruled out the original plan to procure 1,000 Swifts shared between UK and Benelux firms. As for the Hunter, this was not even in the first group of orders, but in April 1953 contracts were signed in Paris for 450 Hunter F.4s at a cost of $182 million. Most were for the RAF, but those for Benelux included 64 for Belgium and 48 for the Netherlands, in each case made in the recipient country (larger numbers of additional Benelux Hunters werè locally funded).

Many of the planned OSP contracts were never fulfilled. One of the difficult ones was the Italian-built F-86K Sabre, a simplified gun-armed version of the F-86D. In the event, most of the 221 examples assembled by Fiat at Turin were made from parts shipped from North American Aviation, which made the costings complicated. In contrast, Dassault did better than expected. Whereas the original plan had been to order the Mystère IIC, which Davies had dived beyond Mach 1, what actually happened was that the French company—with a rapidity which was to become famous, and to lead to a detailed USAF investigation in the 1960s to find out how the company was managed—produced the greatly improved Mystère IVA. Thus, at the same ceremony in Paris at which the Armée de l'Air paid for 150 IICs, the MSA signed away dollars to pay for 225 of the new IVAs. Dassault delivered them to the Armée de l'Air ahead of schedule.

The year 1953 brought a marked change in the political climate. The Korean War ended, and Britain began to sell Comets and Viscounts to a growing number of the world's airlines, including the Comet 3 to PanAm and the Viscount to Capital Airlines of Washington. Rather quickly it appeared that the needy ally had become the commercial competitor, and rumblings on Capitol Hill against OSP had become deafening. By June 1954 British OSP already stood at over $620 million, and unfulfilled contracts took the total by 30 June 1955 to $913.9 million. The whole concept began to fall apart on 29 June 1954, when several Congressmen lobbied hard against it. Perhaps the most powerful opponent was the formidable Carl Hinshaw, who among other things said: 'The competition from the British is getting far too tough.' The House obviously agreed with him, because when it came to the vote the split was 85-50 to delete the outstanding $75 million that was Britain's share of OSP for Fiscal 1955.

By this time the British aircraft industry had, as noted earlier, largely recovered from its terrible weakness of 1951. Indeed, it comprised almost thirty companies, most of whom had far too much work on far too many projects. It had long been self-evident that there ought to be some kind of overall direction and planning in British aircraft manufacture. A few lone voices cried in the wilderness, and Sir Roy Fedden even got a book published (*Britain's Air Survival* was not exactly one of Cassell's best-sellers, because nobody wanted to be told). I'll touch on this theme again. Meanwhile, I could not help being amused at one of the things Congressman Hinshaw said on 29 June 1954: 'We have been too busy concentrating on the output of military planes to concentrate on civil transports.' For one thing, Britain's competition had reduced the US market share from 99.3 per cent to a mere 98.8. Secondly, what he said had for years been a parrot-cry of politicians in Britain!

39

10 January 1954

No Fatigue Problem

One of my happy memories is of working as an undergraduate in the Structures Department at the RAE, Farnborough, in the summer of 1949. I learned much, and one of the things I learned was that 'There is no fatigue problem in aircraft'. The Principal Scientific Officer who told me this then added, 'At least, that has been the official view throughout my lifetime. The rule of thumb has always been that, if the structure or part is strong enough to bear the fully factored static loads, then that will take care of any fatigue.' But he went on to add that he was personally uneasy. He said there was evidence that a Stinson Model A in Australia, which had fallen out of the sky in 1945 killing ten, had suffered failure of welded steel tube wing structure following the growth of a crack over a period reckoned to be many weeks or even months. At almost the same time that he said this, his boss, the head of the department Dr P.B. Walker, announced that in future designers would have to consider fatigue life as well as static strength and stiffness.

This was a bit of a shock. Static tests are done by applying the load once only. In most cases the load is gradually increased until the part breaks. In contrast, in fatigue testing the load is applied in one direction, then in the reverse direction, and so on for maybe a few thousand or even million times. Where the load can only be applied in one direction, as in the case of a pressurized cabin, the load is applied, then removed, then reapplied and so on. Whereas some fatigue specimens can have the load reversed over 100 times a second, the inflation and deflation of a pressure cabin takes quite a long time, and 20 applications of full pressure in a working day might be good going, at least when air was used as the inflating medium.

In static testing, the part deforms almost imperceptibly under load until, at a point depending upon the material, it flows plastically and breaks with a load bang. In contrast, a fatigue crack begins with the separation of small groups of crystals and progresses very slowly. After a few weeks it may still be only a small fraction of an inch long, but eventually it will reach a critical length. The longer the crack, the greater the stress concentration at its end and the faster it grows (assuming that the applied load remains the same on each flight). At the critical value, if there is nothing else to carry the loads, the crack suddenly rips right across the rest of the part, which can be bad news for the aircraft. Today's structural designers must find it very hard to imagine a time when fatigue was ignored.

Before the war designers had certainly worried about strength, though standard handbooks—such as, in Britain, Air Publication 970—gave plenty of rule-of-thumb guidance. But fatigue was not even thought about. Aircraft flew at low speeds, lurching gently through 'air pockets' and 'bumps', and seldom piled up more than about thirty hours in a month. An aircraft that had flown 500 hours, military or civil, was quite exceptional. In World War Two the environment of front-line operations, the need to fly in bad weather and enemy action brought down average airframe life still further. At the risk of turning a serious essay into a mere joke, I like the story about the first Airbus meeting attended by German representatives. A white-haired German stood up and said he was unhappy about the fatigue life of the proposed A300B wing, designed at Hatfield. The leader of the wing design team, Jock Macadam, on being told that the critic was 'The great Dr Willy Messerschmitt', likewise stood up and said: 'Herr Messerschmitt, I believe the fatigue life of the Bf 109 was about 50 hours, providing it didn't meet a Spitfire!'

I'm not sure about 50 hours being a typical fatigue life for a World War Two fighter, but not many of them got much beyond that. Today's restorers, and especially the racers, have to inspect their structures with meticulous detail because restored aircraft often fly far more hours than any similar aircraft did back in the war. But as soon as the war was over, aircraft began to pile on the hours. One of the most important lucky chances in aviation was John K. Northrop's predeliction for multi-spar stressed-skin wings. From the Northrop Alpha of 1929 onwards Northrop's multi-spar wings went on a host of aircraft, including the DC-1. This led naturally to the DC-2 and then the DC-3, which via various military versions has made more transport flights all over the world than any other aircraft. Dozens of aircraft of this family are still flying today, and I have never heard of a serious fatigue problem.

Again it was sheer (bad) luck that the British designers tended to prefer single-spar wings. As a result, in 1950 the first of at least three Doves crashed from fatigue failure, usually of the lower spar boom. In 1951 a Viking main-spar lower boom was found to be completely severed after months of cracking. Much later, in 1968, the RAF was faced with the complete re-sparring of the wings of its Pembrokes (it nearly junked them instead). Many other British types, military as well as civil, have required expensive re-sparring or other structural rework in order to keep flying. So did aircraft designed in other countries.

The immediate post-war era accentuated the previously dormant fatigue problem. Aircraft speeds were suddenly multiplied by about two, so that encounters with bumps—henceforth given the more scientific name of gusts, with measured vertical velocities—changed from being a soft lurch to being a sharp hammer-blow, which at times could be really vicious. Wing loadings (weight W divided by wing area S), which had been rising since 1903, had been predicted before the war to level out, one gazer into a crystal ball in 1936 proclaiming 'Several factors, not least the problem of landing speed, will force designers generally to keep wing loading below 25 lb/sq ft'. What actually happened was that W/S went through the proverbial roof, and kept right on going. For example in the F-101 Voodoo of 1954 it reached 139 lb/sq ft, while even in the rather pedestrian Vanguard turboprop airliner it reached 96. This had a corresponding effect on material stresses, and not only in the wings. Another factor was the introduction of new light alloys. Older alloys were soft, and stretched (elongated) before fracture. The new ones were stronger, but they were harder and more brittle, and could break with little warning.

The greatly increased indicated airspeeds naturally demanded thicker skin gauges throughout, even where these were not required for reasons of structural strength. Higher speeds also meant greater impact energy from birds and hailstones, rising as the square of the speed, though the most severe such impacts are to this day well outside the design envelope, which means that damage, possibly very severe damage, will result. Another factor that suddenly made life arduous was the impingement on structure of noise from jets, and especially from jets with afterburners. The energy from such intense noise fields was found sufficient to cause fatigue damage within a few hours. A typical example concerned the flaps of the B-52, whose skin and internal structure began to break up in one case within four hours after being subjected to the noise field behind paired J57 engines on takeoffs with water injection (early B-52s, with no water, lasted much longer).

Other causes of increased fatigue damage were numerous. Small grass fields had given way to gigantic airfields with runways up to three miles long. Though the surfaces might be generally smoother than grass, the enormously greater distances modern aircraft travel on the ground result in prolonged periods of rapid load reversal which affect all parts of the structure. Cycling of landing gear, flaps, slats, spoilers, and other movable parts all results in local stresses which can be extremely large and highly variable. And, not least, the introduction of pressurized cockpits and then of complete pressurized fuselages resulted in extremely large hoop and tensile stresses, mainly in the fuselage skin, which are applied and then removed completely once on every flight.

This should all have been obvious back in the 1930s. Both my college library and RAE Structures Department had plenty of dusty tomes in which could be found treatises on 'thin-walled cylinders under internal pressure'. I recall reading some Proceedings of 1906, I believe by a Prof Stewart, which included calculations of the ideal shape for a cutout in such a pressurized cylinder. We have had such things for nearly 200 years in the form of inspection manholes in steam boilers. Such a shape is approximately an ellipse with the major axis perpendicular to the axis of the cylinder, like the windows of a Viscount or F27. Such calculations were dusted off in, I think, 1946, and the ideal shape again published with the name 'neutral hole'. But you don't positively have to make cutouts this shape. Fokker, for example, had beautiful wide-vista ellipses on the F27, but on the Fokker 50 has decided instead to follow the thoughtless multitudes—who had all previously followed Boeing—and uses small rectangular windows with rounded corners. An even more extraordinary choice is seen on the beautiful Gulfstreams. I believe the G IV's dP (maximum pressure differential) of 9.45 lb/sq in is higher than that of any other civil aircraft except Concorde, yet the windows are huge ellipses with the major axis *horizontal*. Maybe Allen Paulson's engineers really do believe nothing tears along the perforations.

Of course, nobody can even think of fatigue in aircraft without thinking of the Comet, and to this day I am bemused at the whole affair. The de Havilland DH.106 Comet was something that had never happened before. It was a beautifully engineered and well thought out commercial transport propelled by turbojets, and designed (within the technology of the times) to reap full benefit from such propulsion in speed and cruising altitude. It had large integral-tank fuel capacity, unprecedented cabin pressure, fully powered flight controls and many other advanced features. It was also the first time the British industry had produced a 'mainline' commercial transport that was not merely competitive but years ahead of all the competition. In fact there simply was no competition, nor could there be any for many years.

Near the end of my time at RAE Structures I walked outside and there she was, a poem in gleaming polished metal, newly arrived for the 1949 SBAC Show. Apart from the giant single mainwheels, which were known to be only temporary, this aircraft, G-ALVG, was, to a greater degree than any other aircraft I could think of, an aircraft of the future. I wondered if anything could possibly go wrong. So too, I am sure, did R.E. Bishop and all the fine team of engineers under him at Hatfield.

As the world knows, the first production Comet 1 for BOAC, G-ALYP, callsign Yoke Peter, opened the civil jet age on 2 May 1952 when, dead on time at 3.30 pm, she left Heathrow for Johannesburg. This pioneer jet-propelled revenue service did not only 'halve the size of the world' (to quote BOAC's Sir Miles Thomas) but it also introduced passengers to a completely new kind of air travel. Instead of ploughing through the clouds and weather in a vehicle that thundered, thumped, and vibrated, passengers could now travel on a kind of magic carpet, far above everything except clear-air turbulence in a vehicle that seemed virtually without noise or vibration. As a result they arrived refreshed in half the time, after having had a wonderful vista of our world that one might call a bird's-eye view, except for the fact that birds don't fly so high. It was this intense passenger appeal that really worried Lockheed, Douglas, and other rivals. They might pretend the Comet 1 to be 'uneconomic', but the Comets were flying with almost every seat filled, and every passenger departed saying 'I don't want to go back to DC-6s and Super Connies'. And, of course, the de Havilland company was coming on fast with the Comet 2 and Comet 3, which were bigger, more powerful and a real force to contend with.

There were a few snags. Two Comets simply failed to leave Mother Earth, the second occasion killing all on board. The cause was found to be over-eager pilots hauling back too soon, putting the aircraft into a nose-high attitude which reduced engine inlet efficiency and caused high drag, so that speed simply stopped increasing. One wonders whether perhaps this possibility might not have been thought of during the flight test programme in 1949-51? Is it not part of a test pilot's job to sit in his armchair at home and think 'What can the other guys do that could get them into difficulty?' Perhaps what I am saying is that manufacturers ought to let customer pilots, and especially pilots who are inexperienced or teetering on the brink of being failed by the Training Captains, fly their new aircraft at the earliest possible date. This just might avoid some accident investigator, years later, saying 'Whoever would have thought he'd do that?'

Less easily explained was Comet 1 Yoke Victor, which, exactly a year after the start of BOAC services, disintegrated climbing out of Calcutta. It was thought to have entered a giant Cu-Nim, the most violent kind of storm cloud, and the kind of Cu-Nims you find in that part of the world can rip apart any commercial transport ever built. The Comet 1 had no radar, which would have warned of the hazard ahead.

Much worse was to come. On 10 January 1954 Yoke Peter left Rome and climbed hard en route for London. Capt Alan Gibson had promised to pass the height of the cloud tops to colleague Capt J.R. Johnson who was ploughing along in an

Argonaut far below. Gibson flicked his transmit switch and said 'George How Jig from George Yoke Peter, did you get my . . .' And at that instant something catastrophic happened to Yoke Peter, something obviously so overwhelming that it took the captain by surprise in mid-sentence. Whatever it was, it happened at about 31,000 ft over the Tyrrhenian Sea near the island of Elba.

BOAC's Comet fleet were grounded, and inspected in the minutest detail. On 10 February a Royal Navy salvage team at last found the main wreckage of Yoke Peter and began a painstaking search for other parts, which after six months had shipped back to RAE Farnborough more than three-quarters of Yoke Peter, a lot of it looking like aluminium cornflakes. My old friends in Structures then tried to put each bit in the right place. Meanwhile, de Havilland and BOAC racked their brains to find the cause. Even at the time it seemed obvious that the favoured theory, that there had been an engine fire, must be utter nonsense. An engine fire would have allowed Gibson several minutes to tell everyone all about it, and could hardly have caused such mid-air disintegration. Nevertheless, of the numerous mostly minor and completely 'blind' modifications made to the BOAC Comet fleet, about half were concerned with engine fires. Unbelievably, the investigators thought of cabin fatigue but failed to think a bit further. When all the modifications had been completed the Comets resumed operations, on 23 March 1954. A mere fortnight later, on 8 April, Yoke Yoke took off from Rome flying south. Her last transmission was a routine 'Climbing on track'. All the evidence showed that Yoke Yoke also had disintegrated at high altitude.

It was almost the end of the Comet. Oliver Stewart said 'Never was bold inventiveness worse rewarded'. This time all Comets were grounded. Though the parts of Yoke Yoke had fallen into water too deep for (at that time) much hope of recovery, Farnborough very soon knew the horrific truth about what had happened to Yoke Peter. Not least of the discoveries was an exact imprint of the dark blue and gold-edged fuselage cheat line far out on the top of one of the wings. It showed where the skin of the fuselage had slammed against the top of the wing as the entire pressurized cabin exploded. If BOAC had waited a week or two longer before resuming operations, Yoke Yoke would never have suffered the same fate as Yoke Peter, 21 people would not have been killed, and the lead established by the Comet would not have been lost. The existing aircraft could have been modified to make them safe, the production line of Comet 2s would have been held up only a matter of a few weeks, and the plans for the big Comet 3 would hardly have been affected, except to remove the lethal parts of the structural design.

Instead, there were two Comet disasters instead of one. The Comet had become famous all over the world, in a way previously unknown for a commercial transport. On its broad wings rode a large part of the hopes of the British nation, and that nation's belief in its technical lead in aviation. The shock of those disasters was immense. Newspapers asked if the Comet would ever fly again. At Hatfield the de Havilland management, in as bad a state of shock as anyone else, discussed the abandonment of all future jetliners. When it was at length decided to go ahead with a still nebulous 'Comet 4', the wisdom of adhering to the same name was debated. It was a time when a lot of decisions were taken on a basis of emotion.

On 17 July 1954 Boeing flew the prototype of a much bigger, faster and longer-ranged jetliner called the 707. It was obvious that, starting with an aircraft designed in 1946-7 and flown in 1949, de Havilland were running a race. There seemed no obvious reason why a thoroughly safe Comet 4 should not be in production by the end of 1954, and in airline service by early 1956. For example, in 1959 the Electra turboprop airliner suffered a succession of catastrophic mid-air breakups whose cause was much less obvious than the cause of the Comet disasters. While Electras remained in operation, but limited to 225 knots, Lockheed and the FAA discovered that minor damage to the engine mountings could lead to 'whirl mode' oscillation of the engine, gearbox and propeller, which could tear off a wing. In six months a cure was devised, and within a year, from 5 January 1961, Lockheed was extolling the virtues of the modified 'Electra II' which quickly resumed full-speed operation.

The difference was that Lockheed was an American company with a totally commercial outlook. In contrast, Britain simply wallowed in the prolonged Comet disaster. Even after the painstaking investigation at Farnborough under Sir Arnold Hall had worked out what had happened, and delivered their *Report* (which measured 13 in × 8.7 in × 4 in), there still had to be a public court of inquiry, at Church House, Westminster. My *Flight* colleague Ken Owen, detailed to cover the inquiry, thought he might be out of the office a day or two at most, but it actually lasted from 19 October to 24 November 1954! After all this, it still took de Havilland years to get back to where they had left off, and eventually the Comet 4 got into service in October 1958, the same month as the Boeing 707. Unbelievably, Britain's seemingly unassailable lead in jetliners had been completely and unnecessarily lost.

So what were these lethal parts of the Comet 1? As soon as it was obvious that the pressure cabin had exploded, a water tank was built in which could be put a complete Comet, the wings projecting through watertight seals on each side so that flight loads could all be simulated. The first tank measured 112 ft long, 20 ft wide, and 10 ft deep, holding 225,000 Imperial gallons. At the same time a tank was constructed for the Britannia holding 400,000 gallons. Water had to be used to cut down the explosive energy of the pressurizing medium. Early tests using air had led to failures exactly like explosions, which were not only dangerous but often destroyed the evidence. Merely filling the cabin with water gives a false difference in dP between the bottom of the cabin and the top; you have to have water inside and out.

The aircraft put into the tank was Yoke Uncle, which had made 1,230 flights. After a further 1,830 simulated flights there was a big 'thump' and it was found that Yoke Uncle's cabin had ripped open along the side, starting at the corner of one of the windows. Sir Arnold's experts searched all the corners of the cutouts in Yoke Peter and, lo and behold, there was a beautiful fatigue crack starting at the corner of one of the two cutouts in the top of the fuselage for the suppressed ADF (auto direction finding) antennas. This was the lethal point that killed that particular Comet. A crack had probably been growing there for months, and if that crack had failed to turn into a catastrophic rip, Yoke Peter would have been killed by another one starting at a passenger window.

The dP of the Comet 1 was 8.25 lb/sq in, just over double that of the DC-6 and Constellation. The de Havilland engineers took the greatest pains to avoid problems, for example by testing major fuselage sections to 11 lb/sq in, and windows to a factor of 10 (83 lb/sq in). All pressurized structure was designed to a factor of 2.5. Some specimens, after undergoing static testing, were put through fatigue programmes without failure. It was suggested in 1954 that a static-strength specimen cannot give a true result in a subsequent fatigue test, but I doubt if the errors are anything like as great as the normal scatter of fatigue-test results. What surprised me very much at the time was that de Havilland exploded a complete fuselage section by inflating it with air, and only then realized that you get the same results less dangerously with water.

What makes it doubly surprising is that Armstrong Whitworth carried out a complete static and fatigue test programme on the fuselage of the Apollo turboprop airliner back in March 1949, using water. I believe this was the first time this had been done. Chief designer Dixie Keen told me they had been careful to establish a minimum radius for the corner of every cutout of 5 in, even though their dP was only 5.5 lb/sq in. Their more successful rival, Vickers, even went so far as to make the main doors on the Viscount elliptical, as you can see on the original V.630 flown on 18 July 1948. Later they decided this was overdoing it, and they switched to rectangular doors but with generous radii at the corners. Whatever possessed them at Hatfield?

As an aside, when the Comet 1 was new I was a staff man on *Flight*. The people at Hatfield considered themselves superior to lesser mortals, and visiting Hatfield could be an ordeal. For one thing, any attempt to describe the Comet's design features, other than those externally obvious, was absolutely forbidden. I remember how disconcerted we were when our rival, *The Aeroplane*, published what at first glance looked like a cutaway. In fact it was a sepia wash drawing (by Leslie Carr, I believe, who was an artist rather than a technical artist) and it showed no structure or systems detail whatsoever. The idea, of course, was to prevent all those lesser mortals from learning de Havilland's secrets. But surely the boot was on the other foot? Perhaps one of the lesser folk might have said, 'Are you sure about your square cutouts?'

It all comes back to the amazing decision of de Havilland to cut *square* holes in the thin-skinned high-pressure Comet, with totally inadequate corner radii. It was known in the nineteenth century that a cutout with a sharp corner radius concentrates the stress in a sheet subjected to a tensile load. When the maker and the airline went over the Comet with a fine tooth comb in January and February 1954, why did nobody point out the danger of all the stress-raising corners? Really, all the Comet did in the longer term was to teach the world's air travellers that jets are serene and comfortable as well as fast, and to teach the world's planemakers that they have to take fatigue very seriously indeed. But we didn't have to go through any of it.

40

10 November 1955

Without a Struggle

In the second Christopher Hinton lecture in 1982 Sir George Edwards—'GRE' back in the 1950s, and surely the greatest leader the British aircraft industry has ever had—said: 'I have often been asked what I thought was the biggest setback that the industry suffered. Certainly on the civil scene I am sure it was the cancellation of the V.1000 transport six months before it was due to fly . . . A military cancellation does not show if you do not have a war, whereas the battle with the enemy never stops on the civil front. If you miss one stage by a cancellation then you are lost.' The V.1000 was actually being built for the RAF, but it was the civil derivative that really mattered.

Today I doubt if many aviation enthusiasts have even heard of the V.1000, but they can hardly be unaware of Boeing. Starting off with about 2,000 'Big Jets' of basically 707 design, they went on to deliver nearly 2,000 727s, and are now far beyond the 2,000 mark with the 737 and edging towards the first 1,000 747 'Jumbos' which sell for about $150,000,000 each and have no competitor. The 757 and 767 are extras. It's quite nice business, and I don't begrudge Boeing a cent of it. I just regret that we never gave them the competition that the V.1000 promised. Put another way, there are not many things in the aircraft industry that can be predicted with certainty, but one is that if you cancel a major programme then your share of that market will be zero (that sounds like a GRE quote). What's more, it is almost certain to be zero, or very near to it, for ever afterwards.

The Vickers-Armstrongs V.1000 had its roots in an earlier programme, the V.660 long-range jet bomber, designed and built with great rapidity and assurance to meet Specification B.9/48. The prototype flew on 18 May 1951. Production orders soon followed, and Vickers delivered 108, named Valiant, in one of the best programmes in post-war Britain. There was just one major mistake. On 4 September 1953 Vickers flew the Type 673 Valiant B.2, for some reason painted black. This had a completely revised structure specially designed for sustained operations at low level. Maximum speed at sea level was 552 mph, whereas the production bomber was limited to 414 mph at sea level because its structure was *not* designed for low-level operations. So in October 1964 the entire force of Valiants had to be grounded and scrapped because, as they had had to switch to low-level operations, their airframes were cracking all over the place. The Ministry explained that this was entirely because the aircraft had not been designed for low-level operation. At the Press conference announcing the premature demise of the Valiants—which threw the RAF into a panic, because among other things it meant they suddenly had no tankers—I asked why the production order had not been for the B.2 version. The people on the platform looked at each other, and one who shall be nameless said: 'I don't know what Mk 2 version you are referring to, next question.'

Back in 1951 discussions had begun regarding a possible transport aircraft using Valiant technology. Compared with the pioneer Comet 1 this would have been bigger, heavier, carried much greater payloads for much longer range, used far more efficient axial or 'bypass jet' engines (what we today would call low-bypass-ratio turbofans) and, having swept wings and tail, would be about 60–70 mph faster. Such a development seemed absolutely obvious. Boeing had wanted to do the same, but its bombers were totally unsuitable as a basis for a transport. Vickers, however, to quote GRE again, could 'use the same basic technology and aerodynamics'. The ITP (Instruction to Proceed) was given in December 1952, and in the following year Vickers revealed that it was working on the V.1000 and had an order for a prototype. Shortly afterwards an order was placed for six production aircraft for RAF Transport Command.

In January 1954 it was announced that the first flight was expected in the summer of 1955, but 18 months later it was clear the programme had slipped slightly. To some degree this was because nobody had appreciated the enormous challenge of such a big and advanced aircraft, but the main reason was that, like virtually every programme for the RAF, the customer had seldom adhered to a decision or requirement longer than a few weeks before it was altered, usually to ask for a bit more. Basic dimensions did not change, the most basic of all being the fuselage diameter of 150 in (which compared with 148 in for the 707). The wings would have been extremely efficient, with a section profile more advanced than that chosen for the 707 and with curved Küchemann tips. The principal demands that kept being increased were range and payload, without any relaxation in the very severe demand that the V.1000 should operate from 6,000-ft runways, even in the tropics, and this necessitated very powerful double-slotted flaps on a wing with an area of 3,267 sq ft (compared with intermittently broken flaps on a wing of 2,433 sq ft for the 707–120). Other severe demands included a giant hydraulically powered cargo lift able to hoist large items of cargo and vehicles into the fuselage, and a floor stressed to accept a load of 150 lb/sq ft.

It can thus be seen that in many respects the V.1000 was a more capable aircraft than the original 707 or DC-8, and that the planned VC.7 civil version, without the massive cargo hoist or freight floor, and (any sensible person would say) designed to the same runway length as the US rivals, ought to be a world-beater. One reason for its superior performance was its engine. Instead of the Pratt & Whitney JT3C-6 (wet rating 13,000 lb, weight 4,401 lb, cruise specific fuel consumption about 0.92) the British aircraft was designed to use the Rolls-Royce Conway, the world's pioneer modern production turbofan (in this version, wet rating 15,000 lb, weight 4,075 lb, sfc 0.67). The contrast was startling in its magnitude. The Conway began its flight development in early 1954 with a podded RCo.5 engine slung under an Ashton Mk 3 testbed. About twenty years later Lindsay Dawson, the original Conway Development Engineer, told me: 'Despite its very advanced design the Conway went very well. From about 1954 we could see our way in stages to at least 20,000 lb thrust, which of course we achieved.' It is worth bearing this in mind.

In theory the national airline BOAC had been involved from the outset, with a view to drawing up the detailed specification of the VC.7 civil version. Surely that's one of the national airline's important functions? By 1953 the project team at Weybridge had almost completed the design of the Type 1001 for the RAF (except that the customer kept changing his requirements), the VC.7 Type 1002 for BOAC and the 1003 for civil export customers, of which TCA (Trans-Canada Airlines) was prominent. Unfortunately, BOAC appeared to have very little real interest in such an aircraft. Vickers said nothing in public, but another project for a long-range civil jet was the Handley Page HP.97, based on the Victor. This was nothing more than a brochure, but any professional airline would obviously have kept in the most intimate touch with HP to see how the project stacked up against such others as the Avro Atlantic (another paper aircraft, based on the Vulcan) and the VC.7. It so happened that one of the HP directors, Air Commodore A. (later Sir Arthur) Vere Harvey, was also a very active MP. In 1954 he said in the House of Commons. 'My firm has had the greatest difficulty in persuading Sir Miles Thomas or his technical assistants to come . . . and discuss the civil version. Yet Sir Miles has stated in the current BOAC Annual Report that the Corporation has continued to be in close and constant touch with the manufacturers in order to assess the probable capabilities of such aircraft as the proposed civil versions of the three types of V-bomber. I am astonished that he dare put those words into a public report.' In fact, it seemed to me perfectly obvious what Sir Miles meant. For the past forty years Britain's chief flag carrier has been perfectly happy to equip its mainline fleets with any kind of aircraft so long as they are American. Right now, as I write, British Airways (successors to BOAC) is one of the most important of the team of airlines trying to help Boeing find a way of producing a rival to the world-beating Airbus 330. We are told BA means Boeing Always. So what Sir Miles meant all those years ago— later I confirmed this—was that he had kept in 'close and constant touch' with Boeing and Douglas.

Let's just look at the situation as the Farnborough airshow opened in September 1955. Vickers had completed the engineering design of the Type 1001, and the first aircraft, XE294, was fast taking shape at Wisley, Weybridge and Foxwarren. As related, in most respects it promised to outperform either the planned 707-121 or the DC-8-10, despite the severe handicap of having a huge wing sized to much shorter field lengths. There was, so far as I could see, no reason to doubt the ability of the Vickers-Armstrongs design staff, nor the validity of their figures. Thus, we appeared to be extremely well placed, with a highly competitive military transport similar in timing to the USAF Boeing KC-135 tanker/transport (first flight August 1956) and a derived civil jet similar in timing to the 707 (first flight December 1957). There were of course differences, such as the basic fact that while the RAF was buying six V.1000s the USAF was buying an initial 732 KC-135s.

At Farnborough Rolls-Royce exhibited a Conway, revealing the thrust of that (earlier) version as 13,000 lb, 'with the lowest specific fuel consumption of any type-tested turbojet'. *Flight* reported 'Considerable congestion was caused by this eagerly awaited exhibit'. It was obvious that the Conway was a world-beating engine for large aircraft in the Mach 0.8 class, as outlined previously in the comparison with the JT3C-6. The V.1000 seemed a solid programme, but it was at this show that I learned of an apparent lack of BOAC interest, electrical engineer Harry

Zeffert saying 'We'd like to propose a different generating system for the VC.7 but we can't even get an answer to our letters.'

I was totally unprepared for the announcement on the next day, 10 September 1955, which said: 'The future of the V.1000 in its military and civil forms is under consideration in the light of the probable performance of the aircraft and the general transport aircraft situation here and overseas.' This came from the Ministry of Supply. I called them, and Press Officer Charles Huntly, a dour Scot (deep inside he had Walter Mitty dreams of emulating Juan Fangio, but that was only very late in the evening), said: 'I can only tell you the V.1000 is in trouble. Confidentially, it is common knowledge it will be scrapped.'

I could think of no reason for such a staggering decision. Neither could Charles Gardner and the good folk at Weybridge, but a little light (or perhaps darkness) was shed by a further amazing announcement in the same month: 'The Goverment consider that, in view of recent American developments in the field of large jet transports, the potential market for a developed civil version has been considerably reduced.' For many months I had those words taped to my office wall. They were absolutely in line with the strange inability of the British Government ever to regard aeroplanes as products, like cars or toothpaste. If your competitor brings out a new car, do you therefore cancel your own? If this was our policy, why did we in the immediate post-war years, in the face of competition from the L-1049 and DC-6, bring out such incomparably inferior aircraft as the Tudor and Hermes, which had zero chance of success on the world market? Yet here we seemed to be about to chuck a *competitive* product on the scrap heap merely because it had competitors!

On 13 October 1955 PanAm ordered 20 707s and 25 DC-8s and thereby launched the Jet Age, and what was popularly called 'the jet buying spree'. Very soon orders reached 55 for the 707 and over 60 for the DC-8, and it was obvious that the VC.7 alone could enable us to compete in this enormous market. Yet BOAC appeared unable to comprehend this. Having suffered severely from problems with Comets and Britannias, to the extent that it had just bought a fleet of piston- engined DC-7Cs to tide it over, the airline was committed to buying an £85m fleet of Comet 4s which, though not designed for such long sectors and incapable of flying them efficiently, were going to be launched on the North Atlantic, in a childish 'race' with PanAm's more capable 707. It was also committed to a further fleet of a longer-ranged version of the Britannia, the Series 312, which certainly could operate on the North Atlantic but with propellers. Obviously BOAC would have to buy Big Jets, especially as Boeing and Douglas had announced heavier and more powerful versions of the 707 and DC-8 which, by 1959, would, in the absence of the VC.7, sweep away all other competition on the North Atlantic.

Boeing and Douglas have never been noted for making predictions or promises they couldn't keep, but for some reason not far removed from wishful thinking many people in Britain pretended the long-range jets were incapable of realization. In Filton House, Bristol, I was assailed by technical and PR people who, with one voice, insisted 'They'll never be able to build 707s and DC-8s for the North Atlantic . . . If they ever do get round to it, it will be with bigger aircraft, with six engines' (Scout's honour, that's what they said). This after the Big Jets had been bought by PanAm, Air France, KLM, and others, all with the North Atlantic in view.

By November 1955 it was 'common knowledge' (quote *Flight*) that the V.1000 was dead. The decision was actually taken on 10 November, and announced two days later. The Ministry of Supply said: 'The plans for re-equipping Transport Command with the Vickers-Armstrongs long-range V.1000 transport aircraft have been under review in the light of the probable delivery dates of the aircraft and the general transport aircraft situation. As a result it has been decided to cancel the orders for the development and production of this aircraft. The contracts cover the production of one prototype and six production aircraft for Transport Command, whose needs will now be met by the purchase of the Bristol Britannia 250LR.' Note, this time they said nothing about 'the performance of the aircraft'. Pressed, the Minister, Reggie Maudling, elaborated on the decision (at the time his remarks were non-attributable, which has long been the British way of avoiding the American practice of actually making particular people responsible for particular decisions). He said: 'It has taken longer than was hoped to overcome the problems of meeting the specification . . . As the design and construction of the prototype progressed, the weight rose, and finally increased to such a figure that, in spite of the rise in the thrust of the Rolls-Royce Conway bypass turbojet, the aircraft would not have been successful. Regarding the proposed VC.7 civil derivative, not only would the increased weight have impaired its operational flexibility, but its sales prospects would have been poor. One could not expect operators to buy so large and expensive a machine unless it was used by BOAC, *and Sir Miles has said its existing purchases will fill their requirements well into the 1960s.*' The Air Ministry threw in its two-penn'orth by adding: 'The point is, the RAF cannot wait until 1958.' So they bought lumbering Britannias, and got the first one on 4 June 1959.

To give them their due, I am convinced the various decision-takers were too ignorant to understand what they had done. Moreover, when GRE tried to explain what had been done his words carried little weight, because he was the manufacturer. He said: 'We have abandoned to the Americans, without a struggle, this highly important market. How important this market is can be seen from the fact that the orders so far placed by a very few operators for big jets total over £200 million [as he spoke the total went to £260m and a week later to £340m]. The future size of the market could be of the order of £1,000 million. I think the decision to cancel Britain's only contender in this market is a national decision we shall regret for many years to come.' And so we would, if anybody had thought about it.

Before returning to the enormous implications of that cancellation, let's look briefly at each detailed point. First, increased weight tends to increase flexibility rather than reduce it. You don't always have to operate at maximum weight, but if you do then you get extra payload/range capability. Part of the trouble was that the V.1000 began life as a smaller and lighter aircraft in the 195,000 lb class, which was then burdened by ever-increasing RAF demands until it grew to 230,000 lb at the time the contract was signed, and to 248,000 lb at cancellation. This was made to seem a reason for cancellation, whereas any sensible customer would have said, 'Can you bring it up to 350,000 lb in ten years?' Two weeks before the V.1000 was cancelled Douglas had announced that it would build the DC-8 at two weights, 265,000 lb Domestic and 287,500 lb Intercontinental, and with less powerful (and much less fuel-efficient) engines than the V.1000 and a wing only 84 per cent as large. Ten years later the DC-8 had been developed to 350,000 lb, but the people who cancelled our only big jet would have completely failed to understand why.

In Story 35 George Miles makes some pertinent comments on how the political mind works. We can sit in on the final meeting on 10 November 1955, and hear what is said: 'Vickers, they've got plenty of work, they don't need the V.1000 . . . Sir Miles is adamant, he won't have anything to do with it . . . In my view the right policy is to build on success; we have the Comet, Viscount and Britannia, and these are what we must concentrate on . . . Excellent, but we must have the Britannias made in Belfast, because with the Swift and Comet 2 cancellations Shorts need the work . . .'

That's pretty much how it was, and nobody appeared to realize that we were throwing away our own stake in a billion-pound market. And if the loss of our Big Jet was a disaster, I can only say that from then on people offered explanations which appeared to be nonsensical. Cornered on a BBC TV programme on 14 November Sir Miles explained why he had no interest in the VC.7: 'The Comet 4 will be much more suitable for the Empire routes . . . the few aircraft of VC.7 type needed just for the transatlantic service—say six—is too small to justify production . . . The VC.7 would in any case have been very demanding as to airport requirements.' By airport requirements I (and I assume everyone else) took him to mean runway length. The V.1000 was to carry its 25,000 lb payload a still-air distance of 5,400 miles with an ISA sea-level takeoff distance of 7,400 ft. (From Heathrow it could in theory have been loaded up to 286,000 lb.) Thus, its takeoff distance at maximum weight of 248,000 lb was 7,400 ft, compared with 10,200 ft for the 707–120 and 9,440 ft for the light Domestic DC-8. Pity these figures were not known to the BBC interviewer. And this must have been the first time an airline rejected a type on offer because of the small number needed. Did Boeing and Lufthansa cancel the 737 because only ten were needed? No, and now they're nudging 3,000.

Sir Miles went on to reaffirm that the airline's requirements would be 'fully met by the Comet 4 and Britannia'. Pressed on the question of competition from the 707 and DC-8, likely to be on the Atlantic routes by 1959, he said 'I am not in the least worried about such competition. It won't be until 1962 at the earliest that the Americans will have these aircraft in non-stop transatlantic service. We have no intention of buying American jets. Indeed, I am confident that the British aircraft and engine industries will in due course surmount US jet competition.' In the *Financial Times* he wrote that his Board were 'very interested in the proposed Super Britannia planned by Bristol and General Dynamics with Orion turboprops; indeed we have placed an order for 60 Orion engines'.

On 2 December 1955 Robson Brown, Member for Esher, asked the Minister: 'Will you review your decision in view of the V.1000 performance figures released by the manufacturer, since these reveal that the civil version of this aircraft is potentially superior to any projected long-range US jet transport, in that it has more power, shorter takeoff, better operating economics, and was designed around the most suitable type of engine for this work yet produced?' Maudling replied: 'I regret I can do nothing where BOAC have no requirement for it.' He added, 'I do not share the gloomy view about future British prospects in jet transports.'

The previous month we had had a formidable competitor in the Big Jet race, so there was then no reason to feel gloomy. Now we had destroyed it, and with it any hope of competing, so from whence came Mr Maudling's inspiration? It could hardly come from Hatfield, where, as well as rushing to supply Comet 4s to BOAC, the Project Design staff were drawing an idea called the Comet 5. This was in essence a Comet 4 which tried to behave like the VC.7. As the drawing on page 122 shows, it had four Conway RCo.10 engines buried in the roots of the swept wing, just like the VC.7, and it also had a swept tail very like that of the VC.7. However, it retained the narrow 10-foot-diameter fuselage of earlier Comets, which alone made it completely uncompetitive with the American jets, holding seating capacity to 84 (or 105 tourist) in 21 rows, compared with up to 152 for the VC.7. It was an altogether smaller aircraft, with a wing area of 2,750 sq ft.

The drawing was dated 13 July 1956, though de Havilland did not disclose it at that time. But in September of that year, after prolonged efforts, I managed to discuss the Big Jet situation with Sir Miles Thomas and his two top technical men, Alan Campbell-Orde (Development Director) and Charles Abell (Chief Engineer). It was strictly off the record, but so much water has gone under the bridge that I have no hesitation in repeating what was said. First, it was confirmed that Britain's national airline had never had any interest in the VC.7, nor in any other British jet except those emanating from Hatfield. I completely failed to pin anyone down to any shortcoming in the VC.7, and even gained the feeling that the disinterest had nothing to do with the aircraft itself. Each time I tried to enquire about the VC.7 the answer was to extol the virtues of the Comet 5. I learned that, for some reason, this obviously uncompetitive project was the subject of urgent talks between BOAC and the Ministry of Supply to try to get the thing funded and, about five years later than the VC.7, into BOAC service. What I did not learn was that BOAC and de Havilland were aware of the shortcomings of the Comet 5 and were trying to develop it into an all-new aircraft called the D.H.118. This would have been a perfect reinvention of the VC.7, with the same fuselage diameter, but with pod-mounted engines as adopted by the 707 and DC-8. This replaced the Comet 5 as a Hatfield project in October 1956, and BOAC even announced that it was 'urgently discussing' the D.H. paper aeroplane with the various ministries. By this time the airline had actually realized that it had destroyed Britain's only competitive Big Jet and that, in the absence of any possible alternative, it would have to buy either the 707 or DC-8. I recall how bothered Alan Ponsford, BOAC's deputy chief PR man, was at the prospect of having to announce such an order, after rejecting the VC.7 and saying they had no interest in US jets.

Back in December 1955 the MP for Sunderland South, Paul Williams, had forecast: 'I believe in the early 1960s BOAC will inevitably have to buy American jets for its transatlantic services.' In this prediction he was totally wrong. They bought American jets on 24 October 1956, and it was not six 707s but fifteen, all powered with the same Conway engines as planned for the VC.7. GRE said he found it hard to take when, in the House of Commons, Minister of Transport Harold Watkinson said 'This is because no suitable new British aircraft can be available for the purpose. The purchase is an exceptional measure to bridge the gap.' GRE recalls: 'It was no great surprise when I was sent for by the relevant Minister and told BOAC had asked permission to buy 707s. Was I going to be troublesome? Or could I reactivate the V.1000? I said I could not do the latter as we had pulled up the jigs, and as far as the former was concerned I had other things to do with my adrenalin.'

Can you wonder that for forty years I have felt there's nothing wrong with the British aircraft industry except the Government and British Airways?

41

4 April 1957

The Royal Ground Force

Just over thirty years ago the British Goverment announced a policy so incredible that it is hard to believe it really happened. Yet it was announced with no fanfare of trumpets, there was no storm in the media, and most people who thought about it at all were left wondering whether perhaps the policy was right. The policy was, in a nutshell, to do away with military aircraft, except for transports, trainers, and some naval types!

Posterity regards the policy as the brainchild of one man, Duncan Sandys (pronounced 'sands'), later Lord Duncan-Sandys. In 1940, as a Major, he took command of the first Z-battery of 3 in unguided but spin-stabilized rockets, one of which actually downed a German bomber near Cardiff on 7 April 1941. From that time on, Sandys was, in the words of one of his closest aides in the 1950s, 'A nut case on rockets. He seemed to love them all, guided or not. He was convinced they would inherit the Earth, making other weapons obsolete.'

As Parliamentary Secretary, Ministry of Supply, he was charged in April 1943 with investigating reports of German secret weapons, especially rockets. On 20 June 1944 he became Chairman of the Crossbow Committee for reporting on the effects of German missiles and Allied countermeasures (Story 32). On 7 September 1944 he issued a statement to the Press which began: 'Except possibly for a few last shots, the Battle of London is over.' About 2,300 of the hated flying bombs had got through, and everyone now breathed a huge sigh of relief. Just 24 hours later the first A4 ('V2') rocket fell on London, to be followed by 1,114 others. Mr Sandys never quite got over this inept timing, but it strengthened his belief that rockets and missiles were the only things in sight.

In the early 1950s Sandys was Minister of Supply, and in between cancelling the Brabazon, Princess, and many other things, he perhaps got the impression that aeroplanes are complicated, take a long time to perfect, and invariably cost much more than anyone had expected. Thus the stage was set for some pretty dramatic changes. In October 1954 he was appointed Minister of Housing and Local Government, and quite a lot of people in the RAF and aircraft industry wish he'd stayed there. But his missionary work was tireless, and by 1956 even a former Chief of the Air Staff (Sir William Dickson) was very concerned about it. I won't quote him, but he saw the writing on the wall clearly enough. His successor, Sir Dermot

Boyle, was likewise keenly aware of the rumblings but less inclined to get bothered—outwardly at any rate. I had great respect for him, and he let it be known that the upper echelons of the RAF, definitely including the Air Staff, were split right down the middle. I got a strong impression that the 'air marshals' could be divided into the professionals, who thought only about the tasks facing the RAF and how they could best be accomplished, and the political animals who thought only about how they could further their careers. It is said that the quickest way to further your career is 'Find out what your boss wants and give him lots of it'. The political air marshals found out that Sandys wanted missiles instead of aeroplanes, and so an influential clique determined to 'give him lots of it'.

Rumblings of the coming storm surfaced in late 1956. The aeronautical press noted that Fairey had been told they would not get an order for the OR.329 fighter based on scaled-up aerodynamics of the world-record FD.2 (Fairey used to hold memorable Christmas parties in their London office at 24 Bruton St, and at the 1956 event they strenuously denied this, saying they were the front runner). Hunter orders were cut, the promising Gloster G.50 'thin-wing Javelin', with Olympus engines, was cancelled, and it was announced that the Royal Auxiliary Air Force would soon be disbanded. In a leading article on 25 January 1957 *The Aeroplane* dared to touch on the subject that, to avoid rocking the boat, had previously been ignored. It said merely 'It is hard to imagine any reliance being placed on guided missiles for offence.' I thought that this missed the point, and that it was also untrue. If you have a fixed target, such as an airfield, a missile is the ideal and obvious way to wipe it off the map. The writer, probably Phillip Robins or Thurstan James, seemed to feel far more strongly about the disbandment of the Auxiliaries. He reminded his readers of the old Latin proverb, 'Those whom the Gods wish to destroy they first make mad', and went on: 'Britain's own end must be very close, for what could be madder than to discourage those who wish to allocate their spare time to serving their country?'

The argument over the RAuxAF centred on the belief of the politicians—at least I suppose it was the politicians—that part-time pilots could not possibly manage modern complicated fighters. I was myself briefed to this effect by Andrew Peggie, the senior PR officer at the Ministry of Supply, and he seemed irritated when I asked on what evidence the opinion was based. I need not go on about this, except to remind today's British Government that our American allies never did anything so stupid as to disband the Air National Guard. Today's ANG is much bigger than the RAF and is made up of part-time chaps who, with utter professionalism, fly the same aircraft as the regular USAF, far more complicated than anything thought of in the mid-1950s.

The RAF had actually been to war in November 1956. Like most 'peacetime wars' it did not conform to preconceived ideas; for example one Valiant captain was embarrassed by being given accurate homings from the tower of the Egyptian airfield he was about to bomb. It was also a war in which missiles, of any kind, would have been of very limited use, whereas the many types of aeroplane and helicopter involved operated around the clock. This campaign had no apparent influence on the policymakers in Whitehall. I thought then, and I think today, that behind all of their thinking was a vague belief that by replacing aircraft by missiles it would be possible to save a tremendous amount of money. The talking went on through December 1956, and in the New Year the three appointments were announced of the men who were to steer the new policy through Parliament and sell it to the country, if this were needed. They were: The Hon George Ward, Secretary of State for Air; Aubrey Jones, Minister of Supply; and Duncan Sandys, Minister of Defence.

On 4 April 1957 English Electric Chief Test Pilot 'Bee' Beamont thundered out of Warton on the first flight of the P.1B, the first P.1 prototype to look outwardly like the future Lightning; he had a thrilling ride, in the course of which he was cleared to go to Mach 1.2 (soon Mach 2 was permitted). On the same day, about 200 miles to the south, Duncan Sandys rose to his feet in the House of Commons and presented to Parliament *Outline of Future Policy*, the breathlessly awaited White Paper on Defence (Cmnd 124, price ninepence). To everyone's surprise the section on the RAF said nothing startling at all; in fact it was boring. Everyone began to wonder what all the fuss had been about.

The sting was in the tail. Tucked away under the heading 'Research and Development' was the following: 'An adequate effort on research and development must be continuously maintained. Shortage of scientists and technicians in civil industry makes it imperative to restrict the military programme to absolutely essential projects. High priority will be given to the development of British nuclear weapons for delivery by bombers and rockets. Nuclear weapons are being evolved for defensive guided missiles . . . Having regard to . . . likely progress with rockets and missile defence the Government has decided not to proceed with the supersonic manned bomber, which could not be brought into service in much under ten years. In view of the good progress made towards the replacement of the manned aircraft of Fighter Command with a ground-to-air guided missile system, the RAF are unlikely to have a requirement for fighter aircraft of types more advanced than the supersonic P.1, and work on such projects will stop.' Regarding the P.1 (Lightning) itself, it was later officially stated that this had 'unfortunately, already gone too far to cancel'.

It was a decision so enormous in its implications, both for the defence posture of Britain and for the health of the aircraft industry, that many people who knew a bit about the subject could hardly believe what they heard and read. But, though some daily papers sought (completely in vain) for a 'Revolt of the Air Marshals', the idea that there was going to be a huge row and public debate just fizzled out like a damp squib. The attitude of the media in general was 'We aren't experts on all this, if the air marshals don't mind then there's no story in it'. The 'air marshals' didn't mind. Sir Robert Saundby published his review of the White Paper in which he said 'The disappearance of manned fighters and long-range bombers will have a profound effect on the future of the RAF, and undoubtedly involve some risk, but few will doubt that these decisions are right . . . the Government are to be congratulated on the production of a realistic document.' Today I feel like printing this in italics and adding 'my italics', to show the staggering disbelief that today attaches to every word.

So, if the mass media quickly dropped the subject, what did we of the so-called aeronautical technical press think? For a start, we recognized that we were not privy to all the facts and figures at the disposal of the Government. Second, we found it very hard to believe that, on so weighty a matter, the Goverment could have got everything completely wrong. Third, if one didn't think too much about it, it seemed quite a plausible idea for missiles to 'take over', perhaps at the expense of armoured vehicles and some ships as well as of aircraft. To argue against the imagined futuristic 'push-button warfare' tended to brand one as a dyed-in-the-wool old reactionary who couldn't move with the times. I was reminded of the words of George M. Bunker, who two years earlier had been President and Board Chairman of Martin. This famous company had been one of the world pioneers of aircraft manufacture, but when the last B-57 and P6M-2 went out of the door in Baltimore and the gigantic new plant at Denver was ready to build Titan intercontinental missiles, Bunker said Martin had 'Sloughed off its emotional attachment to the airplane'. It wasn't going to built them any more, and I rejoiced in Bunker's choice of words.

Ought we not to do as the Government said and, at least where military aircraft were concerned, slough off our emotional attachment too? Every evening the *Flight* editorial staff would leave their desks—seldom before 7 pm incidentally—and repair to the Brunswick Arms next door. Here we would meet up with anyone who happened to be in town, from Tex Johnston or George Schairer of Boeing to top people of our own industry. A few days after 'The Sandystorm', Sir Roy Dobson dropped in. He typified the tough, ebullient, no-nonsense kind of man who had built Britain's aircraft industry. We were amazed to find him very subdued. The Hawker Siddeley Group, of which Dobbie was Chairman, had received a strongly worded letter expressing the Government's great displeasure at something his Managing Director, Sir Frank Spriggs, had said in public: 'If the cancellation [of the Avro 730 supersonic bomber] is not put back, or if some supersonic long-range bomber, manned, of another type, is not ordered, then this country is completely written off for a supersonic civil aircraft for the rest of its days.' In fact I thought this badly expressed, and it proved also to be untrue, and to miss the main point of the 'missiles instead of aircraft' policy, but I was keenly interested in the Government's sharp reaction. Dobbie—I am sure for the first time in his life—was adopting the policy of not daring to say or do anything that might offend his biggest customer. He even said 'I have given my top PR man at Avro, Phillip Kidson, strict instructions not to give the slightest hint that we disagree with Government policy.'

Even at the time I felt that the people one might have expected to offer informed and impartial comment either failed to do so or else latched on to trivialities and side issues. To my surprise the leading article in our rival paper for 12 April, headed 'Over to Artillery', merely concentrated on the British nuclear deterrent and said, in effect, 'Oh well, so it's going to be delivered by missiles instead of bombers, no big deal.' Our own leader for the 19th said: 'Criticism has been largely directed at the decision to cancel the Avro supersonic bomber . . . Speed is but a single factor in reducing the bomber's vulnerability; among other possible means to the same end are the attainment of extreme altitude and the avoidance of the target area . . . Possibly of greater consequence, our V-bombers will be carrying (unless one of the most appalling blunders in Service history is committed meanwhile) a guided bomb . . . It is to this bomb, then . . . that we must turn for our reassurance, just as the demands hitherto placed upon the manned fighter will now be progressively transferred to the missile it carries.'

I didn't write this. I felt this was yet another concentration on side issues. It overlooked the fact that the original mission of the Avro 730 had been strategic reconnaissance, using among other things the impressive Red Drover SLAR (side-looking airborne radar). How was a missile going to fly that mission? As for the guided bomb, this was to have an extremely short operational career, being withdrawn as soon as the V-bombers took to operating at very low level with conventional bombs. The leader writer overlooked flight at treetop height as a far more effective means of reducing vulnerability, and we never even thought of 'stealth' (Story 19). The words 'appalling blunders' showed that we knew how to express strong feelings, but nobody used such language in connection with doing away with manned military aircraft!

On 12 April, at Westminister, C.I. (later Sir Ian) Orr-Ewing, Parliamentary Under-Secretary of State for Air, said: 'It is totally untrue to deduce that we are trying to create the Royal Ground Force . . . The P.1 has several years work to do; and Fighter Command is only one part of the RAF, and even when manned aircraft do yield to guided missiles . . . there will still be many vital jobs in the air which a machine alone cannot do.' Geoffrey Dorman, who had been active in aviation since 1914, wrote: 'Surely the end of fighter aircraft isn't in sight . . . There will be an air space between missile level and the ground which someone is going to use. If we are to scrap fighters, what is going to prevent enemy bombers with H-bombs coming over at supersonic speed in that empty space? And if the Government wakes up and provides an adequate air transport force, as an alternative to antiquated troopships, who will protect these air transports if we have no fighters?'

A little later, on 9 May 1957, Lord (and Marshal of the RAF) Tedder observed: 'If the development of these mystic or misguided missiles proves to be slower than anticipated, the failure to develop the supersonic manned bomber and the successor to the P.1 might well result in leaving us facing a dangerous gap in our defences.' On the same day George Ward opened the Commons Debate on the Air Estimates. Amazingly, he contrived to skate over all the controversial 'no more manned aircraft' policy in 200 words, taking perhaps one minute. For the next hour he droned on about trooping and other aspects of Transport Command—without, incidentally, answering Dorman's question about what would protect the transports. Even more extraordinary was the fact that the subsequent debate totally failed to address the central problem of what we were going to do when we had no more fighters or bombers. Even Geoffrey de Freitas, a leading Opposition spokesman on aviation, concerned himself only with the RAF trade structure, while 'Laddie' Lucas asked only about RAF publicity and advertising! The Air Ministry, perhaps getting the idea that the RAF might no longer appeal to young men with 'the right stuff', had previously put out a press release emphasizing that the run-down in pilots would 'be spread over several years'.

Throughout 1957—the media said—RAF chaps greeted each other with 'Hallo, old chap, got the chop yet?' The magazine *Punch* produced an issue (4 September 1957) during the Farnborough Airshow whose content seemed completely polarized around the replacement of aeroplanes by missiles. But at the Society of British Aircraft Constructors Show Dinner on the same date Saunders-Roe Chief Test Pilot John Booth got to his feet and put in a quick plug for his firm's mixed-power fighter, saying 'It flies faster than missiles and it flies further. Usually it gets back home, and its guidance system weighs 200 lb and drinks gin.'

So what about the long-term effects of all this nonsense? One thing that hardly anyone commented upon was that little or nothing had been said about the 'mystic or misguided missiles' which were supposed to take over the offensive and defensive duties of the RAF. The Blue Steel 'stand-off bomb' has already been mentioned. This short-range cruise missile served with a total of five V-bomber squadrons from 1962 and was withdrawn from 1973. Several planned advanced versions of it were cancelled. The weapon intended to replace the Avro 730 supersonic bomber was an LRBM (long-range ballistic missile), Blue Streak. This never even got into service, being cancelled in May 1960. Sir Geoffrey de Havilland, concerned at the large force of talented designers suddenly put out of work, said 'Let's built an executive jet', hence the famous 125. Blue Streak was cancelled because of a marvellous American missile called Skybolt, so we ordered this, but then the Americans cancelled it. One got the impression our 'credible deterrent' had yet to become credible.

As for the missiles to replace fighters, the only one known to me is Bloodhound. This entered service in Mk 1 form in 1958, but only to protect V-bomber bases. In 1964 the improved Mk 2 entered service, and for many years two squadrons, 25 and 85, have deployed this missile from sites near the East Coast to protect some RAF airfields. Range varies with target height up to about 50 miles, so this one-mission weapon cannot exactly replace fighters. It cannot, for example, fly most of the way to Iceland in order to check on the identity and registration letters of an unknown intruding aircraft. On the two occasions after 'The Sandystorm' when I was able to talk to the man himself I asked him about this kind of mission, but he brushed it off with 'We have to consider what would happen in a war. We would not be concerned with identifying individual aircraft.' And he repeatedly stressed, as if people might not believe him, 'I cannot force my beliefs down the throats of the Air Staff. I have to respond to the views of the Air Staff.'

Around 1961 I remember seeing a mention of a 'Bloodhound 3' on the BAC stand at Farnborough. This was the planned new-generation missile with greatly increased range, advanced semi-active guidance, and passive homing, but it was cancelled in 1962. So I have been left wondering about all the 'mystic and misguided missiles' that don't seem to have happened. Another thing nobody explained was whether all the financial saving was based on replacing aircrraft by missiles one-for-one. As even military aircraft might fly 50 or 100 missions, surely the replacement ratio should have been 50- or 100-for-one?

Perhaps the most serious effect of the whole business was on the British aircraft industry. For one thing, it destroyed the essential continuity of the design, testing, and manufacturing process. Like the cancellation of the V.1000 (preceding story) the cancellation of all new fighters and bombers made it very difficult indeed ever to recover the lost capability. It destroyed morale, and destroyed the faith of overseas customers. Federal Germany, for example, was convinced that the Saunders-Roe SR.177 mixed-power fighter would be superior to any version of the Mirage III or F-104, and I am certain they were right. But how could they commit the Luftwaffe to something that had been cancelled by its own government? Conversely, Britain's amazing policy had a big effect on the government of Canada, which wanted to save money. The huge programme for the Avro CF-105 Arrow—unquestionably the most advanced and capable long-range interceptor ever flown in the West, though of course its avionics have since been overtaken by new technology—stood out like a sore thumb. In January 1959 Premier Diefenbaker cancelled it, even refusing to let any of the existing Arrows be put to good use, (when asked, he shouted 'Melt it down!'). Instead he bought American IM-99B Bomarc missiles, which accomplished nothing and were soon withdrawn. Canada lost for ever its ability to design its own fighters. Avro Canada, described by a USAF general (Lauris Norstad) as 'just about the best team anywhere', vanished completely, and the morale of the whole industry has even today not recovered.

With enormous reluctance the Government conceded that the Air Staff might need a 'Canberra replacement' to meet Operational Requirement 339, which resulted in a project called TSR.2. It was decreed that the engines had to be developed by a merger of at least two companies, and the same applied to the aircraft itself, so we had arguments between groups of Chief Designers and Chief Test Pilots, and, in the event, really serious arguments over where the first flight should take place. The story is told later (No 43).

When Michel Wibault hit on a rather clumsy way of driving four centrifugal blowers to lift a tactical strike fighter vertically off the ground he took it to NATO in Paris. As Bristol Aero-Engines made the Orpheus turbojet, used in NATO G91 strike fighters, NATO took the idea to Bristol. There Dr Stanley Hooker and his team turned the original idea into a much simpler and more elegant one, a single turbofan engine with vectored nozzles, later called the Pegasus. The British Treasury utterly refused to have anything to do with it, saying 'It must be for a manned military aircraft, and manned military aircraft are prohibited'. So the MWDP (the US-funded Mutual Weapons Development Program) paid for 75 per cent of the engine's development, and Sir Reginald Verdon Smith—one of our most farsighted, courageous and patriotic leaders of industry—said Bristol would pay the rest. As for the aircraft that was to pioneer single-engined jet lift, Hawker produced this as the P.1127 after the company board had boldly said they would finance two prototypes. It was not until 18 months later that the Ministry of Aviation (the name changed every few months) agreed to provide funding, provided that it was clearly understood that the P.1127 was for pure research and had nothing whatever to do with the forbidden idea of a manned combat aircraft.

Much later we got the Harrier properly off the ground, and this pure research aircraft came in quite handy in the Falklands. We also gradually got back into the business of building combat aircraft, but only as partners in collaborative programmes. I suppose you could say that, via the Hawk T.1, an outstanding basic design, we have now in the Hawk 100 and 200 actually got back in the combat aircraft business on our own account, because, so far as I know, nobody in Whitehall today says that this is forbidden. Perhaps our political lords and masters have finally added up all the F-104s, F-5s, Phantoms, Mirages, MiG-21s, and Heaven knows what else that have been sold to the world's 150 land-based air forces, and what kind of business has been lost to Britain.

But I doubt it. Barring Mrs T, policiticans are seldom around long enough to notice anything. During 'The Sandystorm', in the course of a big Commons debate, one wag got up and pointed out 'This Government has so far had seven Ministers of Defence. They don't last long enough to find the way out of their office without help.'

42

20 June 1958

Obvious

I don't want to bring Newton and Einstein into it, but there are not many rules that don't have exceptions. 'Ah,' you will say, 'but it is the exception that proves the rule.' Fair enough, but my lifetime in aviation has taught me something extra. As soon as something is obvious, taken for granted, and accepted by everyone, you can be pretty sure it isn't so at all.

By the end of World War Two the experts on engines knew that there was not much future for the aircraft piston engine. Small lightplanes might continue to be piston-engined, but even here the gas turbine was clearly going to work its way down the power spectrum until the only field left for pistons (by about 1950, said one sage) would be in the bracket under 100 hp. What actually happened was that in the post-war era Pratt & Whitney and Wright sold *twenty times* the piston-engine horsepower that they had sold in the 1930s. Pratts sold over 28,000 piston engines of over 2,000 hp after the end of World War Two. Wright delivered the first Turbo-Compound in March 1950 and then followed it with a further 12,000. All over the world big piston engines are hard at work in agricultural aircraft, and new engines for this market are still in production, notably in Poland. Canadair recently sold 125 CL-215 amphibians powered by Double Wasps. Britain lost the entire market, because we knew that big piston engines were obsolete.

In the immediate post-war era the experts thought there might be a limited market for jet transports for relatively short stage-lengths. Obviously, the high fuel consumption of such aircraft made a long-range jetliner impossible, so for long hauls the choice lay between the turboprop (possibly with a heat exchanger) and the compound engine. Several reports by the top authorities in Britain (RAE) and USA (NACA) predicted the possibility of short-haul jets but pronounced that long sectors would be flown exclusively by propellers. What actually happened was just the opposite. While Vickers sold 438 short-haul turboprop Viscounts, Boeing and Douglas absolutely cleaned up the global long-haul market with jets. Indeed, the impact of the 707 and DC-8 was so tremendous that the Britannia was stopped in its tracks, and soon the turboprops were considered obsolete as a class.

During the first half of the 1950s Vickers and Lockheed studied the prospects for advanced short-haul jets and turboprops. Both decided on the turboprop, because such aircraft were lighter, smaller, quieter, burned less than half as much fuel, and took only a very few minutes longer on each trip. The result was the Vanguard and Electra. Both were excellent aircraft, but if you emerge into a world that knows turboprops are obsolete you can't win, so both production lines were short (only 43 for the Vanguard) and lost money. So by 1960 the situation was clear: the turboprop was obsolete. The unfortunates who had brought them wrote 'Jet Power' on the tail, and airbrushed out any suggestion of propellers in their marketing brochures.

In 1960 I doubt if a single aircraft expert would have believed that 30 years later aircraft factories all over the world would be churning out short-haul turboprops at the rate of 500 a year, while Canadair is marketing a Regional Jet 'to break into a sector of the market currently dominated by turboprop aircraft'! So, to recap: 1950, jets for short hauls, turboprops for the rest; 1955, no, turboprops for short hauls, jets for the rest; 1960, no, jets for everything; 1980, no, jets for long hauls, turboprops for short hauls; 1989, no, maybe jets are good for short hauls too. How about the propfan, chaps?

Two stories of wonderful new ideas, that everyone knew would sweep the board, are too long to be skated over here: VG 'swing wings' and jet-lift V/STOL. They simply went out of fashion. So I'll just sound off on the centrifugal compressor.

In the years immediately following World War Two every gas-turbine expert (and they were rather thin on the ground) knew that the centrifugal compressor would disappear from the scene very quickly. This was actually despite some of the evidence: for example, in 1950 the centrifugal Rolls-Royce Tay had been type-tested at 6,280 lb thrust and weighed 1,961 lb, while after years of heartbreaking effort the axial Avon RA.2 had just managed to scrape through a type test at 6,000 lb for a weight of 2,502 lb. The experts would have said 'That's the last of the centrifugals compared with the first of the axials, it won't be like that in a few years' time'.

Rolls were then just getting into production with the Dart turboprop. It used two centrifugal compressors in series, so was universally derided as (to quote Sir Denning Pearson, then R-R managing director) 'crude agricultural machinery'. In April 1955 I happened to be at Derby when the RB.109 was run for the first time. Later named the Tyne, this was the exact opposite of the Dart: it was the most advanced turboprop R-R could devise. It had two axial spools, the first having six stages and the HP nine, giving a pressure ratio of about 13. Other features included a can-annular combustion chamber and air-cooled turbine blades. A senior figure at Rolls-Royce said on that first run: 'The RB.109 takes over where the Dart leaves off.' The implication was that there wouldn't be very many more Darts, and (I quote the same speaker) that the centrifugal compressor was 'as dead as the Dodo, except possibly for small engines such as those made by Turbomeca'.

Well, what happened was that not many Tynes were sold, while the crude old Dart stayed in massive production for a further 32 years! But this was almost entirely because of the aircraft programmes, not because of any unsuspected technical superiority of the Dart. In fact when the last complete new-build Dart came off the line in 1987 it did represent a bygone style of technology. Certainly I had no doubt in the mid-1950s that, except for the smallest engines, below 1,000 hp, the centrifugal compressor had 'had it'. Why was it still attractive in small engines? Partly because tiny axial compressor blades, as small as the nail on your little finger, are vulnerable to FOD (foreign-object damage) and almost impossible to seal all round against leaks (put another way, the gaps that have to be left are

relatively far bigger and more serious than with blades bigger than playing cards).
Second, the supposed better fuel economy of the high-pressure axial was less
important with little engines. Third, capital cost was relatively more important, and
the one thing nobody could take away from the centrifugal was that it was cheaper.

In June 1953 General Electric received a contract for the XT58, a small shaft
engine in the 800 shp class. Its outstanding feature was its ten-stage axial
compressor, with three rows of variable stators. Pressure ratio was to be 8.3. This
seemed to me a big straw in the wind, but I was not prepared for what happened
on 20 June 1958. On that date Allison received a military (USAF/Army) contract
for the T63, a very small engine in the 250-hp class. Allison announced it would
also develop a civil version, the Model 250, as both a turboshaft for helicopters and
also a turboprop. This little engine had a mass flow of only 3 lb/sec. Yet it was
announced that its compressor would be a seven-stage axial, with a centrifugal
impeller added to the HP end merely to fling the air outwards to enter the two
combustion chambers. The Allison 250 seemed to be the writing on the wall for
the centrifugal, and that soon there would be none left, not even in the smallest
sizes.

Well, of course, by now you know what's coming. We were all wrong, and for
the past 25 years the derided centrifugal compressor has been hard at it replacing
axials! To some degree this is because the technology of centrifugals has made big
advances; it also reflects the fact that today we have open minds, better able to judge
on the basis of evidence, rather than on mere fashion and what seems to be obvious.

To a first approximation, the pressure ratio you can get from a centrifugal is a
function of the square of the rotational speed. It also naturally depends on the shape.
Until well into the 1960s most centrifugal impellers were made of aluminium alloy
and had straight radial guide vanes. But Garrett (then called AiResearch) and one
or two others were busy with stronger yet lighter impellers made of titanium alloy.
These could spin at much higher speed yet still have guide vanes that formed 3-D
curves across their front face. This eventually led to centrifugals that really give
axials a run for their money.

For example, whereas the mass-produced Pratt & Whitney Canada PT6A,
designed originally in 1958, has three axial stages leading to a centrifugal (just put
there to throw the air out around the reverse-flow combustor), the much bigger and
more powerful PW100 family, designed around 1978, has two centrifugals in series,
just like the ancient Dart which it replaces. In the early 1980s the US Army wanted
a completely new engine, the T800, to power the LHX helicopters. This engine has
to look modern in about the year 2020. The winning design has two centrifugal
compressors in series, with no axial stage. But what the 'centrifugals are dead as
the Dodo' fraternity must find really hard to swallow is that the Allison 250 has now
been developed in newer and much more powerful versions with the axial spool
thrown away. There is now just a single centrifugal, and it typically handles much
greater airflow with a pressure ratio of 8.4, compared with 7 to 7.2 for the original
engines with an extra seven axial stages!

So don't forget. When next you find something that is obvious, that 'everyone
knows', and that is taken for granted, say to yourself 'It probably isn't so.'

43

6 April 1965

TSR.2

It's not easy to begin this story. I have to ask myself if I really have the desire, the stamina, the sheer willpower, to rake over a story of the ten most dreadful years in the history of any modern industry? The story is one of two completely opposite factions. On the one side was the British aircraft industry, as always patriotic, dedicated, highly competent, and devoted to working day and night to meet the demands of the customer, especially when that customer was the British Government. On the other side were the knockers, the denigrators and the instant experts of the media who told the public all about it, together with the British Labour Party which in 1964 was elected to form a government.

The reason I shrink from this story is that, instead of being a plain tale of some technical or even political problem, it is a quite extraordinary history of acrimony between many groups of people who, throughout those years from 1957 until 1967, never for a moment tried to use their brains to find the best answers for Britain. The RAF hated anything to do with the Royal Navy, and to some degree the compliment was returned. The Ministry of Defence hated military aircraft. The pundits of the media—newspapers, radio, and TV—consistently went for the totally negative and thus controversial 'story' that would get the public's attention and further their careers (a view utterly at variance with the technical aviation magazines, who were naïve enough to try to find out the facts, which was not easy). The Labour Party saw that there was good political capital and a lot of votes in attacking the British aircraft industry. It all added up to a lot of the most influential people riding a tiger. At times a few realized what they were doing, but nobody could get off. They rode it to the end, to the decimation of the British aircraft industry. But we didn't have a war, so it didn't *seem* to matter.

One of the funny features of the whole tragic saga is that, throughout, numberless officials of the huge Ministry of Aviation were engaged in endless meetings to make sure everything was all right. After it was all over, and we had nothing left, more officials organized vast enquiries into the aircraft industry to try to find out how it should be managed. One of the main conclusions of one of these huge probes, headed by Lord Plowden, was basically that as a nation we should give up making aircraft. Reluctantly, it was admitted we might be allowed to take part in multi-national projects, but should never do anything on our own. These people get *paid* for coming up with ideas like this.

One could say the saga began in July 1952 with the issue by the Ministry of Specification B.126T. This was in my view the most farsighted specification ever written in Britain, so of course nothing came of it. It called for a bomber to fly missions to targets 2,500 nautical miles (2,879 miles) away, staying under 500 ft for 80 per cent of the round trip. I never understood the need for 80 per cent; my map of Europe suggests that 40 per cent would have been more than adequate, and the very high fuel burn at low level enormously enlarges the aircraft and makes it less attractive, but B.126T was farsighted in recognizing that future bombers would have to fly at tree-top height (as did the solitary Valiant B.2 prototype). Avro, Bristol, Handley Page, and Vickers proposed advanced bombers, all characterized by having a canard foreplane and very high wing-loading. All were developed to meet the later B.156 requirement. The resulting aircraft would have been extremely impressive, and still look modern today, but as they were not built the chief effect of these requirements was to ensure that the Royal Navy likewise knew about the need to fly at low level. Back in June 1952 the Admiralty had drawn up NAST.39 (Naval Air Staff Target), and this actually got built. The prototype Blackburn Buccaneer first flew on 30 April 1958. It was an aircraft of great potential and significance.

I don't know if the Canadians have got something in their notion of a single armed force, but we (rather like the Americans) have suffered through not having one. Ever since 1912, when their Lordships at the Admiralty refused to have anything to do with the Royal Flying Corps, and developed their own air power, we have had one side or the other automatically refusing to show an interest in an aeroplane simply because it belongs to the opposition. From the beginning, it would have been clear to anyone with an impartial brain that the Buccaneer was worthy of extremely careful evaluation by the RAF. It was also clear that it was an outstanding basis for prolonged further development. Sadly, when in 1955 the RAF first formally drew up its ideas for a replacement for the Canberra, and among other things realized that such an aircraft would have to be designed to fly virtually all its missions at low level, the Buccaneer was never for a moment considered. Indeed, the Air Staff rather resented the fact that it was being 'pushed' in their direction, by such people as the First Sea Lord (Mountbatten), and that in consequence they had to go to the bother of inventing all sorts of reasons why it was totally unsuitable.

Gradually the Air Staff drew up General Operational Requirement 339. When 'The Sandystorm' hit in April 1957 this was the only thing left, so everyone made the most of it. But surely manned aircraft were forbidden? At an off-the-record luncheon in December 1957 Sandys said: 'If the RAF find they now do in fact have a requirement for a new aircraft there is absolutely no reason why it should not be put forward and discussed.' Over the next three years it was indeed put forward and discussed, not forgetting the numberless officials. As GOR.339 was the only project in sight, these officials, and the Air Staff, were able to give it their undivided attention. Moreover, as it was the only new goody the RAF could look forward to they made jolly sure it was, in the words of the media, 'an all-singing, all-dancing aircraft'. Again, because it was the only new project, the officials carefully totted up the cost of every new thing in it—and every bit of it had to be new—and charged it to the programme.

Yet another result of this being the only new military project was that the

Government thought it would be a good idea to use it as a carrot—some would say shotgun—to force the industry into mergers. The scurrying around may be imagined. Had the media latched on to it they'd have had a field day, predicting everyone hopping into bed with everyone else, but the horsetrading went on for a full year. This was just one aspect of the whole affair, when every major firm in the British industry was forced under duress to bare its soul and its innermost financial secrets to all the most hated rivals. At last, in late 1958, the contractors were picked. The aircraft prime contractor was to be Vickers-Armstrongs, with exactly half the work to be done by English Electric Aviation, pending a full merger of the two giants' aviation interests. The engines would be developed by Bristol Siddeley Engines, formed by Bristol Aero-Engines and Armstrong Siddeley Motors.

At an early stage, in May 1958, the Air Council did a remarkable thing. Having failed to say a word during the months leading up to 'The Sandystorm', or in the period immediately following, the Air Staff appeared to gain some kind of collective courage, enabling it to sound forth on air power to invited audiences. It was called *Exercise Prospect,* and was a two-day event. On the first day the audience was exclusively Service (and a few Government) personnel with Security clearance. On the second day everybody who was anybody of supposed importance was invited, from Prince Phillip down through Top Brass and MPs to such lowly beings as aviation editors. Sir Wallace Kyle, ACAS(OR), explained why a new manned aircraft was needed. It had to fly every kind of attack and reconnaissance mission, operating from short unpaved strips anywhere in the world and able to penetrate the most modern defences at very low level. In his closing address the CAS, Sir Dermot Boyle, said: 'We in the Royal Air Force, if you ask for our professional advice, are convinced that we will require manned aircraft as far as we can see, to supplement the missile in both the offensive and defensive roles.'

As I said earlier (Story 41) Boyle was a man of considerable stature. Today it seems hardly credible that, by saying the RAF was going to need manned aircraft, he was virtually putting his career on the line. How right he was is seen by the fact that today the RAF has nothing else but manned aircraft in the offensive role and almost nothing else in the defensive role, but in 1958 his words were heresy. Sandys, who accepted the invitation to *Prospect* and then failed to turn up, was extremely angry, and there were various recriminations. In particular, the RAF was told it must never again take part in anything so embarrassing to the Government.

In the course of the horsetrading English Electric made a joint submission with Shorts, the former offering an aircraft called the P.17A and the Belfast firm the remarkable P.17D vertical lift platform (with 60 lift jets and 10 propulsion engines!) to get the heavy, small-winged P.17A off the ground and back when dispersed away from airfields. A few years before (Story 40) Shorts had been the good boys for whom the Government were prepared to kill off our only big jetliner. By 1958 the capricious politicians had exactly reversed their allegiances. Purely in order to ensure that Shorts were replaced by Vickers, the RAF was told to reissue OR.339 as the slightly revised OR.343, written around the submissions of English Electric and Vickers-Armstrongs.

It was not easy to prepare the submissions because, with so many people having nothing else to do, even the revised OR.343 changed day by day, mostly by being upgraded. Starting as a rather simple aircraft, by August 1958 OR.343 asked for just about everything that a manned aircraft could do. At last came an official statement, by Air Minister George Ward on 17 December 1958. He just said: 'It has been decided to develop a new strike/reconnaissance aircraft as a Canberra replacement. This will be capable of operating from small airfields with rudimentary surfaces, and have a very high performance at all levels.' The 'very high performance' included sustained speeds of Mach 1.1 at 200 ft and a design M_{max} of 2.75 at 35,000 ft. Radius of action, initially thought of as 600 to 700 miles, progressively escalated to 1,000 nautical miles (1,150 miles), of which 100 in each direction were to be at Mach 2.05 and 200 nm into and away from the target were to be at Mach 0.9 at 200 ft, with 1.1 in the target area. Bristol Siddeley's Dr Hooker met the Vice-Chief of Air Staff, Sir Geoffrey Tuttle, and asked him 'Geoffrey, why do you insist on a 1,000-mile radius? It is clearly a number carved out of the sky. Do you realize that the final 100 miles will cost you something like £1 million a mile for engineering development?' The air marshal waved his arms in a gesture of despair. Of course, this demanding mission had to be flown on internal fuel. Ferry range, again without external fuel, had to be 2,800 nm (3,224 miles); with two tanks it was 4,300 miles. At first the takeoff run was fixed at 500 yards (1,500 ft), and even with the almost doubling in weight that resulted from the upgrading in mission radius this figure was only relaxed to 1,800 ft, and from a rough strip.

On top of this the OR.343 requirement called for a powerful multi-mode forward-looking radar, a separate terrain-following radar linked to the flight-control system for automatically following the undulations of the ground, a sideways-looking reconnaissance radar, a battery of cameras, an infra-red linescan sensor, inertial platform, doppler radar, powerful digital computer, internal weapon bay and integral tankage for 5,588 Imperial gallons of fuel. Moreover, to meet the STOL demand the aircraft had to have exceedingly powerful blown flaps, and to meet the Mach 2.75 demand the engine had to be made of steel and titanium and be installed in a duct starting with a fully variable power-driven inlet and ending with a fully variable convergent/divergent nozzle, all of which were things never previously produced in Britain (though they would have been needed for the cancelled Avro 730 and privately funded Hawker P.1121).

Thus, whereas in the USA there continued to be an unbroken process of design and development by a large number of companies producing a large number of types of advanced supersonic aircraft, in Britain we had just the one programme. Everything was charged to it, from the entire spread of avionics devices to the vacuum-melted steel used in the landing gear and the Silcodyne H fluid used in the 4,000 lb/sq in hydraulics. Anyone able to think for a few seconds would naturally have been able to see that this was going to be a very expensive programme, because it was going to have to bear all the costs of an entire generation of new technology far more advanced than anything previously attempted in Britain. Perhaps aware of this, the Minister of Supply, Aubrey Jones, said the new aircraft would be 'not fantastically complicated' and that the development estimate was 'under £40 million'. A little later, on the first day of 1959, he announced that the new aircraft was known as TSR.2, 'a tactical support and reconnaissance aircraft . . . incorporating modifications which will greatly increase the usefulness of the aircraft in limited operations and for close support of the Army, particularly by reducing the length and strength of runways required for takeoff'. Back in the 1930s TSR had meant 'torpedo spotter reconnaissance', and the TSR.2 was none other than the famous Stringbag (Fairey Swordfish). Now we had a new meaning for the same initials, and the odd thing is that ever afterwards the letter S has been assumed to stand for 'strike', not support.

In his 1 January 1959 announcement Jones announced the main contractors. Vickers-Armstrongs (Aircraft) and English Electric Aviation were to merge completely, and in fact when they formed British Aircraft Corporation (BAC) it also embraced Bristol Aircraft and Hunting Aircraft. A very large part was played by the jet fighter designers from the former Supermarine design organization at Hursley Park, and their George Henson was appointed Chief Project Engineer under the two programme directors, Henry H. Gardner at Weybridge and Freddie Page at Warton. Sir George Edwards, who became BAC Managing Director, said the 'one-year run-in period', from the design contract of June 1959 to the development contract signed on 7 October 1960, had been 'most valuable. It paved the way at the working man's level . . . for the formation of BAC and for the creation of TSR.2 out of the two projects.' The latter were the Supermarine (Vickers) 517 and the English Electric P.17A. He added: 'At one time the Vickers STOL study and the P.17A with a tiny low-level wing seemed irreconcilable', but, by splicing the long and densely packed Weybridge fuselage to the high-lift wing, rear fuselage and tail from Lancashire, 'the two teams have hammered out an extraordinarily good aeroplane'.

One problem was that, after most careful assessment, both teams unanimously picked a Rolls-Royce engine. But, as stressed elsewhere in this book, such secondary considerations as the best engine for the aircraft don't count in the world of politics. When I wrote the first detailed description of TSR.2 on 31 October 1963 I was permitted to say that 'The Ministry of Supply regarded an advanced version of the Olympus turbojet as the optimum choice'. I was not permitted to add 'in the face of the unanimous recommendations of the aircraft designers, and for the purely political reason that Rolls-Royce had not merged with anyone'.

Another rather minor problem was that, despite the fact that the pioneer work on advanced VG (variable geometry) 'swing wings' had been done under Sir Barnes Wallis at Weybridge, when English Electric designed the P.17A wing they could not find sufficient backup information on such things as slow-moving but heavily loaded bearings, and so did not put such a wing on TSR.2. In April 1957 the VG Swallow project was cancelled, said Sandys, 'because it was related to the supersonic bomber. It was a post-SSB. The case for having VG in the research programme now is that we shall have to study its applicability to the strike role.' As the reader will have been made aware, the usual procedure in British aviation has been 'think of something new, put a lot of effort into developing it, cancel it just when it's coming good and then insist that everything is sent to the USA'. In this case the Weybridge VG was sent to John Stack at the newly formed NASA, and to Richard E. Horner, Assistant Secretary (R & D) USAF. NASA acknowledged the British input in their own programme, which in turn supported the General Dynamics F-111, which in the context of TSR.2 is ironic.

I won't comment on the subsequent pre-flight development of TSR.2, which is available in many unclassified places, beyond noting that the very few words about the programme said in public contained a high proportion of errors. For example the 1959 Defence White Paper said TSR.2 would 'carry air-to-air missiles', while in late 1960 Defence Minister Harold Watkinson said it would 'carry an air-launched ballistic missile' (Douglas hastily said 'Not Skybolt' and we never did hear what missile was in the Minister's mind). At the political level, however, one got the impression that about ten thousand people were latching on to this highly visible programme, a few in order to help it, a much bigger number in order to destroy it, and a few thousand because it was their job to manage and take decisions and there was nothing else they could get their teeth into. Test pilot Beamont recalled (in *Phoenix into Ashes*): 'It seemed that TSR.2 was receiving the undivided attention of all the inmates of St Giles Court. At one progress meeting which I attended the Chairman insisted on a count being taken, and, on establishing that there were 52 people in the room, requested that strenuous attempts be made to cut this down in future; at the next meeting the count was 61.' After describing 'day, night and weekend work on the avalanche of design appreciations, technical specifications and test notes which poured in endlessly', Bee went on to note how thoroughly the project flight-test team understood the aircraft, but 'often the recommendations made were turned down subsequently at the official Ministry of Aviation Cockpit Co-ordination Committee, at which 20 to 30 three-year-tour personnel would often debate for half a day the position of a switch and the label to put under it—and then get it wrong, as demonstrated subsequently by flight experience'.

Even the basic mission of TSR.2 seemed a matter for argument. Back on 23 February 1959 Minister Jones made it quite clear: 'The TSR.2 is not a deterrent weapon. It is not a bomber in the conventional sense of the word, but an aircraft intended to give strike support to ground forces. The reason for the delay in deciding on it was the redesign of the aircraft to make it suitable for limited-war contingencies overseas.' I wondered how such a basic and obvious requirement could possibly have been overlooked in the original OR.339. Anyway by February 1963 all the ministers had played musical chairs a few times, so Mr Jones perhaps didn't even notice what the new Air Minister, Hugh Fraser, had to say: 'TSR.2 will operate in the strategic role, both before and after the introduction of Polaris submarines.' So it *was* a deterrent weapon, and *was* a bomber. These facts just made it even more a target for the Labour Party.

I don't need to point out that the basic objective of politicians is not to help their country but to get elected. When they are in opposition they look for ammunition they can use against the party in power, and there is seldom any shortage of subjects. In 1964, with a General Election due in October, the Labour Party decided they could get a tremendous amount of mileage out of TSR.2, and the British aircraft industry generally. They began this campaign back in early 1963. While the Minister of Defence, who that week was Peter Thorneycroft, increased the number of aircraft on order from nine to twenty, and authorized long-lead materials for the aircraft for squadron service, the Australians urgently weighed up whether to replace their Canberras with TSR.2s, Vigilantes, Mirage IVAs, Phantoms, or F-111s. In many respects the British aircraft was way out in front, but the British Labour Party then announced that, if they were returned to power in October 1964, they would cancel the TSR.2 programme. To help matters a bit further, the CIGS (Chief of the Imperial General Staff), Lord Mountbatten, said he was sure TSR.2 would 'never go into service'. So the RAAF selected the F-111, and on 24 October 1963 their Air Minister, David Fairbairn, signed for 24 F-111Cs at US$90,749,040, which seemed a good deal. What actually happened was that the marvellous

American aircraft were *ten years* late in delivery and cost a little over US$300 million.

In 1963-4 none of this could be known, and the Labour Party lost no opportunity to ram home the message that, while TSR.2 was a completely useless aircraft whose cost had mounted to outrageous levels, the F-111 was a wonderful aircraft that would save the British public hundreds of millions. The Labour campaign was the outstanding example, in my lifetime at least, of a carefully planned campaign against a major British industry for party political ends. Part of the trouble was that TSR.2 could be sold to the public as an anachronism, an undesirable instrument of British imperialism and nuclear sabre-rattling (but no campaign was mounted against the Polaris submarines). The biggest factor was that, by the 1960s, the costs of advanced military aircraft seemed to have reached astronomic levels. The Labour Party correctly reasoned that the average voter would have no yardstick for comparison, and would therefore believe that the supposed prices were outrageous. And a third factor was Britain's love of secrecy, providing a perfect breeding ground for rumour and argument.

The Conservative Government was just as inclined to do almost anything for political ends. On 28 October 1963 there was still almost a year to go to first flight, and the aircraft would normally have remained under wraps, but on that day Julian Amery, Minister of Aviation, held a big Press conference at which all was revealed. This was purely to try to counter the very effective opposition campaign, but it cut no ice whatever. Led by Dicky Worcester and Mary Goldring, the London Press corps were soon united in the knowledge that TSR.2 was a rotten aircraft in a mismanaged and wasteful programme. This again was an interesting psychological phenomenon. While the American and French journalists had every reason for running down the British product, why did the British media take such a strange idea on board, and with such enthusiasm?

Back in 1958 Beamont had found himself opposite a journalist at a luncheon celebrating the initial trials of the Lightning. He was foolish enough to ask her opinion. 'Without moving a facial muscle she began a tirade that did not stop until the next course, to the effect that it was all a disgrace, a dreadful waste . . . it should all be done with rockets, and the Lightning was a useless aeroplane anyway, everybody knew this . . . In subsequent years the lady persistently denigrated on TV, radio and in her gossip column, most major British aircraft programmes . . . She was nothing if not consistent in attacking every aircraft project of importance when it became the subject of any attempt to build up confidence and morale in the aviation industry of this country . . . while advocating the outright purchase of American equipment.' There were many prominent media 'experts' who didn't want to know anything about TSR.2 or any other British aircraft, because they had made up their minds already. Without them the Labour party's task in destroying British aircraft would have been much harder, if not impossible to carry out.

Another prominent knocker was Andrew Wilson, who made his special target the Concorde programme. His paper, *The Observer*, published a big attack on TSR.2, starting that at £20 million per aircraft the cost of 50 would be £1,000 million. Next day this supposed 'fact' was used by Mr Healey in a vehement speech, in the course of which he said: 'TSR.2 is becoming the biggest scandal in British politics since the South Sea Island Bubble' (his history erred; there was no *island*).

The Government said the total programme cost was still £400 million, and hadn't changed for three years; as nothing had ever been revealed before one couldn't judge, but it was clear we were in for a few years of pointless arguments about hundreds of millions, where you crank in any figure you like. Sir Geoffrey Tuttle, who had got his bowler hat and joined BAC, had an uphill job trying to convince everyone that the Corporation's signed contracts amounted to just £50 million, while Amery got virtually no Press mileage when he described Mr Healey's £20 million as 'an exaggeration by about a factor of ten'.

Bee Beamont and navigator Don Bowen made the first flight in the first TSR.2, XR219, at Boscombe Down on 7 September 1964. From the start it was clear they had a superb aircraft, though at first the flying rate was depressed by persistent troubles with the engine and landing gears. In October 1964 the Labour party did indeed win the election, helped enormously by their 'patriotic and fearless campaign against the wasteful aircraft industry'. Nobody on the new Government Front Bench knew anything about aviation (if they had, they'd never have admitted it). Healey, after two years foaming at the mouth against the British aircraft factories, found that the average 'man in the street' had been roused almost to the point of throwing stones at the factory windows. He therefore said he had no intention of taking such an unpopular post as Minister of Aviation, and instead became Minister of Defence. The unpopular job went to another suitably smooth and competent man, Roy Jenkins. When the two ministries had got their act together a top-level team, headed by Prime Minister Harold Wilson, went to Washington, and also to see General Dynamics in Texas. They calmly told the Americans we were ditching all our own programmes, and would like to buy American aircraft instead. Their hosts probably said 'Have a nice day!'

First to go were the two Hawker Siddeley aircraft. The Hawker P.1154 supersonic jet-lift V/STOL multi-role fighter was replaced by the F-4 Phantom, which cannot operate except from long paved runways, or a carrier if you happen to have one. Stopped at the same time, in January 1965, the Hawker Siddeley HS.681 V/STOL jet transport was replaced by the C-130 Hercules, which also isn't a V/STOL jet. Wilson said he would not take a decision on TSR.2—which the newspapers called 'this inherited monster . . . which has gone on long enough'—until June 1965. But the obvious brilliance of the performance of TSR.2, as manifest in the flight-test results, made it clear that the programme had to be stopped much sooner, before any of this excellence leaked out, so the announcement was tucked in the Budget speech on 6 April 1965, in between an extra sixpence on cigarettes and four shillings on a bottle of whisky.

BAC was instructed to destroy the two completed and five almost completed aircraft, as well as all tooling and anything else related to the programme. Weybridge, Hurn, and Itchen (Southampton) were in full production delivering fuselages in green primer; everything was chopped up. Preston, Samlesbury, and Warton were in full flow with rear fuselages, wings and the extremely advanced tails (with no fixed portion) in white anti-flash paint; everything was chopped up. It was tough on the thousands of devoted people who had toiled (many day and night) to get this far. Ollie Heath, later 'Mr Tornado', said 'Whatever the rights and wrongs of cancelling the main programme . . . the rejection of the limited flight-test programme . . . was unforgivable.' Sir Ian Orr-Ewing said: 'At least the third aircraft should have been kept flying to prove the reconnaissance, navigation and attack systems . . . this urgent wish to destroy everything suggests . . . a pathological hate . . .'

As I said, we were in for a long bout of how many hundreds of millions had been saved by stopping TSR.2 and instead buying 55 American-made F-111Ks. Nobody seemed to notice that, if we kept on with TSR.2, all the money stayed in Britain, to the benefit of our economy, whereas if we bought American aircraft the money all went across the Atlantic. Indeed, in the former case the Government would itself get about 40 per cent of it back in taxes. But none of this was cranked into the multitude of rather sterile and inconclusive arithmetic which for several more years sought to prove that cancelling TSR.2 was a wise move, or a foolish one. Sir George Edwards once said that, if you don't have a war, cancelling a military aircraft hardly shows. (If you do have a war, you're in desperate trouble. Could you imagine us fighting the Battle of Britain over again whilst relying on our aircraft coming from Fort Worth, Texas?) Eventually we cancelled the F-111K as well, thereby saving ourselves having to pay between three and four times the attractive price that Mr Wilson said would 'save £300 million', though we did have to fork out about $130 million in cancellation charges and various other costs.

Why were the 'corridors of power' in Britain so hooked on the F-111? One answer is that, like British Airways, many of the most senior officers in the RAF were, to quote a very eminent Briton, 'absolutely fascinated by anything American'. To begin with, there was an overall belief that, if it was American, it must be superior. If it showed itself to be riddled with faults, there was a touching belief that the sheer might of American technology would just trample the shortcomings to death. There is an old saw, 'The grass is always greener on the other side of the street'; pity this is a one-way street, and so far I have yet to meet a single American who automatically thinks any British aerospace or defence item must be better than his own, to the point where he wishes to junk the homegrown product. The disease seems to be uniquely British. Few people are as well qualified to compare the TSR.2 and F-111 as test pilot Beamont. He recently recalled: 'The nearest rival was the F-111 development programme, which, though similar in military role capability, was less capable in many aspects of performance than TSR.2. The F-111 did, however, eventually have one significant advantage: it was not cancelled . . .'

I'm doubtful that any useful purpose is served by repeating many of the opposing financial figures. In 1972 I got the MoA to state in writing that the 'total cost of the TSR.2 programme was £192 million', but what did that include? Certainly vacuum-melted steel research and development of Silcodyne H (for example), but one of Mr Healey's estimates went so far as to lump in (said Dr Geoffrey Williams, Higher Defence Studies, University of Southampton) 'much general research at Government establishments which would have been done anyway, even including work on flying boots'. On Healey's own figures it was possible to work out that the target price for manufacture was £575 million for a run of 158, or £3,640,000 per aircraft. At the time this seemed high—Prime Minister Wilson likened it to 'a pre-war battleship' to increase the public blood pressure—but looking back from today my feeling is that there was no way BAC could have produced TSR.2s at that price. We just have to revise our ideas, like the US Congressman who, appalled at the deal struck on Block 5 of Grumman's F-14A production, declaimed 'Never again will this nation buy a 20 million dollar fighter!' Today we can see how right he was; they don't come that cheap any more. And in the same way, today £3,640,000

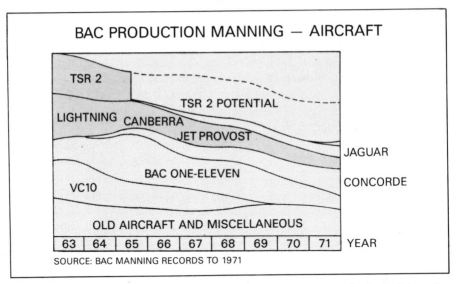

BAC PRODUCTION MANNING — AIRCRAFT

TSR 2

TSR 2 POTENTIAL

LIGHTNING   CANBERRA

JET PROVOST

JAGUAR

BAC ONE-ELEVEN

VC10

CONCORDE

OLD AIRCRAFT AND MISCELLANEOUS

| 63 | 64 | 65 | 66 | 67 | 68 | 69 | 70 | 71 | YEAR |

SOURCE: BAC MANNING RECORDS TO 1971

Having cancelled TSR.2, Defence Minister Denis Healey made out that he had done the British aircraft industry a good turn, by forcing them 'to put their money into producing spares and aircraft they had already developed'. He might have found this graph of manning (which means employment) hard to reconcile with his cosy belief.

would certainly not even pay for a TSR.2's avionics.

One of the things politicians most dislike is being reminded of their past words or deeds. In justification of cancelling TSR.2 Mr Healey said: 'Even the Americans are now coming to realize that aircraft like the TSR.2 and F-111 are just not good buys, because you cannot afford enough of them to make sense.' A unit price of between £3 million and £5 million made it, he said, 'far too expensive'. He said this in 1972, since when we have had a fair amount of inflation, but I wonder how Mr Healey views the B-1B at a unit price which certainly exceeded the published figure of $283 million (before the additional 18 months of work on the avionics), 100 of which were delivered? What would he think of the B-2, with a planned buy of 132 at a unit price likely to exceed the published figure of $600 million? I'm reminded of Sir Kenneth (now Lord) Keith, who as chairman of one of the biggest merchant banks had formed the view that £5 million was a lot of money. Sir Stanley Hooker of Rolls-Royce observed: 'After a few weeks on the RB.211 he soon came to understand that £50 million is peanuts.'

At the start of this story I said loss of the TSR.2 'decimated' the industry. That's a good emotive word. It comes from a traditional Roman army punishment (for mutiny, for example): every tenth man is put to death. A lot of people erroneously think it means you only have one-tenth left. In fact, loss of TSR.2 took away much more than one-tenth of the British industry's workload. Sir George Edwards recalls:

It was no joke pulling BAC together after the sudden loss of such a large part of the forward programme. The production and development teams at Warton and Preston were both very badly hit. Amongst the documents circulating at that time was a Ministry of Aviation official paper saying that there was no way that these two plants could be kept in business and they should both be shut. When one considers that those teams under Sir Frederick Page have played the absolutely dominant part in the design and manufacture of the Tornado and Jaguar, the idea that this could, even for a short space of time, become official policy, was at its lowest unreal. In the end, we had to close a factory, and in the way that these things go we closed Luton, a highly efficient low-cost little factory that had nothing to do with TSR.2, but the work had to go up to the North in order to preserve the capability of the factories there and their military expertise.

Yet in 1972 Mr Healey actually announced that killing off TSR.2 had done the industry a good turn. In his view, 'There was a saying in the Ministry, "The only way to make money in the aircraft industry is never to produce an aircraft . . ." After the cancellation of TSR.2 and the other two projects the production and foreign earnings of the industry just rocketed, because they put their money into producing spares and aircraft they had already developed.' He appeared not to understand that such production is geared to the demands of customers.

To me there are several fundamental factors which added together produce this disgraceful story. One is that if you cancel an entire activity (in this case in 1957), and then try to restart it with a project of exceptional challenge, then you cannot help having to foot the bill for all the things that were not done during the 'minus' period. Another is that it never does any harm to try to be objective and weigh things up correctly, instead of childishly rejecting something (I'm thinking of the Buccaneer, of course) just because it was developed for the rival mob. Now that tempers have cooled I'm sure that most of the army of TSR.2 knockers and denigrators would today admit that perhaps they had got things a little wrong, and that it is seldom a good idea to make up one's mind before you have found out anything about the subject. For example, is there a single person alive today who considers it sensible to suppress all information relative to a new aircraft's flight-test programme in order that none of the general public should learn of its brilliant performance and superb handling?

Not least, I don't have the slightest compunction in describing the basic philosophy of ditching all British programmes and replacing them with 'cheap' hardware from the United States as not just lunacy but dangerous lunacy. Nobody wants to get involved in a shooting war but it can happen in the most unexpected way, as in the Falklands in April 1982, and, to put it mildly, it helps if you make your own kit. As to the notion of saving money, well I think the track record of US products (the F-111 for example) must by now have killed that idea stone dead.

But I doubt it. If people have made up their minds in advance, they don't want to consider the facts.

44

1984

How to Destroy a Prosperous Industry

The year 1984 will forever be remembered as the title of a chilling book about a world in which, for example, 'black is white, falsehood is truth', and so on. The once prosperous GA (general aviation) industry, at least in the United States, did indeed enter such a world in that year—it had a few warning signals earlier—but this world is a real one. We are still living in it, and it means, in effect, that, if you are in the United States, you had better not make any kind of aircraft, fly any kind of aircraft and certainly never design any kind of aircraft, unless it is either your own property or of the kind that sells for about 100 million dollars.

To give a rough idea of the size of the problem, in the 1970s Cessna was the No 1 planemaker to the world. In the calendar year 1979, for example, Cessna's commercial sales exceeded 8,400 aircraft. But total sales for 1987 amounted to just 187 aircraft, and the 1988 figure was only 161. Whatever happened? The answer has nothing to do with either the aircraft or the customers but rests entirely on clever lawyers who know how to take advantage of the deeply flawed legal procedures of the United States.

Most of us have heard almost unbelievable stories of plaintiffs in the United States obtaining large sums by suing anyone who has a lot of money, or seems likely to have a lot of money. One of the most tasteless concerned the lady who shampooed her poodle and then thrust the dog into her microwave to be dried. She successfully sued the microwave manufacturer, for a large sum, for not explicitly warning her not to do such a thing. It is just faintly conceivable that this lady was genuinely surprised at what happened to her pet, but there have been countless cases more recently where any reasonable person—such as the proverbial 'man on the Clapham bus'—would come to the conclusion that the whole thing—the act, the result, and the subsequent litigation—was a put-up job, arranged from the start in order to obtain a lot of money from a defenceless company.

In the United States there are many thousands of highly professional lawyers. They know that, within the existing framework of the American legal system, it almost always pays to target someone who has what looks like a deep pocket (such as an aircraft manufacturer), concoct a case against them, and then bring it to court. The jury will invariably decide for the plaintiff, without necessarily having the slightest idea what the case was about or whether the action was justified. The jury also has the power to name the sum to be awarded in damages, and for about fifteen years the sums awarded have been utterly unrelated to what happened, or what the lawyer tried to pretend happened, but instead to pure emotion. The ruling emotion is: 'Here's a big company, it's got lots of money, let's make them pay out a million or two.'

If you think this is overstating the case, try these three examples: A US manufacturer was successfully sued for $1.75 million for 'negligent design and construction' of an aircraft which they had built in 1954, which had had at least thirteen owners and had been modified at least nine times, on each occasion without the slightest reference to the unfortunate original maker; the same company was done for over $2 million by the family of a pilot who, in a state of intoxication, flew the perfectly serviceable aircraft into a mountain; another US manufacturer had to fork out $2.5 million for 'negligent design and construction' despite the fact that the actual aircraft had been twice tested by the FAA and found to comply with all Federal Aviation Regulations! As one man from Cessna commented: 'I don't know what we can do, short of go completely out of business. It might help if we stuck a big label in every cockpit in every Cessna in the world: WARNING, THIS AIRPLANE MIGHT KILL YOU.'

Not only the big names in GA manufacture are vulnerable. So too are the purveyors of plans and kits to the world's homebuilders. Many of these suppliers are mere individuals, often with an overdraft at the bank, but that does not stop them being hauled into court by some idiot who has failed to follow the plans, introduced his own modifications and then suffered inflight failure of some kind.

So what have the planemakers done? First, they have stopped making all aircraft except those at the top 'up-market' end of the price bracket, such as big twins, turboprops and business jets. Second, they have tried to protect themselves with product-liability insurance. And it is the amount of insurance necessary that has driven most companies out of business, especially those which make simple aircraft for ordinary private owners. For example, in the 1950s Beech were never sued to the extent of $1 million (total) in a year; the smart lawyers had not then got into action. But in 1985 Beech had to pay out over $210 million, of which (on my reckoning) over $208 million was completely unjustified. So in 1986, to cover an expected bill of $240 million, Beech had to add $80,000 in totally unncessary liability costs to the price of each of the 300 aircraft produced.

In the case of Cessna the arithmetic is even more ridiculous. If they were once more to build a Cessna 172 or Skyhawk they could sell it for $50,000. On top of that they would have to add a further $60,000 to cover their product liability. The answer is self-evident: for six years Cessna has built no 172s or Skyhawks, nor any other small piston-engined aircraft, and neither has its French associate Reims Aviation. But that only solves a small part of the problem. What is even worse is that the lunatic US legal system encourages plaintiffs to sue with so-called 'historic claims' involving aircraft made ten, twenty, or even fifty years ago. Cessna have sold about 177,500 aircraft (though now the total is climbing very slowly indeed). The company can hardly buy them all back again, yet at any moment they may face a ridiculous claim involving an ancient Cessna subjected to all kinds of unauthorized modification of which the Cessna Aircraft Company was not even aware.

The situation is indeed a terrifying one. Merely stopping production provides no defence, though going bankrupt would help enormously—bright lawyers don't sue bankrupts. An alternative is to try to take refuge under the wing of a giant corporation, with not only lots of money but also lots of lawyers and political clout of its own. Thus in 1985, Cessna became a wholly owned subsidiary of General Dynamics. I would not be surprised if the company had been bought for $1.

Today many once-prosperous US general-aviation builders, such as Rockwell, Bellanca, Champion, and Helio, have disappeared from the scene. The entries for Piper, Beech, and Cessna in *Jane's* make dismal reading. Much of each entry comprises a list of types the production of which has been suspended. And there is absolutely no point in anyone—certainly not any company responsible to stockholders—taking the trouble to design a new and superior lightplane, unless it is going to be sold exclusively outside the United States.

The situation hits not only the builders but also the operators, airshow organizers, and almost anyone who has anything to do with flying. For example, in 1985 the EAA (Experimental Aircraft Association) had to find an *extra* $150,000 in third-party insurance for that year's Oshkosh fly-in. Since then the extra premiums have roughly doubled. Even in the UK the insurance premiums are almost crippling. If you want to fly your microlight at an RAF open day you must take out insurance to indemnify the Crown to the tune of £2 million. The simplest answer, of course, is just to stop all flying altogether.

Will it ever change, and sanity return? So far there is not much real sign of this happening, but we are told 'hope springs eternal'.

For several years a bill to change the lunatic product-liability laws has been pending in the US Supreme Court in Washington, but as this is written there seems no sign of much happening in the short term. Cessna's view is that they do not expect to resume production of their famous lightplanes until late 1991 at the earliest. But their Chairman and CEO, Russ Meyer, who is a lawyer, has gone on record as saying 'If ever the product-liability laws return to normality we will be in production again within 24 hours.'

So far the only company to put a bold face on the situation is Piper. On 12 May 1987 this famous firm was taken over—everyone says, for a dollar, though I rather doubt this—by Californian businessman M. Stuart Millar. In the depths of surrounding gloom, he restarted production and shook his fist at the lawyers, saying 'I will sell any Piper airplane to anyone with the cash to pay for it . . . and if anyone attempts to impose an excessive and undeserved liability claim on Piper I will fight it and win.' He gathered a team of 'the meanest, ornariest lawyers that could be found'. So far most litigants have avoided Piper and sued someone else. Quite a few 'had a go', and so far Millar has won every case except one. That one, unfortunately, was for $20 million—and in my opinion totally unjustified. I think the penny is gradually dropping, and that even the American lawyers are beginning to realized that their profession has been brought into utter disrepute around the world.

45

8 April 1985

McDonnell Douglas v Northrop

On this date two of the world's leading high-tech aerospace companies, named above, announced that they had settled their differences. A lot of people interested in big business and finance hardly noticed. As for 'aircraft enthusiasts', I doubt if any of them gave the matter a second thought. So here are some second thoughts.

When two big companies like McDD and Northrop sew up a big deal together they really do it properly. Each has an army of lawyers; anyone who knows the Damon Runyon stories will recall the Old Doll who had so many potatoes she was always surrounded by an army of lawyers to protect her, especially from each other. Big corporations, as well as the US armed forces, certainly do their bit to use up the world's forests, because the amount of paperwork involved is mind-boggling. It is all deadly serious, because huge sums are at stake. But sometimes the agreements are not worth the millions of sheets of paper they are written on.

I first encountered the problem in a big way when writing the official history of Nadgeco, the great 14-nation multi-national which, led by Hughes of the USA, designed, built and commissioned the gigantic Nadge (NATO Air Defence Ground Environment) air-defence system which stretches in a vast arc from North Cape at the top of Norway through Central Europe to eastern Turkey. Every one of the thousands of contracts was drawn up by more lawyers than I knew existed. Every clause was drafted, amended, re-amended, and finally printed after being approved by everyone. But what nobody had bothered to write into the clauses was what to do if things didn't go according to plan. To cite a simple example, one clause (probably called something like II-1/B-100/He 51185a) stipulated that, for Nadge sites in Greece 'all final working drawings shall be approved or rejected within 90 days of submission'. What actually happened was that, two years after submission, about three drawings had been approved and about 30,000 hadn't. The Greeks said 'digital electronics experts aren't very common in Athens' (this was about 1972) so they had nobody able to approve the drawings. This is the kind of thing armies of lawyers can overlook.

What about the Nadge book? Well, again the lawyers didn't look ahead. I wrote it, and thought it one hell of a fine story. Then, on the final meeting by the 14 companies to agree the manuscript, one little chap stood up and said 'Of course, the book can't actually be published!' All heads turned in his direction as he continued, 'We have to stay in business, and this is not merely NATO with the lid off but NATO with the lid off written *with authority*. It's dynamite on every page.' So I had to see my solicitor and submit a sworn affidavit that I had destroyed not only my manuscript but even my notes and references. What's more, I really did. Too bad.

At least I got paid, though I have on many occasions completed major jobs without the question of my fee even being discussed. I have been quite happy because the customer and I know each other, trust each other, and perhaps need each other, so there's no problem. In sharpest contrast, I have also signed the most detailed contracts with publishers or packagers who, when they've got my work, either just don't pay (one said 'Sue me') or, more often, choose to go bankrupt and start again under another name. Would you believe, I've let one man do that to me four times! So you will gather I am utterly unimpressed by carefully drawn up legal agreements.

Nevertheless, I suppose you have to give lawyers work to do, even in the USA where they are overworked suing lightplane builders (preceding story). So when big companies get together in a joint programme it has to be sewn up very carefully indeed. I won't rake over the whole history, because it's in plenty of books and magazine articles, but today's F/A-18 Hornet had its roots in a US Navy programme called VFAX, from fixed-wing fighter attack experimental, in April 1974. The objective was a small, low-cost but extremely modern aircraft that could replace the F-4 in the fighter role and the A-7 in the attack role—and far outperform both. Northrop put in two proposals, one based on the YF-17 (a candidate for the USAF ACF, Air-Combat Fighter, programme) and the P-630 based on the P-530 Cobra. McDonnell Douglas submitted an all-new, and very good, proposal called Model 263. The Navy was deep into the scoring process, to see who should be announced as the winner, when on 28 August 1974 Congress, mindful of saving money, directed the Navy to terminate VFAX and instead pick an NACF, a naval version of one of the USAF ACFs. This restricted the choice to either the General Dynamics F-16 or the Northrop F-17.

This left McDonnell Douglas out in the cold, but James S. and son Sanford N. McDonnell had a way of never being out there for long. They even examined a scheme to ensure that they would have 50 per cent of whichever NACF was chosen, but not even their army of lawyers could sew that idea up! So they had to make a choice, and they chose Northrop. To cut an extremely long story short, they reached agreement with Northrop Corporation that the partners would jointly redesign the YF-17 into the F/A-18 Hornet to meet the NACF specification. The prime contractor was to be McDonnell Aircraft (MCAIR) at St Louis, to whom Northrop would supply design engineers, to help turn the YF-17 into the F/A-18, and later production centre and aft fuselages and tail units made in California. Northrop's share of the programme was fixed at 'about 40 per cent'. As I have stressed, everything was put into legal language to make it watertight, and prevent any future arguments.

Unfortunately, arguments were just what everyone got, almost from the word go. There were several points at issue. One was simply 'Who invented the F/A-18, Northrop or McDonnell Douglas?' Another was that Northrop, seeing a big global market opening up for such an excellent twin-engined multirole aircraft—which, unlike the F-16, had a radar that could illuminate targets for big radar-guided medium-range missiles, such as Sparrow—reasoned that, except possibly for France, nobody would want a carrier-based version. Accordingly, Northrop began marketing the F-18L, L for land-based, which compared with the F/A-18 promised 'empty weight 2,200 to 2,600 lb lighter, payload/range 40 to 100 per cent greater, 8 per cent faster turn rate, 25 per cent faster transonic acceleration, 10 per cent lower fuel burn rate, and reduced maintenance and failure rates'. Sounds marvellous, and Northrop was rather put out when Canada, Australia, and Spain all signed for the heavy and penalized carrier-based version.

Nevertheless Northrop kept on pushing the F-18L, and increasingly felt that its partner was hogging the market. It looked at the world market for fighters equipped with powerful radars for all-weather interception and missile guidance and decided it could put together a 'monopolization' case. It was rather like a rerun of the Jaguar programme, where BAC in Britain and Dassault-Breguet in France put together a joint company called SEPECAT to market the Jaguar, and BAC then found that Dassault was doing all it could to stop anyone buying Jaguars so that they could sell them Mirages instead! Neither Northrop nor McDonnell Douglas ever tried to damage the prospects for the F/A-18, but Northrop certainly found itself in a no-win situation, in which all the prospective customers for the F-18L instead went to St Louis where the product was the F/A-18. So after briefing its own army of lawyers it decided in mid-1979 it could try to get its partner on various counts, notably violation of the anti-trust laws 'in that McDonnell Douglas Corporation has attempted to monopolize the state-of-the-art jet fighter market and various submarkets thereof. Northrop Corporation is seeking damages and injunctive relief for the injury to the business or property of Northrop Corporation suffered by it, as a result of the overt acts engaged in by McDonnell Douglas Corporation in furtherance of its attempt to monopolize.' And so on.

I got involved as an expert witness on behalf of poor little hard-done-by Northrop. Gradually I built up some large bundles of papers. The early letters, all from firms of lawyers, were headed rather grandly 'Northrop Corporation versus McDonnell Douglas Corporation, United States District Court, Central District of California, Civil No 79-04145-R'. Progressively this was whittled down until, in spring 1985, I was getting letters headed 'N v McDD'. Somewhere along the way McDonnell Douglas decided that attack was the best form of defence, and filed a counter-claim 'that Northrop wrongfully misappropriated F-18A data, particularly in the areas of display symbology and switchology, for use in Northrop's F-20A'. A bevy of fresh lawyers got to work, and in fact about half my tome of paper on the overall dispute is concerned with this counter-claim that Northrop pinched the technology of the F/A-18 cockpit.

I wasn't too bothered about losing the case for Northrop at the hands of some slick lawyer in LA—I was reassured on that point—but I was increasingly bothered at the fact that I was legally forbidden to 'speak to, write or in any other way' communicate with McDonnell Douglas. They happen to be friends of mine, and I often have to do business with them, so after a lot of negotiating I was released from my involvement in the litigation. Of course, I am still not permitted to disclose a lot of things learned during the action which might still make 'the fur and feathers fly'. And, as it happened, it was all settled out of court. On 8 April 1985 the litigants announced that they had kissed and made up. McDonnell Douglas paid Northrop $50 million—carefully explaining to their stockholders this would not affect 1985 earnings—and would henceforth be prime contractor for all versions of the Hornet, 'including versions designed only for land-based use'. The deal was to some degree made possible by the certainty that the F-20A would not go into production (I believe McDonnell Douglas were on to a loser on that one, anyway). A completely new contractual agreement was drawn up, and all claims under the giant lawsuit were dismissed.

The good news was that production of the various version of the Hornet was never affected. And today Northrop has two potentially gigantic programmes to worry about, the YF-23A Advanced Tactical Fighter and B-2 Advanced Technology Bomber, and has no time to spare on such trivialities as billion-dollar lawsuits.

Index